VOLTERRA STIELTJES-INTEGRAL EQUATIONS

NORTH-HOLLAND
MATHEMATICS STUDIES **16**

Notas de Matemática (56)
Editor: Leopoldo Nachbin
Universidade Federal do Rio de Janeiro
and University of Rochester

Volterra Stieltjes-Integral Equations

Functional Analytic Methods; Linear Constraints

CHAIM SAMUEL HÖNIG
Instituto de Matemática e Estatística, São Paulo, Brazil

1975

NORTH-HOLLAND PUBLISHING COMPANY – AMSTERDAM • OXFORD
AMERICAN ELSEVIER PUBLISHING COMPANY, INC. – NEW YORK

North-Holland ISBN for this Series: 0 7204 2700 2
North-Holland ISBN for this Volume: 0 7204 2717 7
American Elsevier ISBN: 0 444 10850 5

Publishers:
NORTH-HOLLAND PUBLISHING COMPANY – AMSTERDAM
NORTH-HOLLAND PUBLISHING COMPANY, LTD. – OXFORD

Sole distributors for the U.S.A. and Canada:
AMERICAN ELSEVIER PUBLISHING COMPANY, INC.
52 VANDERBILT AVENUE
NEW YORK, N.Y. 10017

PRINTED IN THE NETHERLANDS

INTRODUCTION

This work presents the results we obtained in the study of linear Volterra Stieltjes-integral equations with linear constraints i.e. in the study of systems of the form (K), (F) where

$$\text{(K)} \quad y(t)-y(t_o) + \int_{t_o}^{t} d_\sigma K(t,\sigma)\cdot y(\sigma) = f(t)-f(t_o) \qquad t\in \,]a,b[$$

$$\text{(F)} \quad F[y] = c.$$

These systems are studied in all their generality (see Remark 3 at the beginning of Chapter III); we give a Banach space X, $y,f\in G(]a,b[,X)$ (the space of regulated functions– see the index for this and other definitions) and

$$K: \,]a,b[\times]a,b[\, \longrightarrow L(X),$$

that satisfies natural conditions defined in §1, Chapter III.

$$F\in L[G(]a,b[,X),Y],$$

where Y is a locally convex space, is called a linear constraint. In the item A of §1, Chapter III, we show how linear differential equations, linear Volterra integral equations, linear delay differential equations, etc. are reduced to the type (K). As particular instances of linear constraints we have the initial conditions, boundary conditions, periodicity conditions, discontinuity conditions, multiple point conditions, integral conditions, interface conditions, conditions at infinite points etc. (see item B of §3, Chapter III).

We give necessary and sufficient conditions for the existence of a Green function for the system (K), (F) i.e. a function $G: \,]a,b[\times]a,b[\, \longrightarrow L(X)$ such that for f continuous and $c = 0$ the solution y of the system is given by

$$\text{(G)} \qquad y(t) = \int_a^b G(t,s)\cdot df(s) \qquad t\in \,]a,b[$$

(see Theorem 3.28 of Chapter III); we also characterize the Green function (see Theorem 3.29 of Chapter III) and show that the solution y is a continuous function of f (and K).

In order to obtain the representation (G) we have to solve preliminarily two important problems; I - Find a resolvent for the equation (K). II - Find integral representations associated to (F).

I - The resolvent of (K) is a function

$$R: \left]a,b\right[\times \left]a,b\right[\longrightarrow L(X)$$

that satisfies

$$(R^*) \qquad R(t,s) = I_X - \int_s^t d_\sigma K(t,\sigma) \circ R(\sigma,s) \qquad s,t \in \left]a,b\right[$$

$$(R_*) \qquad R(t,s) = I_X + \int_s^t R(t,\sigma) \circ d_\sigma K(\sigma,s) \qquad s,t \in \left]a,b\right[$$

and such that the solution of (K) with $y(t_o) = x$ and f continuous is given by

$$(\rho) \qquad y(t) = R(t,t_o) + \int_{t_o}^t R(t,\sigma) \cdot df(\sigma) \qquad t \in \left]a,b\right[$$

(see Theorem 1.5 of Chapter III).

In the particular instance of an integro-differential equation

$$(L) \qquad y(t)-y(s) + \int_s^t dA(\sigma) \cdot y(\sigma) = f(t)-f(s) \qquad s,t \in \left]a,b\right[$$

the existence of the resolvent (called harmonic operator in this case) was proved by Wall [W] and specially by Mac-Nerney [M] under the restriction that A is locally of bounded variation (and continuous). In this case Mac-Nerney also proved that there is a one-to-one correspondence between the space of coefficients A and the harmonic operators. We extend this correspondence to the general case (Theorems 2.1 and 2.3 of Chapter III) and prove that it is bicontinuous in a natural way. The proof in the general case however is much more difficult than the proof given in [M] where one applies directly the Banach fixed point theorem. In the general case in order to prove the existence of the resolvent and specially that it satisfies (R_*) we had to replace the natural norm of the space of resolvents by an equivalent one (Theorem 1.12 of Chapter III) and give a laborious proof that now we can get a contraction. By the way, this proof is made directly for the resolvent of (K) and this generalization explains why, for the resolvent of (L), we have to prove first the semivariation properties with respect to the second variable and only afterwards with respect to the first variable. This generalization also keeps the symmetry between the equations (R^*) and (R_*) satisfied by the resolvent, a symmetry that does not exist for differential equations or Volterra integral equations when they are written in their usual form. For equations of type (K) we also prove that there is a natural bicontinuous correspondence between the space of kernels K and the space of resolvents R (Theorems 1.27 and 1.30 of Chapter III) and we show that the solution y of (ρ) is a continuous function of f, x and K. We mention that part of the results of §2 of Chapter III on (L) have been extended by Maria Ignez de Souza [S] to the case where A allows discontinuities; this generalizes results of Hildebrandt [H-ie] in this direction.

II - The integral representation associated to F is necessary essentially in order to prove an identity of the form

$$F\left[\int_a^b \chi_{[a,t]}(s)R(t,s)\cdot df(s)\right] = \int_a^b F[\chi_{[s,b]}(t)R(t,s)]\,df(s);$$

this identity (the Dirichlet formula) is necessary in order to obtain the Green function for the system (K), (F) - item D and E of §3, Chapter III; in the item B we do a formal (algebraic) study of the system not using the integral representation for F. Both for this representation as for (K) we need the notion of function for bounded semivariation.

The present work has its origin in our attempts to extend our results of [H-IME], where we studied systems of the form

$$L[y](t) = y'(t) + A(t)y(t) = f(t) \qquad t \in]a,b[$$

$$F[y] = c$$

with $y \in G^{(1)}(]a,b[,X)$, $f \in G(]a,b[,X)$, $A \in G(]a,b[,L(X))$ and $F \in L[G(]a,b[,X),Y]$. We wanted to extend the results to the case where the coefficient A and the functions f and y allow discontinuities. Initially we tried to work with functions that were locally of bounded variation but in this case we had no integral representation for the linear constraint F; the same was true for other "natural" classes of functions. Afterwords we realized that the regulated functions, or their equivalence classes (see the end of §3, Chapter I), are the adequate ones since in this case we obtained good representation theorems for the elements $F \in L[\tilde{G}([a,b],X),Y]$, $F \in L[G(]a,b[,X),Y]$ etc. (Theorems 5.1, 5.6, 6.6 and 6.8 of Chapter I). In the numerical case $(X = Y = \mathbb{R})$ and for closed intervals this representation is due to Kaltenborn [K]; it requires the interior or Dushnik integral (see §1, Chapter I). We also obtain other representation theorems (see theorems 5.10, 5.11, 6.10, 6.12 and 6.16 of Chapter I); Theorem I.6.12 is a particular case of more general theorems on measure spaces (see [D]). For these and other results we need convergence theorems of the Helly type (theorems 5.8, 5.9, 6.3 of Chapter I). Of fundamental importance too are the formulas of Dirichlet and of substitution ((6), (10), (11), (12) and (13) of Chapter II) which are deduced from Theorem II.1.1; in the numerical case (i.e. $X = Y = \mathbb{R}$) and for continuous functions this theorem is essentially due to Bray [B].

All these results use a quite complete study we made in Chapter I of the functions of bounded semivariation (first defined by Gowurin, [G]), of the interior integral (due to Dushnik - see [H-ti] p.96) and of the regulated functions. We give much more results, specially in Chapter I, than we need in the rest of the work. These additional results or others that may be read only in the moment they are applied are given in smaller print and/or in appendices.

For other versions of the formulas of Dirichlet and of substitution see [H-DS]. For an unified presentation of the representation theorems mentioned above see [H-R]. For an abstract of the main results of these notes see [$H\text{-}BAMS_2$]. For related results see [Ca], [H] and [R].

The notation (III.2.5) refers to 2.5 of Chapter III; for a result in the same chapter we write only 2.5.

These notes were witten for the Analysis Meeting organized by the Sociedade Brasileira de Matemática at the Universidade de Campinas, from 15 to 25 July, 1974. They reproduce an advanced graduate course we gave at the Instituto de Matemática e Estatística da Universidade de São Paulo during the first semestrer of 1974. The audience of this course was very stimulating.

Special thanks are due to my colleague Prof. L.H.Jacy Monteiro who took in charge the publication of these notes and without whose help they would not have been ready for the Meeting.

CONTENTS

§ 0 - NOTATIONS

A - We always consider vector spaces over the complex field **C**, but all our results, with obvious adaptations, are valid for real vector spaces.

For intervals we use the usual notation, $]a,b[$, $[c,d]$ etc. $|c,d|$, where $c < d$, denotes any of the intervals $]c,d[$, $]c,d]$, $[c,d[$ and $[c,d]$; $\{c,d\}$ denotes the interval $[c,d]$ if $c \leqslant d$ and the interval $[d,c]$ if $d \leqslant c$.

Given real numbers s, t we write $s \wedge t = \mathit{inf}(s,t)$ and $s \vee t = \mathit{sup}(s,t)$.

Given a function $h: (t,s) \in B \times A \longmapsto h(t,s) \in Y$, for every $t \in B$, h^t denotes the function $s \in A \longmapsto h(t,s) \in Y$ and for every $s \in A$, h_s denotes the function $t \in B \longmapsto h(t,s) \in Y$.

Given a function $f: X \longmapsto Y$ and $A \subset X$, $f_{|A}$ denotes the restriction of f to A. I_X denotes the identical automorphism of X. Given an $A \subset X$, χ_A denotes the characteristic function of A: $\chi_A(x) = 1$ if $x \in A$ and $\chi_A(x) = 0$ if $x \in X$ and $x \notin A$. $Y: \mathbb{R} \longmapsto \mathbb{R}$ denotes the Heaviside function $Y = \chi_{[0,\infty[}$. We define $sg: \mathbb{R} \longrightarrow \{-1,0,1\}$ by $sg\, t = 1$ if $t > 0$, $= 0$ for $t = 0$ and $= -1$ if $t < 0$.

If X and Y are topological spaces, $\mathcal{C}(X,Y)$ denotes the set of all continuous functions of X into Y. If a sequence x_n converges to x in a topological space X, we write

$$x_n \xrightarrow{X} x \quad \text{or} \quad x_n \longrightarrow x.$$

If the sequence $t_n \in \mathbb{R}$ tends to t and is decreasing we write $t_n \downarrow t$; in an analogous way we define $t_n \uparrow t$ and $\delta \downarrow 0$. For $\alpha:]a,b] \longmapsto X$, $\alpha(t-)$ denotes the limit at the left, when it exists. In an analogous way we define $\alpha(t+)$.

Given $f: [a,b] \longrightarrow X$, where X is a normed space, $\|f(\ )\|$ denotes the function $t \in [a,b] \longmapsto \|f(t)\| \in \mathbb{R}_+$ and unless otherwise specified $\|f\|$ denotes $\mathit{sup}\{\|f(t)\| \mid a \leqslant t \leqslant b\}$.

The notion of summable series is defined in the sense of Bourbaki.

B - Given a closed interval $[a,b] \subset \mathbb{R}$ a *division* of $[a,b]$ is a finite sequence $d: t_0=a<t_1<t_2<\dots<t_n=b$. We write $|d| = n$ and $\Delta d = sup\{|t_i - t_{i-1}| \mid i = 1,2,\dots,|d|\}$. $\mathbb{D}_{[a,b]}$, or simply $\mathbb{D}$, denotes the set of all divisions of $[a,b]$. For $\varepsilon > 0$ we write $\mathbb{D}_\varepsilon = \{d \in \mathbb{D} \mid \Delta d < \varepsilon\}$; the class $\mathcal{D}_\Delta = \{\mathbb{D}_\varepsilon \mid \varepsilon > 0\}$ is a filter basis on $\mathbb{D}$.

Given two divisions $d_1, d_2 \in \mathbb{D}$ we denote by $d_1 \vee d_2$ the division of $[a,b]$ obtained by all points of d_1 and d_2. Given $d_1, d_2 \in \mathbb{D}$ we say that d_2 is *finer* than d_1, and we write $d_1 \leqslant d_2$, if every point of d_1 is a point of d_2. The relation $\leqslant$ is an order relation on $\mathbb{D}$ that makes it filtered on the right. For every $d \in \mathbb{D}$ we define

$$\mathbb{D}_d = \{d' \in \mathbb{D} \mid d \leqslant d'\};$$

the class $\mathcal{D}_\leqslant = \{\mathbb{D}_d \mid d \in \mathbb{D}\}$ is a filter basis on $\mathbb{D}$ which is finer than the filter basis $\mathcal{D}_\Delta$ and hence

0.1 - *Let* X *be a topological space and* $f: \mathbb{D} \longmapsto X$; *the existence of* $\lim_{\Delta d \to 0} f(d)$, *that is the limit over the filter basis* $\mathcal{D}_\Delta$, *implies the existence of* $\lim_{d \in \mathbb{D}} f(d)$, *that is, the limit over the filter basis* $\mathcal{D}_\leqslant$, *and both are equal.*

If X is a seminormed space and $f: [a,b] \longrightarrow X$, for $A \subset X$ we define the *oscilation* of f on A

$$\omega_A(f) = sup\{\|f(t) - f(s)\| \mid s,t \in A\};$$

for $d \in \mathbb{D}$ we write $\omega_i(f) = \omega_{[t_{i-1},t_i]}(f)$, $i = 1,2,\dots,|d|$ and $\omega_i^\bullet(f) = \omega_{]t_{i-1},t_i[}(f)$, $\omega_d(f) = \sup_{1 \leqslant i \leqslant |d|} \omega_i(f)$, $\omega_d^\bullet(f) = \sup_{1 \leqslant i \leqslant |d|} \omega_i^\bullet(f)$ and for $\delta > 0$ we write

$$\omega_\delta(f) = sup\{\|f(t) - f(s)\| \mid s,t \in [a,b],\ |t-s| \leqslant \delta\}.$$

$\mathcal{D}$ or $\mathcal{D}_{[a,b]}$ denotes the set of all pairs (d,ξ) where $d \in \mathbb{D}_{[a,b]}$ and $\xi = (\xi_1,\dots,\xi_{|d|})$ with $\xi_i \in [t_{i-1},t_i]$, $i = 1,2,\dots,|d|$. $\mathcal{D}^\bullet$ denotes the set of all pairs $(d,\xi^\bullet)$

where $d \in \mathbb{D}$ and $\xi^{\bullet} = (\xi_1^{\bullet}, \ldots, \xi_{|d|}^{\bullet})$ with $\xi_i^{\bullet} \in \,]t_{i-1}, t_i[$.

We say that a function $f\colon [a,b] \longrightarrow X$ is a step function, we write $f \in E([a,b], X)$, if there exists a $d \in \mathbb{D}$ such that f is constant in $]t_{t-1}, t_i[$, $i = 1,2,\ldots,|d|$.

C - A *bilinear triple* (BT) is a set of three vector spaces E, F, G, where F and G are Banach spaces, with a bilinear mapping $B\colon E \times F \longrightarrow G$; we write $x \cdot y = B(x,y)$ and denote the BT by $(E,F,G)_B$ or simply (E,F,G). A *topological* BT is a BT (E,F,G) where E too is a normed space and B is continuous; we suppose that $\|B\| \leqslant 1$.

EXAMPLES - Let W, X and Y be Banach spaces.

1. $E = L(X,Y)$, $F = X$, $G = Y$ and $B(u,x) = u(x)$.
2. $E = L(X,Y)$, $F = L(W,X)$, $G = L(W,Y)$ and $B(v,u) = v \circ u$.
3. $E = Y$, $F = Y'$, $G = \mathbf{C}$ and $B(y,y') = \langle y, y' \rangle$.
4. $E = G = Y$, $F = \mathbf{C}$ and $B(y,\lambda) = \lambda y$.

0.2 - a) Ex.1 is a particular instance of Ex.2: take $W = \mathbf{C}$.

b) Ex.3 is a particular instance of Ex.2: take $X = \mathbf{C}$ and $W = Y$.

c) Ex.4 is a particular instance of Ex.2: take $X = W = \mathbf{C}$.

Given a BT $(E, F, G)_B$ for every $x \in E$ we define

$$\|x\|_B = \sup\{\|B(x,y)\| \mid \|y\| \leqslant 1\}$$

and

$$E_B = \{x \in E \mid \|x\|_B < \infty\};$$

we endow E_B with the norm $\|\ \|_B$ and we say that the topological BT (E_B,F,G) is *associated* to the BT (E,F,G).

D - Let E be a vector space and Γ_E a set of seminorms defined on E such that $p_1, \ldots, p_m \in \Gamma_E$ implies

$$\sup[p_1, \ldots, p_m] \in \Gamma_E.$$

Γ_E defines a topology on E: the sets

$$V_{p,\varepsilon} = \{x \in E \mid p(x) < \varepsilon\} \quad p \in \Gamma, \quad \varepsilon > 0$$

form a basis of neighborhoods of 0; the sets $x_o+V_{p,\varepsilon}$ form a basis of neighborhoods of $x_o \in E$. Endowed with this topology E is called a locally convex space (LCS).

A LCS E is separated if and only if $p(x) = 0$ for every $p \in \Gamma_E$ implies $x = 0$.

A sequence x_n of a LCS E is called a *Cauchy sequence* if for every $p \in \Gamma_E$ and every $\varepsilon > 0$ there exists an $n_\varepsilon(p)$ such that for $n,m \geq n_\varepsilon(p)$ we have $p(x_n - x_m) < \varepsilon$. A separated sequentially complete LCS (SSCLCS) is a separated LCS in which every Cauchy sequence is convergent. A Frechet space is a SSCLCS whose topology can be defined by a countable set of seminorms (and is therefore metrisable).

EXAMPLES

LCS 1 - Every normed or seminormed space E is a LCS.

LCS 2 - If X is a LCS and K a compact space there is a natural structure of LCS on $E = \mathscr{C}(K,X)$: for every seminorm $p \in \Gamma_X$ we define a seminorm $p \in \Gamma_E$ by $p(f) = \sup_{t\in K} p[f(t)]$, where $f \in E = \mathscr{C}(K,X)$; we obtain on $\mathscr{C}(K,X)$ the topology of uniform convergence on K. If X is a Banach or a Frechet space, so is $\mathscr{C}(K,X)$.

LCS 3 - Let X be a normed space; $E = \mathscr{C}(]a,b[, X)$ becomes a LCS when endowed with the family of seminorms

$$\|f\|_{[c,d]} = \sup_{c\leq t\leq d} \|f(t)\|$$

where $[c,d]$ runs over all closed intervals of $]a,b[$. If X is complete, i.e. a Banach space, E is a Frechet space; its topology may be defined by the countable set of seminorms $\| \ \|_{\left[a+\frac{1}{n},\, b-\frac{1}{n}\right]}$, $n \in \mathbb{N}$.

LCS 4 - Let X be a LCS; $E = \mathscr{C}(]a,b[, X)$ becomes naturally a LCS when endowed with the family of seminorms

$$p_{[c,d]}[f] = \sup\{p[f(t)] \mid c \leq t \leq d\}$$

where $p \in \Gamma_X$ and $[c,d] \subset]a,b[$.

For LCS X and Y, $L(X,Y)$ denotes the vector space of all continuous linear mappings from X into Y; in order that a linear mapping $f: X \longrightarrow Y$ be continuous it is sufficient that it is continuous at the origin and hence for every $q \in \Gamma_Y$ there is a $p \in \Gamma_X$ and $a > 0$ such that $q[f(x)] \leqslant ap(x)$ for every $x \in X$.

LCS 5 - If X is a normed space and Y a LCS, on $L(X,Y)$ we consider the topology defined by the seminorms

$$p(f) = \sup\{p[f(x)] \mid x \in X, \|x\| \leqslant 1\}, \quad p \in \Gamma_Y.$$

If Y is a SSCLCS so is $L(X,Y)$.

If X is a LCS and $f: [a,b] \longrightarrow X$ for every $q \in \Gamma_X$ we define the oscilations as in B: for $A \subset X$ we write

$$\omega_{q,A}(f) = \sup\{q[f(t)-f(s)] \mid t,s \in A\}$$

and for $d \in \mathbf{D}$ we write

$$\omega_{q,i}(f) = \omega_{q,[t_{i-1},t_i]}(f), \quad \omega^{\bullet}_{q,i}(f) = \omega_{q,]t_{i-1},t_i[}(f),$$

etc.

A *locally convex* BT (LCBT) is a set of three vector spaces E, F, G, where F is a Banach space, G a SSCLCS, with a bilinear mapping $B: E \times F \longrightarrow G$.

E - In chapter III we will use the following

THEOREM 0.3 - *Let* X *be a complete metric space and* I *a topological space. For every* $i \in I$ *let* $T_i: X \longrightarrow X$ *be such that:*

1) $(T_i)_{i \in I}$ *is locally a uniform contraction, i.e., for every* $i_o \in I$ *there is a neighborhood* J *and a constant* $c_J < 1$ *such that*

$$d[T_i x, T_i y] \leqslant c_J d(x,y)$$

for all $x,y \in X$ *and every* $i \in J$.

2) *For every* $x \in X$ *the function* $i \in I \longmapsto T_i x \in X$ *is continuous.*

Then, if for every $x \in X$, x_i *denotes the fixed point of* T_i

(which exists by Banach contraction mapping theorem), the mapping $i \in I \longmapsto x_i \in X$ *is continuous.*

PROOF. Obviously it is enough to prove that the mapping is continuous at i_o. We have

$$\begin{aligned} d(x_i, x_{i_o}) &= d[T_i x_i , T_{i_o} x_{i_o}] \\ &\leqslant d[T_i x_i , T_i x_{i_o}] + d[T_i x_{i_o}, T_{i_o} x_{i_o}] \\ &\leqslant c_J d(x_i , x_{i_o}) + d[T_i x_{i_o}, T_{i_o} x_{i_o}] \end{aligned}$$

hence

$$d(x_i, x_{i_o}) \leqslant \frac{1}{1-c_J} d[T_i x_{i_o}, T_{i_o} x_{i_o}]$$

that by 2) goes to zero when $i \to i_o$.

CHAPTER I

THE INTERIOR INTEGRAL

§1 - *The Riemann-Stieltjes integral and the interior integral*

Let (E,F,G) be a BT, $\alpha: [a,b] \longrightarrow E$ and $f: [a,b] \longrightarrow F$. For $(d,\xi) \in \mathcal{D}$ and $(d,\xi^\bullet) \in \mathcal{D}^\bullet$ we write

$$\sigma_{d,\xi}(f;\alpha) = \sum_{i=1}^{|d|} [\alpha(t_i) - \alpha(t_{i-1})] f(\xi_i)$$

and

$$\sigma_{d,\xi^\bullet}(f;\alpha) = \sum_{i=1}^{|d|} [\alpha(t_i) - \alpha(t_{i-1})] f(\xi_i^\bullet).$$

We define

$$\int_a^b d\alpha(t)\cdot f(t) = \lim_{\Delta d \to 0} \sigma_{d,\xi}(f;\alpha)$$

and

$$\int_a^b \bullet d\alpha(t)\cdot f(t) = \lim_{d \in \mathbf{D}} \sigma_{d,\xi^\bullet}(f;\alpha)$$

if these limits exist. The first one is called *Riemann-Stieltjes integral* and the second one, the *Dushnik* or *interior integral*.

1.1 - *If* $\int_a^b d\alpha(t)\cdot f(t)$ *exists then there exists*

$$\int_a^b \bullet d\alpha(t)\cdot f(t) = \int_a^b d\alpha(t)\cdot f(t).$$

PROOF. Follows from $\mathcal{D}^\bullet \subset \mathcal{D}$ and 0.1.

THEOREM 1.2 - *Let* (E,F,G) *be a topological BT and*

$$\alpha: [a,b] \longrightarrow E, \quad f: [a,b] \longrightarrow F$$

bounded functions such that there exists $\int_a^b \cdot d\alpha(t)\cdot f(t)$; *if* α *or* f *is continuous there exists*

$$\int_a^b d\alpha(t)\cdot f(t) = \int_a^b \cdot d\alpha(t)\cdot f(t).$$

The proof is given in the appendix of this §.

THEOREM 1.3 - Integration by parts - *Given a BT* (E,F,G), $\alpha: [a,b] \longrightarrow E$ and $f: [a,b] \longrightarrow F$ *there exists*

$$\int_a^b d\alpha(t)\cdot f(t)$$

if and only if there exists $\int_a^b \alpha(t)\cdot df(t)$ *and then we have*

$$\int_a^b d\alpha(t)\cdot f(t) = \alpha(b)\cdot f(b) - \alpha(a)\cdot f(a) - \int_a^b \alpha(t)\cdot df(t).$$

PROOF. It follows immediately from

$$\sum_{i=1}^{|d|} [\alpha(t_i)-\alpha(t_{i-1})]\cdot f(\xi_i) = \alpha(b).f(b) - $$
$$- \alpha(a)\cdot f(a) - \sum_{j=1}^{|d|} \alpha(t_j)\,[f(\xi_{j+1})-f(\xi_j)]$$

where $\xi_o = a$ and $\xi_{|d|+1} = b$ (and $t_j \in [\xi_j, \xi_{j+1}]$).

FOR THE INTERIOR INTEGRAL THE INTEGRATION BY PARTS FORMULA IN GENERAL IS NOT VALID, UNLESS α OR f IS CONTINUOUS (Cf. Theorem 1.2).

See also Theorems 4.21 and 4.22.

THEOREM 1.4 - *Given* $c \in]a,b[$ *there exists* $\int_a^b \cdot d\alpha(t)\cdot f(t)$ *if and only if there exist* $\int_a^c \cdot d\alpha(t)\cdot f(t)$ *and* $\int_c^b \cdot d\alpha(t)\cdot f(t)$

and then we have

$$(\alpha) \qquad \int_a^b \bullet d\alpha(t)\cdot dt = \int_a^c \bullet d\alpha(t)\cdot f(t) + \int_c^b \bullet d\alpha(t)\cdot f(t).$$

PROOF. The existence of the second member of (α) implies the existence of the first since the set of all divisions $d\in \mathbb{D}_{[a,b]}$ that contain c is cofinal with the ordered filtered set $\mathbb{D}_{[a,b]}$ of all divisions. The other implication is trivial.

Even in the numerical case (i.e. $E = F = G = \mathbb{R}$) the analogous of Theorem 1.4 is not true for the Riemann-Stieltjes integral (unless α or f is continuous) as shows the example $\alpha = \chi_{[c,b]}$ and $f = \chi_{]c,b]}$: there exist $\int_a^c d\alpha(t)\cdot f(t)=0$ and $\int_c^b d\alpha(t)\cdot f(t) = 0$ but $\int_a^b d\alpha(t)\cdot f(t)$ does not exist.

APPENDIX

THEOREM 1.2 - *Let* (E,F,G) *be a topological BT, and*

$$\alpha: [a,b] \longrightarrow E, \qquad f: [a,b] \longrightarrow F$$

bounded functions such that there exists $\int_a^b \bullet d\alpha(t)\cdot f(t)$; *if* α *or* f *is continuous there exists*

$$\int_a^b d\alpha(t)\cdot f(t) = \int_a^b \bullet d\alpha(t)\cdot f(t).$$

PROOF. Since there exists $\int_a^b \bullet d\alpha(t)\cdot f(t)$, for every $\varepsilon > 0$ there is a $d_\varepsilon \in \mathbb{D}$, $d_\varepsilon: a = t_0^\varepsilon < t_1^\varepsilon < \ldots < t^\varepsilon_{|d_\varepsilon|} = b$, such that for $d \geqslant d_\varepsilon$ we have $\|\sigma_{d,\xi^\bullet} - \sigma_{d_\varepsilon,\xi_\varepsilon^\bullet}\| \leqslant \varepsilon$. Hence it is enough to prove that given $\varepsilon > 0$ there is a $\delta > 0$ such that for $d\in \mathbb{D}$ with $\Delta d < \delta$ we have

$$(\alpha) \qquad \|\sigma_{d,\xi} - \sigma_{d_\varepsilon,\xi_\varepsilon^\bullet}\| \leqslant 3\varepsilon.$$

I - Let us first consider the case when f is continuous and take $\delta > 0$ such that $\omega_\delta(f) \leqslant \dfrac{\varepsilon}{4|d_\varepsilon|\,\|\alpha\|}$. For $d \in \mathbb{D}$ with $\Delta d < \delta$ we define $\bar{d} = d \vee d_\varepsilon$ and we take $\bar{\xi}_j = \xi_i$ if $(\bar{t}_{j-1}, \bar{t}_j) = (t_{i-1}, t_i)$; then we have

$$(\beta) \qquad \|\sigma_{\bar{\alpha},\bar{\xi}} - \sigma_{d,\xi}\| \leqslant 2|d_\varepsilon|\cdot 2\|\alpha\|\omega_\delta(f) \leqslant \varepsilon.$$

Let us define a $\bar{\xi}^{\bullet} = (\bar{\xi}_1^{\bullet}, \ldots, \bar{\xi}^{\bullet}_{|d|})$ such that

$$(\gamma) \qquad \|\sigma_{\bar{d},\bar{\xi}} - \sigma_{\bar{d},\bar{\xi}^{\bullet}}\| \leqslant \varepsilon$$

and then, since we have $\bar{d} \geqslant d_\varepsilon$, it follows that

$$(\delta) \qquad \|\sigma_{\bar{d},\bar{\xi}^{\bullet}} - \sigma_{d_\varepsilon,\xi^{\bullet}}\| \leqslant \varepsilon$$

and from (β), (γ) and (δ) follows (α). In order to define $\bar{\xi}^{\bullet}$ we take $\bar{\xi}_j^{\bullet} \in \,]\bar{t}_{j-1}, \bar{t}_j[$ such that

$$\|f(\bar{\xi}_j^{\bullet}) - f(\bar{\xi}_j)\| \leqslant \frac{\varepsilon}{2|\bar{d}|\,\|\alpha\|}$$

which implies (γ).

II - Let us now consider the case when α is continuous. We take $\delta > 0$ such that

$$(a) \quad \omega_{2\delta}(\alpha) \leqslant \frac{\varepsilon}{4|d_\varepsilon|\,\|f\|} \qquad\qquad (b) \quad 2\delta < \inf_{1 \leqslant i \leqslant |d_\varepsilon|} |t_i^\varepsilon - t_{i-1}^\varepsilon|.$$

Again for $d \in \mathbb{D}$ with $\Delta d < \delta$, we define $\bar{d} = d \vee d_\varepsilon$ and we take $\bar{\xi}_j = \xi_i$ if $(\bar{t}_{j-1}, \bar{t}_j) = (t_{i-1}, t_i)$. Then by (a) we have

$$(\beta') \qquad \|\sigma_{\bar{d},\bar{\xi}} - \sigma_{d,\xi}\| \leqslant 2|d_\varepsilon|\cdot 2\|f\|\omega_\delta(\alpha) \leqslant \varepsilon.$$

Let us define a $(\tilde{d}, \tilde{\xi}^{\bullet})$ with $\tilde{d} \geqslant d_\varepsilon$ such that

$$(\gamma') \qquad \|\sigma_{\bar{d},\bar{\xi}} - \sigma_{\tilde{d},\tilde{\xi}^{\bullet}}\| \leqslant \varepsilon.$$

Since $\tilde{d} \geqslant d_\varepsilon$, we have

$$(\delta') \qquad \|\sigma_{\tilde{d},\tilde{\xi}^{\bullet}} - \sigma_{d_\varepsilon,\xi_\varepsilon^{\bullet}}\| \leqslant \varepsilon$$

and (β'), (γ') and (δ') imply (α).

Definition of $(\tilde{d},\tilde{\xi}^\bullet)$:

(i) Let $\bar{t}_j$ be a point of $\bar{d}$; if $\bar{t}_j \neq t_i^\varepsilon$ for $i = 1,2,\ldots,|d_\varepsilon|-1$ and $\bar{\xi}_j = \bar{t}_j = \bar{\xi}_{j+1}$ then we have

$$[\alpha(\bar{t}_j) - \alpha(\bar{t}_{j-1})]\cdot f(\bar{\xi}_j) + [\alpha(\bar{t}_{j+1})-\alpha(\bar{t}_j)]\cdot f(\bar{\xi}_{j+1}) =$$

$$= [\alpha(\bar{t}_{j+1}) - \alpha(\bar{t}_{j-1})]\cdot f(\bar{t}_j)$$

with

$$|\bar{t}_{j+1}-\bar{t}_{j-1}| < \inf_{1\leq i\leq |d_\varepsilon|} |t_i^\varepsilon - t_{i-1}^\varepsilon|$$

by (b). If we eliminate such points $\bar{t}_j$ (and enumerate again the remaining ones) we will have that if $\bar{t}_j \neq t_i^\varepsilon$ for $i = 1,2,\ldots,|d_\varepsilon|-1$ we cannot have simultaneously $\bar{\xi}_j = \bar{t}_j$ and $\bar{\xi}_{j+1} = \bar{t}_j$. We have $|\bar{t}_j-\bar{t}_{j-1}| \leq 2\delta$.

(ii) If $\bar{t}_{j-1} = t_i^\varepsilon = \bar{\xi}_j$ or $\bar{t}_j = t_i^\varepsilon = \bar{\xi}_j$ then we take $\tilde{t}_{j-1} = \bar{t}_{j-1}$, $\tilde{t}_j = \bar{t}_j$ and $\tilde{\xi}_j^\bullet \in]\tilde{t}_{j-1},\tilde{t}_j[$. By (a) we have

$$\|[\alpha(\bar{t}_j)-\alpha(\bar{t}_{j-1})]\cdot f(\bar{\xi}_j) - [\alpha(\tilde{t}_j)-\alpha(\tilde{t}_{j-1})]\cdot f(\tilde{\xi}_j^\bullet)\| \leq$$

$$\leq \omega_{2\delta}(\alpha)\cdot 2\|f\| \leq \frac{\varepsilon}{2|d_\varepsilon|} .$$

(iii) If $\bar{t}_{j-1} \neq t_i^\varepsilon$ for every i and $\bar{\xi}_j = \bar{t}_{j-1}$ we take $\tilde{t}_{j-1} < \bar{t}_{j-1}$ such that $\tilde{t}_{j-1} > \bar{\xi}_{j-1}$ (which is possible by (i)) and such that

$$\|\alpha(\tilde{t}_{j-1})-\alpha(\bar{t}_{j-1})\| \leq \frac{\varepsilon}{2|\bar{d}|\ \|f\|}$$

and $\tilde{\xi}_j^\bullet = \bar{\xi}_j$ and $\tilde{t}_j = \bar{t}_j$, i.e. "we move the point $\bar{t}_{j-1}$ slightly to the left". Then we have

$$\|[\alpha(\bar{t}_j)-\alpha(\bar{t}_{j-1})]\cdot f(\bar{\xi}_j) - [\alpha(\tilde{t}_j)-\alpha(\tilde{t}_{j-1})]\cdot f(\tilde{\xi}_j^\bullet)\| \leq \frac{\varepsilon}{2|\bar{d}|}$$

(iv) In an analogous way if we have $\bar{t}_j \neq t_i^\varepsilon$ for every i and $\bar{\xi}_j = \bar{t}_j$ "we move the point $\bar{t}_j$ slightly to the right".

By (b) between any two points of d_ε there is at least one point of $\bar{d}$ and therefore we have considered all possible cases in which $\bar{\xi}_j$ is not an interior point of $(\bar{t}_{j-1},\bar{t}_j)$.

We have

$$\|\sigma_{\bar{d},\bar{\xi}} - \sigma_{\tilde{d},\tilde{\xi}^\bullet}\| \leq \sum_{j=1}^{|\bar{d}|} \| [\alpha(\bar{t}_j)-\alpha(\bar{t}_{j-1})] f(\bar{\xi}_j) - [\alpha(\tilde{t}_j)-\alpha(\tilde{t}_{j-1})] f(\tilde{\xi}_j^\bullet)\| < \varepsilon$$

because in this sum we have $\leq |d_\varepsilon|$ summands of the type that appeared in (ii) and $\leq |\bar{d}|$ summands of the type that appeared in (iii) and (iv); this completes the proof of (γ').

§2 - *The Riemann integral and the Darboux integral*

In what follows we recall the properties of the Riemann and Darboux integrals for Banach space valued functions. For more details see [H-IME]; appendix of chapter I.

A - Let X be a Banach space and $f: [a,b] \longrightarrow X$; we say that f is *Riemann integrable*, and we write $f \in R([a,b],X)$, if there exists

$$\int_a^b f(t)dt = \lim_{\Delta d \to 0} \sum_{i=1}^{|d|} f(\xi_i)(t_i - t_{i-1})$$

(where $\xi_i \in [t_{i-1}, t_i]$).

We write $R([a,b]) = R([a,b],\mathbb{C})$.

2.1 - $\mathcal{C}([a,b],X) \subset R([a,b],X)$.

2.2 - If $f \in R([a,b],X)$ we have $\|\int_a^b f(t)dt\| \leq (b-a)\|f\|$.

2.3 - If $f_n \in R([a,b],X)$ and $f: [a,b] \longrightarrow X$ are such that $\|f_n - f\| \to 0$, then $f \in R([a,b],X)$ and

$$\int_a^b f_n(t)dt \longrightarrow \int_a^b f(t)dt.$$

Hence $R([a,b],X)$ is a Banach space when endowed with the sup norm.

However $f \in R([a,b],X)$ does not imply $\|f(\ )\| \in R([a,b])$; f and $\|f(\ )\|$ may even be not Lebesgue integrable and even not measurable:

EXAMPLE. We take the Hilbert space $X = \ell_2([a,b])$, that is, the space of all functions $x: [a,b] \longrightarrow \mathbf{C}$ such that

$$\sum_{a\leqslant t\leqslant b} |x(t)|^2 < \infty;$$

e_t denotes the element of $\ell_2([a,b])$ such that $e_t(t) = 1$ and $e_t(s) = 0$ for $s \in [a,b]$, $s \neq t$. Let

$$\psi: t \in [a,b] \longmapsto \psi(t) \in \mathbf{C}$$

be any bounded function; we define $f: [a,b] \longrightarrow \ell_2([a,b])$ by $f(t) = \psi(t)e_t$.

a) $f \in R([a,b], \ell_2([a,b]))$ and $\int_s^t f(\sigma)d\sigma = 0$ for any $a \leqslant s < t \leqslant b$.

PROOF. Let us give the proof for $s = a$ and $t = b$; we have

$$\|\sigma_{d,\xi}(f)\| = \|\sum_{i=1}^{|d|} \psi(\xi_i)e_{\xi_i}(t_i - t_{i-1})\| \leqslant$$

$$\leqslant \|\psi\| \left[\sum_{i=1}^{|d|} |t_i - t_{i-1}|^2\right]^{\frac{1}{2}} \leqslant \|\psi\| (b-a)^{\frac{1}{2}}(\Delta d)^{\frac{1}{2}}$$

(because $|t_i - t_{i-1}|^2 \leqslant |t_i - t_{i-1}|\Delta d$ and therefore $\sum_{i=1}^{|d|} |t_i - t_{i-1}|^2 \leqslant (b-a)\Delta d$) which implies the result.

b) $\|f(\ )\| \notin R([a,b])$ because $\|f(t)\| = |\psi(t)|$ and this function is only supposed to be bounded and not necessarily Lebesgue integrable nor measurable.

If (E,F,G) is a topological BT, $f \in R([a,b],E)$ and $g \in R([a,b],F)$ does not necessarily imply that $f \cdot g \in R([a,b],G)$ nor does it imply

$$(\alpha) \qquad \int_a^b d_t\left[\int_a^t f(s)ds\right]\cdot g(t) = \int_a^b f(t)\cdot g(t)dt.$$

EXAMPLE. We take $E = F = \ell_2([a,b])$, $G = \mathbf{C}$ and

$$B(x,y) = (x|y) = \sum_{a\leqslant t\leqslant b} x(t)\overline{y(t)},$$

the inner product of the Hilbert space $\ell_2([a,b])$. For the function $f \in R([a,b],E)$ of the preceding example we may have $f \cdot f \notin R([a,b])$ since $(f\cdot f)(t) = |\psi(t)|^2$ and $|\psi(\ )|^2$ may be any bounded positive function.

Also by a) of the preceding example the first member of (α) is zero but the second member may not exist or may be different from the first one.

2.4 - Given $f \in R([a,b],X)$ take $g(t) = g(a) + \int_a^t f(s)ds$; for $a \leq s \leq \xi \leq t \leq b$ and S dense in $[s,t]$ we have

$$\|g(t)-g(s)-f(\xi)(t-s)\| \leq (t-s) \sup_{\sigma \in S} \|f(\sigma)-f(\xi)\|.$$

B - Let X be a Banach space and $f: [a,b] \longmapsto X$; we say that f is *Darboux integrable*, and we write $f \in D([a,b],X)$ if f satisfies the Darboux condition:

$$\lim_{\Delta d \to 0} \sum_{i=1}^{|d|} \omega_i(f)(t_i - t_{i-1}) = 0.$$

2.5 - $D([a,b],X) \subset R([a,b],X)$.

2.6 - If X is finite dimensional we have

$$D([a,b],X) = R([a,b],X).$$

For Banach spaces of infinite dimension a Riemann integrable function does not necessarily satisfy the Darboux condition.

EXAMPLES. 1. We take $X = \ell_2(\mathbb{N})$ and let $r_1, r_2, \ldots$ be any enumeration of the rationals of $[a,b]$; we define $f \in R([a,b],X)$ by $f(t) = e_n$ if $t = r_n$ and $f(t) = 0$ if t is irrational; for $a \leq s < t \leq b$ we have

$$\int_s^t f(\sigma)d\sigma = 0 \quad \text{but} \quad \sum_{i=1}^{|d|} \omega_i(f)(t_i - t_{i-1}) = (b-a)\sqrt{2}.$$

2. We take $X = L_\infty([a,b])$ and $f(t) = \chi_{]a,t]}$, $t \in [a,b]$; we have

a) $f \in R([a,b],L_\infty([a,b]))$; indeed, it is easy to verify that for $d \leq \bar{d}$ we have $\|\sigma_{\bar{d},\bar{\xi}}(f) - \sigma_{d,\xi}(f)\| \leq \Delta d$.

b) $f \notin D([a,b],L_\infty([a,b]))$; indeed,

$$\sum_{i=1}^{|d|} \omega_i(f)(t_i - t_{i-1}) = \sum_{i=1}^{|d|} (t_i - t_{i-1}) = b-a.$$

c) f is discontinuous at all points of $[a,b]$; indeed,

for $a < s < t < b$ we have $\|f(t)-f(s)\| = \|\chi_{]s,t]}\| = 1$.

d) f is not measurable (and therefore not Bochner-Lebesgue integrable); indeed, from c) it follows that for $\varepsilon > 0$ there does not exist a compact $K_\varepsilon \subset [a,b]$ with Lebesgue measure $<\varepsilon$ and such that $f_{|CK_\varepsilon}$ is continuous.

This example is important since f is used to represent the identical automorphism of $\mathcal{C}([a,b])$: for every $\phi \in \mathcal{C}([a,b])$ we have

$$\int_a^b \phi(t)df(t) = \phi.$$

This example also shows that the function $\mathcal{I}_f$, where $\mathcal{I}_f(t) = \int_a^t f(s)ds$, $t \in [a,b]$, is absolutelly continuous but is not derivable at any point:

$$\mathcal{I}_f(t)(\sigma) = \left(\int_a^t f(s)ds\right)(\sigma) = (t-\sigma)\chi_{]a,t]}(\sigma)$$

and it is easy to see that

$$\left\|\frac{1}{h}\left[\mathcal{I}_f(t+h) - \mathcal{I}_f(t)\right] - f(t)\right\| = 1.$$

2.7 - $\mathcal{C}([a,b],X) \subset D([a,b],X)$.

2.8 - $f \in D([a,b],X)$ implies $\|f(\ )\| \in D([a,b])$ and $\left\|\int_a^b f(t)dt\right\| \leqslant \int_a^b \|f(t)\|dt$.

2.9 - If $f, f_n \in D([a,b],X)$ are such that $\|f_n\| \leqslant M$ for every $n \in \mathbb{N}$ and $f_n(t) \longrightarrow f(t)$ for every $t \in [a,b]$ then

$$\int_a^b \|f_n(t)-f(t)\|dt \longrightarrow 0 \quad \text{and} \quad \int_a^b f_n(t)dt \longrightarrow \int_a^b f(t)dt.$$

2.10 - If the sequence $f_n \in D([a,b],X)$ converges uniformely to the function $f: [a,b] \longrightarrow X$ then $f \in D([a,b],X)$, $\int_a^b \|f_n(t)-f(t)\|dt \longrightarrow 0$ and $\int_a^b f_n(t)dt \longrightarrow \int_a^b f(t)dt$. Endowed with the sup norm $D([a,b],X)$ is a Banach space.

2.11 - If (E,F,G) is a topological BT, $f \in D([a,b],E)$ and $g \in D([a,b],F)$ imply $f \cdot g \in D([a,b],G)$.

If $\bar{\int}_a^b$ denotes the usual upper Riemann integral for positive, bounded numerical functions we have

2.12 - Given $f: [a,b] \longrightarrow X$ then $f \in D([a,b],X)$ if and only if for every $\varepsilon > 0$ there is a step function $f_\varepsilon \in E([a,b],X)$ such that $\bar{\int}_a^b \|f(t)-f_\varepsilon(t)\| dt \leq \varepsilon$.

2.13 - Let $f_n \in D([a,b],X)$ and $f: [a,b] \longrightarrow X$ be such that $\|f\| \leq M$ and $\bar{\int}_a^b \|f_n(t)-f(t)\| dt \longrightarrow 0$, then $f \in D([a,b],X)$ and

$$\int_a^b f_n(t)dt \longrightarrow \int_a^b f(t)dt.$$

§3 - *Regulated functions*

In this § X denotes a Banach space. We say that a function $f: [a,b] \longrightarrow X$ is *regulated*, and we write $f \in G([a,b],X)$, if f has only discontinuities of the first kind, i.e., for every $t \in [a,b[$ there exists $f(t+)$ and for every $t \in]a,b]$ there exists $f(t-)$.

THEOREM 3.1. *Given* $f: [a,b] \longrightarrow X$ *the following properties are equivalent*

a) f *is the uniform limit of step functions.*

b) $f \in G([a,b],X)$.

c) For every $\varepsilon > 0$ *there exists* $d \in \mathbb{D}$ *such that* $\omega_d^{\bullet}(f) < \varepsilon$.

PROOF. a) $\Longrightarrow$ b). Given $t_n \downarrow t \in [a,b[$ we have

$$\|f(t_n)-f(t_m)\| \leq \|f(t_n)-f_\varepsilon(t_n)\| + \|f_\varepsilon(t_n)-f_\varepsilon(t+)\| +$$
$$+ \|f_\varepsilon(t+)-f_\varepsilon(t_m)\| + \|f_\varepsilon(t_m)-f(t_m)\| \leq$$
$$\leq 2\varepsilon + \|f_\varepsilon(t_n)-f_\varepsilon(t+)\| + \|f_\varepsilon(t_m)-f_\varepsilon(t+)\|$$

and this implies the existence of $f(t+)$.

b) $\Longrightarrow$ c). Given $\varepsilon > 0$, for $t \in]a,b[$ the existence of

$f(t+)$ and $f(t-)$ implies that there exists $\delta_t > 0$ such that $\omega_{]t-\delta_t,t[}(f) < \varepsilon$ and $\omega_{]t,t+\delta_t[}(f) < \varepsilon$; analogously there exists $\delta_a > 0$ such that $\omega_{]a,a+\delta_a[}(f) < \varepsilon$ and there exists $\delta_b > 0$ such that $\omega_{]b-\delta_b,b[}(f) < \varepsilon$. The sets

$$[a,a+\delta_a[,\quad]t-\delta_t,t+\delta_t[,\quad]b-\delta_b,b[$$

form an open convering of $[a,b]$; if

$$[a,a+\delta_a[,\ ]s_1-\delta_{s_1},s_1+\delta_{s_1}[,\ ]s_2-\delta_{s_2},s_2+\delta_{s_2}[,\ldots$$

$$\ldots,]s_m-\delta_{s_m},\ s_m+\delta_{s_m}[,\ ]b-\delta_b,b]$$

is a finite subcovering we take

$$d:\ t_o = a < t_1 < t_2 < \ldots < t_{|d|} = b$$

such that

$$t_o = a,\quad s_1-\delta_{s_1} < t_1 < a+\delta_a,\quad t_2 = s_1,\ldots$$

$$\ldots,\ s_i-\delta_{s_i} < t_{2i-1} < s_{i-1}+\delta_{s_{i-1}},\quad t_{2i} = s_i,\ldots,\ t_{|d|} = b$$

and we have $\omega_d^{\bullet}(f) < \varepsilon$.

c) $\Longrightarrow$ a). If $\omega_d^{\bullet}(f) < \varepsilon$ we define $f_{d,\xi^{\bullet}} \in E([a,b],X)$ by

$$f_{d,\xi^{\bullet}} = \sum_{i=1}^{|d|} f(\xi_i^{\bullet})\chi_{]t_{i-1},t_i[} + \sum_{j=0}^{|d|} f(t_j)\chi_{\{t_j\}}$$

and we obviously have $\|f-f_{d,\xi^{\bullet}}\| \leqslant \varepsilon$.

COROLLARY 3.2. *Given* $f \in G([a,b],X)$ *we have*

a) For every $\varepsilon > 0$ *the sets*

$$\{t \in [a,b[\ \mid\ \|f(t+)-f(t)\| \geqslant \varepsilon\}$$

and

$$\{t \in]a,b]\ \mid\ \|f(t)-f(t-)\| \geqslant \varepsilon\}$$

are finite.

b) The set of discontinuities of f *is countable.*

PROOF. b) follows from a) and a) follows from c) of Theorem 3.1.

3.3 - $\mathcal{G}([a,b],X) \subset G([a,b],X)$.

3.4 - $BV([a,b],X) \subset G([a,b],X)$.

PROOF. See [H-IME], Theorem I.2.7.

a) of Theorem 3.1 implies

3.5 - *The uniform limit of regulated functions is a regulated function.*

Therefore, if we endow $G([a,b],X)$ with the norm

$$\|f\| = \sup_{a \leq t \leq b} \|f(t)\|$$

we have

THEOREM 3.6. $G([a,b],X)$ *is a Banach space; and*

$$G([a,b],X) \subset D([a,b],X).$$

3.7. *If* (E,F,G) *is a topological BT, then* $f \in G([a,b],E)$ *and* $g \in G([a,b],F)$ *imply* $f \cdot g \in G([a,b],G)$.

THEOREM 3.8. *Given* $f,g: [a,b] \longrightarrow X$ *the following properties are equivalent*

a) $f \in G([a,b],X)$ *and* $g(t) = g(a) + \int_a^t f(s)ds$ *for every* $t \in [a,b]$.

b) For every $t \in [a,b[$ *there exists* $g'_+(t) = f(t+)$ *and for every* $t \in]a,b]$ *there exists* $g'_-(t) = f(t-)$.

c) $f \in G([a,b],X)$ *and* g *is a primitive of* f *(i.e.,* g *is continuous and outside of a countable subset of* $[a,b]$ *there exists* $g'(t) = f(t)$*).*

PROOF. a) $\Longrightarrow$ b). We will prove that for $t_o \in [a,b[$ we have $g'_+(t_o) = f(t_o+)$. We have

$$\frac{1}{h}\Big[g(t_o+h)-g(t_o)\Big] - f(t_o) = \frac{1}{h}\int_{t_o}^{t_o+h} f(s)ds - f(t_o+) =$$

$$= \frac{1}{h}\int_{t_o}^{t_o+h} [f(s)-f(t_o+)]ds.$$

The result follows because for every $\varepsilon > 0$ there is a $\delta > 0$ such that for $t_o < s < t_o+\delta$ we have $\|f(s)-f(t_o+)\| < \varepsilon$.

b) $\Longrightarrow$ c). By b) we have $f \in G([a,b],X)$ and therefore by 3.2.a) the subset of points where we have $f(t+) \neq f(t)$ or

$f(t-) \neq f(t)$ is countable; at the other points we have then $g'(t) = f(t)$. g is obviously continuous.

c) $\Longrightarrow$ a). By a) of Theorem 3.1 there exists a sequence of step functions $f_n \in E([a,b],X)$ that converges uniformly to f. We define

$$g_n(t) = g(a) + \int_a^t f_n(s)ds;$$

it is immediate that this sequence g_n converges uniformly to $\bar{g}$ where $\bar{g}(t) = g(a) + \int_a^t f(s)ds$. $\bar{g}$ and g are continuous functions, $\bar{g}(a) = g(a)$, and $\bar{g}$ is a primitive of f (by a) $\Longrightarrow$ b) $\Longrightarrow$ c)), therefore there exists $\bar{g}'(t) = g'(t)$ outside of a contable subset of $[a,b]$. By [C] 3.2.2 we have then $\bar{g} = g$.

Given $f: [a,b] \longrightarrow X$ we write $f \in c_o([a,b],X)$ if for every $\varepsilon > 0$ the set $\{t \in [a,b] \mid \|f(t)\| \geqslant \varepsilon\}$ is finite. It is obvious that

3.9 - $c_o([a,b],X)$ *is a closed subspace of* $G([a,b],X)$.

THEOREM 3.10. *Given* $f: [a,b] \longmapsto X$ *the following properties are equivalent:*

a) $f \in G([a,b],X)$ *and* $\int_s^t f(\sigma)d\sigma = 0$ *for all* $s,t \in [a,b]$.

b) $f \in G([a,b],X)$ *and* $f(t-) = 0$ *for all* $t \in]a,b]$.

c) $f \in G([a,b],X)$ *and* $f(t+) = 0$ *for all* $t \in [a,b[$.

d) $f \in c_o([a,b],X)$.

PROOF. If we take $g(t) = \int_a^t f(s)ds$ the equivalence of a), b) and c) follows from the equivalence of a), b) and c) of theorem 3.8; it is obvious that d) implies b) and c); by c) of Theorem 3.1 b) and c) imply d).

DEFINITION. $G_-([a,b],X) = \{f \in G([a,b],X) \mid f(a) = 0$ and $f(t) = f(t-)$ for $t \in]a,b]\}$.

If we recall that the operators

$$\Phi_a: f \in G([a,b],X) \longmapsto f(a) \in X$$

and

$$\Phi_t: f \in G([a,b],X) \longmapsto f(t)-f(t-) \in X,$$

$t \in]a,b]$, are continuous and

$$G_-([a,b],X) = \bigcap_{a \leqslant t \leqslant b} \Phi_t^{-1}(0);$$

hence

3.11 - $G_-([a,b],X)$ *is a closed subspace of* $G([a,b],X)$.

DEFINITION. $f \in G([a,b],X)$: we define $(I_- f)(t) = f(t-)$ if $t \in]a,b]$ and $(I_- f)(a) = 0$.

THEOREM 3.12. *We have*

a) I_- *is a continuous projection of* $G([a,b],X)$ *onto* $G_-([a,b],X)$.

b) The kernel of I_- *is* $c_o([a,b],X)$.

c) $G_-([a,b],X) \cap c_o([a,b],X) = \{0\}$ *and*

$$G_-([a,b],X) + c_o([a,b],X) = G([a,b],X);$$

more precisely every $f \in G([a,b],X)$ *may be written uniquely as* $f = f_- + f_o$ *where* $f_- \in G_-([a,b],X)$ *and* $f_o \in c_o([a,b],X)$; *we have* $f_- = I_- f$ *and* $f_o = f - I_- f$.

PROOF. a) Let us prove that $I_- f$ is regulated: for every $t \in [a,b[$ we have $(I_- f)(t+) = f(t+)$ because if

$$\| f(t+) - f(s) \| \leqslant \varepsilon$$

for every $s \in]t,t+\delta[$ then also $\| f(t+) - f(s-) \| \leqslant \varepsilon$ i.e. $\| f(t+) - (I_- f)(s) \| \leqslant \varepsilon$ for every $s \in]t,t+\delta[$. In an analogous way we prove that $(I_- f)(t-) = f(t-) = (I_- f)(t)$ for $t \in]a,b]$. Hence $I_- f \in G_-([a,b],X)$. It is immediate that I_- is a projection (i.e. $I_-(I_- f) = I_- f$), is continuous ($\| I_- f \| \leqslant \| f \|$) and is onto $G_-([a,b],X)$ (since $I_- f = f$ if and only if $f \in G_-([a,b],X)$).

b) It follows from the equivalence of b) and d) in Theorem 3.10.

c) It follows immediately from a) and b).

If $\tilde{G}([a,b],X)$ denotes the Banach quotient space

$$G([a,b],X)/c_o([a,b],X),$$

it follows from Theorem 3.12 that

3.13 - $\tilde{G}([a,b],X)$ *is isometric to* $G_-([a,b],X)$.

§4 - Functions of bounded B-variation

A - Given a BT $(E,F,G)_B$ and $\alpha: [a,b] \longrightarrow E$, for every $d \in \mathbb{D}$ we define

$$SB_d[\alpha] = SB_{[a,b],d}[\alpha] =$$

$$= \sup\{\| \sum_{i=1}^{|d|} [\alpha(t_i)-\alpha(t_{i-1})]\cdot y_i \| \mid y_i \in F, \|y_i\| \leqslant 1\}$$

and

$$SB[\alpha] = SB_{[a,b]}[\alpha] = \sup\{SB_d[\alpha] \mid d \in \mathbb{D}\};$$

$SB[\alpha]$ is the *B-variation* of α (on $[a,b]$). We say that α is a *function of bounded B-variation*, and write $\alpha \in SB([a,b],E)$, if $SB[\alpha] < \infty$.

REMARK 1. If α is a function of several variables $s,t,\ldots$ and we calculate the B-variation with respect to t, for instance, we write $SB^{(t)}[\alpha(s,t,\ldots)]$.

The following properties are immediate:

4.1 - $SB([a,b],E)$ *is a vector space and*

$$\alpha \in SB([a,b],E) \longmapsto SB[\alpha] \in \mathbb{R}_+$$

is a seminorm.

4.2 - *For* $\alpha \in SB([a,b],E)$ *we have*

a) The function $t \in [a,b] \longmapsto SB_{[a,t]}[\alpha] \in \mathbb{R}_+$ *is monotonicaly increasing;*

b) $SB_{[a,b]}[\alpha] \leqslant SB_{[a,c]}[\alpha] + SB_{[c,b]}[\alpha]$ *for every* $c \in]a,b[$.

DEFINITION. $SB_o([a,b],E) = \{\alpha \in SB([a,b],E) \mid \alpha(a) = 0\}$.

THEOREM 4.3. *Let* (E_B,F,G) *be the topological BT associated to the BT* (E,F,G) *(see §0.C); we have*

$$SB_o([a,b],E_B) = SB_o([a,b],E)$$

and the functions $\alpha \in SB_o([a,b],E_B)$ *are bounded.*

PROOF. Given $\alpha \in SB_o([a,b],E)$ we have

$$\|\alpha(t)\|_B = \sup_{\|y\| \leqslant 1} \|\alpha(t)\cdot y\| \leqslant SB[\alpha]$$

since $\alpha(a) = 0$. The rest is obvious since the definition of $SB[\alpha]$ depends on no topology on E.

B - If (E,F,G) is a LCTB and $\alpha: [a,b] \longmapsto E$, for $d \in \mathbb{D}$ and $q \in \Gamma_G$ we define

$$SB_{q,d}[\alpha] = \sup\{q\left[\sum_{i=1}^{|d|} [\alpha(t_i)-\alpha(t_{i-1})]\cdot y_i\right] \mid y_i \in F,\ \|y_i\| \leqslant 1\}$$

and

$$SB_q[\alpha] = \sup\{SB_{q,d}[\alpha] \mid d \in \mathbb{D}\}$$

is, by definition, the q-B-*variation* of α. We say that α is a *function of bounded* B-*variation*, and we write

$$\alpha \in SB([a,b],E),$$

if for every $q \in \Gamma_G$ we have $SB_q[\alpha] < \infty$.

REMARK 2. Unless otherwise specified, all the results of this § or, more generally, of this work are valid if we replace the BT (E,F,G) or its particular instances (see item C) by a LCBT $(\bar{E},\bar{F},\bar{G})$ or its particularisations; for this purpose we replace in the proofs the norm of G by the seminorms $q \in \Gamma_{\bar{G}}$.

C - Examples

Ex. $SV([a,b],L(X,Y))$ - Given a normed space X and a Banach space Y we consider the BT $(L(X,Y),X,Y)$ (see ex. 1 of §0,C); then we write $SV[\alpha]$ instead of $SB[\alpha]$ and $SV([a,b],L(X,Y))$ instead of $SB([a,b],L(X,Y))$. The elements of $SV([a,b],L(X,Y))$ are called *functions of bounded semi-variation*.

Ex. $BV([a,b],Y')$ - If we consider the BT $(Y,Y',\mathbf{C})$ (see ex.3 of §0,C) we write $V[\alpha]$ instead of $SB[\alpha]$ and $BV([a,b],Y')$ instead of $SB([a,b],Y')$. We say that the elements of $BV([a,b],Y')$ are *functions of bounded variation*. Obviously we have

$$V_d[\alpha] = \sup\{|\sum_{i=1}^{|d|} \langle\alpha(t_i)-\alpha(t_{i-1}),y_i\rangle| \mid y_i \in Y,\ \|y_i\| < 1\} =$$
$$= \sum_{i=1}^{|d|} \|\alpha(t_i)-\alpha(t_{i-1})\|$$

and we obtain therefore the usual notion of function of bounded variation, i.e., a function α such that its *variation* $V[\alpha] = \sup_{d \in \mathbb{D}} V_d[\alpha]$ is finite. Of course this definition may be given for any normed space. For real functions we obtain the usual notion, i.e., functions that are the difference of two monotonic ones.

REMARK 3. It is immediate that

$$SV([a,b],L(X,\mathbf{C})) = BV([a,b],X').$$

REMARK 4. If X is a Banach space we have

$$R^{(1)}([a,b],X) \subset BV([a,b],X)$$

i.e. if $g(t) = g(a) + \int_a^t f(s)ds$, where $f \in R([a,b],X)$, we have $V[g] \leqslant (b-a)\|f\|$; indeed

$$V_d[g] = \sum_{i=1}^{|d|} \|g(t_i)-g(t_{i-1})\| = \sum_{i=1}^{|d|} \left\|\int_{t_{i-1}}^{t_i} f(t)dt\right\| \leqslant$$

$$\leqslant \sum_{i=1}^{|d|} (t_i-t_{i-1})\|f\| = (b-a)\|f\|.$$

REMARK 5. If (E,F,G) is a topological BT we have

$$BV([a,b],E) \subset SB([a,b],E) \quad \text{and} \quad SB[\alpha] \leqslant \|B\| V[\alpha].$$

Ex. $BW([a,b],Y)$ - If we consider the BT $(Y,\mathbf{C};Y)$ (see ex. 4 of §0,C) we write $W[\alpha]$ instead of $SB[\alpha]$ and $BW([a,b],Y)$ instead of $SB([a,b],Y)$. We say that the element of $BW([a,b],Y)$ are *functions of weak bounded variation.*

REMARK 6. $SV([a,b],L(\mathbf{C},Y)) = BW([a,b],Y)$ obviously.

REMARK 7. It is immediate that

$$SV([a,b],L(X,Y)) \subset BW([a,b],L(X,Y)).$$

THEOREM 4.4. *Given the BT* $(L(X,Y),L(W,X),L(W,Y))$ *of ex.2, §0,C, where* $W \neq \{0\}$, *we have*

$$SB([a,b],L(X,Y)) = SV([a,b],L(X,Y)).$$

PROOF. It is enough to show that $SB_d[\alpha] = SV_d[\alpha]$ for every $d \in \mathbb{D}$; we have

$$SB_d[\alpha] = \sup\{\|\sum_{i=1}^{|d|}[\alpha(t_i)-\alpha(t_{i-1})]\circ U_i\| \mid U_i \in L(W,X),\ \|U_i\| \leq 1\} =$$

$$= \sup\{\sup_{\|w\|\leq 1}\|\sum_{i=1}^{|d|}[\alpha(t_i)-\alpha(t_{i-1})]U_i(w)\| \mid U_i \in L(W,X),\ \|U_i\| \leq 1\}$$

$$\leq \sup\{\|\sum_{i=1}^{d}[\alpha(t_i)-\alpha(t_{i-1})]x_i\| \mid x_i \in X,\ \|x_i\| \leq 1\} = SV_d[\alpha].$$

Reciprocally, given $x_i \in X$, $i = 1,2,\dots,|d|$, with $\|x_i\| \leq 1$ there exist $U_i \in L(W,Y)$ and $w \in W$ such that

$$\|U_i\| = \|x_i\| \quad \text{and} \quad U_i(w) = x_i$$

(by the theorem of Hahn-Banach) and therefore $SV_d[\alpha] \leq SB_d[\alpha]$, hence the equality.

4.5 - *Let* (E,F,G) *be a BT; for* $\alpha \in SB([a,b],E)$ *and* $y \in F$ *we have* $\alpha\cdot y \in BW([a,b],G)$ *and* $W[\alpha\cdot y] \leq SB[\alpha]\,\|y\|$, *where* $(\alpha\cdot y)(t) = \alpha(t)\cdot y$, $t \in [a,b]$.

PROOF. For $d \in \mathbb{D}$ we have

$$W_d[\alpha\cdot y] = \sup\{\|\sum_{i=1}^{|d|}\lambda_i[(\alpha\cdot y)(t_i)-(\alpha\cdot y)(t_{i-1})]\| \mid \lambda_i \in \mathbf{C},\ |\lambda_i| \leq 1\} =$$

$$= \sup_{|\lambda_i|\leq 1}\|\sum_{i=1}^{|d|}\lambda_i[\alpha(t_i)-\alpha(t_{i-1})]\cdot\lambda_i y\| \leq SB_d[\alpha]\,\|y\|.$$

D - Let (E,F,G) be a BT.

THEOREM 4.6. *Given* $\alpha \in SB([a,b],E)$ *we have*

a) For every $f \in \mathcal{C}([a,b],F)$ *there exists*

$$F_\alpha(f) = \int_a^b d\alpha(t)\cdot f(t) \quad \text{and} \quad \|F_\alpha(f)\| \leq SB[\alpha]\,\|f\|.$$

b) $F_\alpha \in L[\mathcal{C}([a,b],E),G]$ *and* $\|F_\alpha\| \leq SB[\alpha]$.

c) For every $(d,\xi) \in \mathcal{D}$ *we have*

$$\|\int_a^b d\alpha(t)\cdot f(t) - \sigma_{d,\xi}(f;\alpha)\| \leq SB[\alpha]\,\omega_{\Delta d}(f).$$

By Theorem 1.2, Theorem 4.6 follows from Theorem 4.12 bellow; for a direct proof of Theorem 4.6 see [H-IME], Theorems I.1.5 and II.1.1.

4.7 - *If* $\alpha: [a,b] \longrightarrow E$ *is a step function with* $\alpha(t) = c_i$ *if* $t \in]t_{i-1},t_i[$, $i = 1,2,\dots,|d|$ *and* $\alpha(a) = c_0$, $\alpha(b) = c_{|d|+1}$, *for every* $f \in \mathcal{G}([a,b],F)$ *there exists*

$$\int_a^b d\alpha(t)\cdot f(t) = \sum_{i=1}^{|d|+1} [c_i - c_{i-1}]\cdot f(t_{i-1}).$$

4.8 - *If* $\alpha \in D^{(1)}([a,b],E)$, *i.e.,* $\alpha(t) = \alpha(a) + \int_a^t \beta(s)ds$ *where* $\beta \in D([a,b],E)$, *then* $\alpha \in SB([a,b],E)$ *and for every* $f \in D([a,b],F)$ *we have*

$$(1) \qquad \int_a^b d\alpha(t)\cdot f(t) = \int_a^b \beta(t)\cdot f(t)dt.$$

PROOF. By the remarks 3) and 4) and by 2.5 we have $\alpha \in SB([a,b],E)$ and by 2.11 the second integral exists. We have

$$\int_a^b \beta(t)\cdot f(t)dt = \sum_{i=1}^{|d|} \int_{t_{i-1}}^{t_i} \beta(t)\cdot f(t)dt =$$

$$= \sum_{i=1}^{|d|} \int_{t_{i-1}}^{t_i} \beta(t)\cdot[f(t)-f(\xi_i)]dt + \sum_{i=1}^{|d|} \int_{t_{i-1}}^{t_i} \beta(t)\cdot f(\xi_i)dt =$$

$$= \sum_{i=1}^{|d|} \int_{t_{i-1}}^{t_i} \beta(t)\cdot[f(t)-f(\xi_i)]dt + \sum_{i=1}^{|d|} [\alpha(t_i)-\alpha(t_{i-1})]\cdot f(\xi_i)$$

where $\xi_i \in [t_{i-1},t_i]$. Since $f \in D([a,b],F)$, from

$$\Big\|\sum_{i=1}^{|d|} \int_{t_{i-1}}^{t_i} \beta(t)\cdot[f(t)-f(\xi_i)]dt\Big\| \leq \|B\|\,\|\beta\| \sum_{i=1}^{|d|} \omega_i(f)(t_i - t_{i-1})$$

follows the existence of $\int_a^b d\alpha(t)\cdot f(t)$ as well as (1).

REMARK 8. More generally (1) is valid if $\alpha \in R^{(1)}([a,b],E)$ and $f \in D([a,b],F)$, or, if $\alpha \in D^{(1)}([a,b],E)$ and

$f \in R([a,b],F)$. However, as is shown by the example that precedes 2.4, (1) is not valid if $\alpha \in R^{(1)}([a,b],E)$ and $f \in R([a,b],F)$.

4.9 - *Let* X *be a Banach space:* $BW([a,b],X) \subset R([a,b],X)$.

PROOF. $\int_a^b \alpha(t)dt = b\alpha(b) - a\alpha(a) - \int_a^b t d\alpha(t)$.

By 4.5 and 4.9 we have

4.10 - *For* $\alpha \in SB([a,b],E)$ *and* $y \in F$ *we have*

$$\alpha \cdot y \in R([a,b],G).$$

By the remarks 5 and 7 and by 4.9 we have

4.11 - $BV([a,b],L(X,Y)) \subset SV([a,b],L(X,Y)) \subset$

$$\subset BW([a,b],L(X,Y)) \subset R([a,b],L(X,Y)).$$

E - The following theorem is fundamental:

THEOREM 4.12 - *Let* (E,F,G) *be a BT,* $\alpha \in SB([a,b],E)$ *and* $f \in G([a,b],F)$:

a) *There exists* $F_\alpha(f) = \int_a^b \cdot d\alpha(t) \cdot f(t) \in G$.

b) $F_\alpha(f)$ *depends only on* f_- *or on the class of* f *in* $\tilde{G}([a,b],F)$.

c) $\|F_\alpha(f)\| \leqslant SB[\alpha]\,\|f_-\|$.

d) $F_\alpha \in L[G([a,b],F),G]$ *and* $\|F_\alpha\| \leqslant SB[\alpha]$.

e) *For every* $(d,\xi^\bullet) \in \mathcal{D}^\bullet$ *we have*

$$\left\|\int_a^b \cdot d\alpha(t) \cdot f(t) - \sigma_{d,\xi^\bullet}(f;\alpha)\right\| \leqslant SB[\alpha]\,\omega^\bullet_d(f).$$

PROOF. a) For every $d \in \mathbb{D}$ we define

$$\Sigma_d = \{\sigma_{\bar{d},\bar{\xi}^\bullet}(f;\alpha) \mid \bar{d} \geqslant d\};$$

these sets form a filter basis and it is enough to show that we have a Cauchy filter basis because by definition the limit is $\int_a^b \cdot d\alpha(t) \cdot f(t)$. We will prove that if $\omega^\bullet_d(f) \leqslant \dfrac{\varepsilon}{SB[\alpha]}$ (Cf.

c) of Theorem 3.1) then diam $\Sigma_d \leqslant 2\varepsilon$; for this purpose it is enough to show that for $\bar{d} \geqslant d$ we have $\|\sigma_{\bar{d},\bar{\xi}^\bullet} - \sigma_{d,\xi^\bullet}\| \leqslant \varepsilon$:

$$(\alpha) \quad \|\sigma_{\bar{d},\bar{\xi}^\bullet} - \sigma_{d,\xi^\bullet}\| = \|\sum_{j=1}^{|\bar{d}|} [\alpha(\bar{t}_j)-\alpha(\bar{t}_{j-1})][f(\bar{\xi}_j^\bullet)-f(\xi_{i(j)}^\bullet)]\| \leqslant$$

$$SB[\alpha]\,\omega_d^\bullet(f)$$

where $i(j)$ denotes that $i \in \{1,2,\ldots,|d|\}$ such that $[\bar{t}_{j-1},\bar{t}_j] \subset [t_{i-1},t_i]$; from (α) and the hypothesis

$$\omega_d^\bullet(f) \leqslant \frac{\varepsilon}{SB[\alpha]}$$

follows the conclusion.

c) From

$$\|\sum_{i=1}^{|d|} [\alpha(t_i)-\alpha(t_{i-1})]\cdot f(\xi_i^\bullet)\| \leqslant SB[\alpha]\,\|f\|$$

and a) follows that $\|F_\alpha(f)\| \leqslant SB[\alpha]\,\|f\|$. For $\varepsilon > 0$ the set

$$F_\varepsilon = \{t \in [a,b] \mid \|f(t)\| \geqslant \|f\_\| + \varepsilon\}$$

is finite since $f-f\_ \in c_o([a,b],F)$ by c) of Theorem 3.12; hence if we take $d \in \mathbb{D}$ such that $d \supset F_\varepsilon$ we have

$$\|\sigma_{d,\xi^\bullet}\| \leqslant SB[\alpha]\,(\|f\_\|+\varepsilon),$$

and this implies c).

b) follows from c) because if $f_1-f_2 \in c_o([a,b],F)$ we have $F_\alpha(f_1-f_2) = 0$ by c).

d) follows from c).

e) follows from (α) because

$$\lim_{\bar{d}\in\mathbb{D}} \|\sigma_{\bar{d},\bar{\xi}^\bullet} - \sigma_{d,\xi^\bullet}\| = \|\int_a^b \bullet d\alpha(t)\cdot f(t) - \sigma_{d,\xi^\bullet}\|.$$

EXAMPLE. Given $u \in E$ for $\tau \in [a,b[$ and $\alpha = -\chi_{[a,\tau[}u$ we have $\int_a^b \bullet d\alpha(t)\cdot f(t) = u\cdot f(\tau+)$ and for $\tau \in]a,b]$ and $\alpha = -\chi_{[a,\tau]}u$ we have $\int_a^b \bullet d\alpha(t)\cdot f(t) = u\cdot f(\tau-)$.

PROPOSITION 4.13. *Let* (E,F,G) *be a BT,* $\alpha \in SB([a,b],E)$ *and* $f \in G([a,b],F)$; *for every* $t \in [a,b]$ *we define*

$$\mathcal{I}_f(t) = \int_a^t \cdot d\alpha(s) f(s).$$

We have $\mathcal{I}_f \in BW([a,b],G) \subset R([a,b],G)$ and $W[\mathcal{I}_f] \leq SB[\alpha]\,\|f\|$.

PROOF. For $d \in \mathbf{D}$ we have

$$W_d[\mathcal{I}_f] = \sup_{|\lambda_i| \leq 1} \Big\| \sum_{i=1}^{|d|} \lambda_i [\mathcal{I}_f(t_i) - \mathcal{I}_f(t_{i-1})] \Big\| =$$

$$= \sup_{|\lambda_i| \leq 1} \Big\| \sum_{i=1}^{|d|} \int_{t_{i-1}}^{t_i} \cdot d\alpha(t) \cdot \lambda_i f(t) \Big\| =$$

$$= \sup_{|\lambda_i| \leq 1} \Big\| \int_a^b \cdot d\alpha(t) \sum_{i=1}^{|d|} \lambda_i \chi_{]t_{i-1},t_i[}(t) f(t) \Big\| \leq SB[\alpha]\,\|f\|.$$

By 4.9 we have $\mathcal{I}_f \in R([a,b],G)$.

PROPOSITION 4.14. *With the notations of the preceding Proposition we have:*

a) Given $t_0 \in [a,b[$ *there exists* $\mathcal{I}_f(t_0+)$ *for every* $f \in G([a,b],F)$ *if and only if for every* $y \in F$ *there exists* $\alpha(t_0+)y = \lim_{t \downarrow t_0} \alpha(t) \cdot y$; *then we have*

$$\mathcal{I}_f(t_0+) - \mathcal{I}_f(t_0) = [\alpha(t_0+) - \alpha(t_0)] f(t_0+).$$

b) Given $t_0 \in]a,b]$ *there exists* $\mathcal{I}_f(t_0-)$ *for every* $f \in G([a,b],F)$ *if and only if for every* $y \in F$ *there exists* $\alpha(t_0-)y = \lim_{t \uparrow t_0} \alpha(t) \cdot y$; *then we have*

$$\mathcal{I}_f(t_0) - \mathcal{I}_f(t_0-) = [\alpha(t_0) - (t_0-)] f(t_0-).$$

c) If α *is* E_B*-continuous on the right (left) at* t_0 *so is* $\mathcal{I}_f$.

d) $\mathcal{I}_f$ *is regulated for every* $f \in G([a,b],F)$ *if and only if* α *is weakly regulated.*

PROOF. It is enough to prove a). In order to show that the condition is necessary we take $f \equiv y$. The rest follows from

$$\mathcal{I}_f(t_0+\varepsilon) - \mathcal{I}_f(t_0) = \int_{t_0}^{t_0+\varepsilon} \cdot d\alpha(t)\cdot f(t)$$

$$= \int_{t_0}^{t_0+\varepsilon} \cdot d\alpha(t)\cdot f(t_0+) + \int_{t_0}^{t_0+\varepsilon} \cdot d\alpha(t)\cdot \left[f(t)-f(t_0+)\right] =$$

$$= \left[\alpha(t_0+\varepsilon)-\alpha(t_0)\right] f(t_0+) + \int_{t_0}^{t_0+\varepsilon} \cdot d\alpha(t)\cdot\left[f(t)-f(t_0+)\right]$$

if we recall that

$\omega_{]t_0,t_0+\varepsilon[}(f)$ goes to zero with ε since f is regulated.

PROPOSITION 4.15. *Let* (E,F,G) *be a* BT, $\alpha \in SB_0([a,b],E)$ *and* $f \in G([a,b],F)$, *then* $\alpha\cdot f \in R([a,b],G)$.

PROOF. By 4.3 we have $\alpha \in SB_0([a,b],E_B)$ and

$$\|\alpha\|_B = \sup_{a\leq t\leq b} \|\alpha(t)\|_B \leq SB[\alpha].$$

By a) of Theorem 3.1 there exists $f_n \in E([a,b],F)$ such that $\|f_n - f\| \longrightarrow 0$. Since $B\colon E_B\times F \longrightarrow G$ is continuous we have $\|\alpha\cdot f_n - \alpha\cdot f\| \longrightarrow 0$; from 4.5 it follows that $\alpha\cdot f_n \in R([a,b],G)$ hence by 2.3 we have $\alpha\cdot f \in R([a,b],G)$.

THEOREM 4.16. *Let* (E,F,G) *be a* BT, $\alpha \in SB_0([a,b],E)$ *and* $f \in G([a,b],F)$; *we have*

$$(2) \qquad \int_a^b \alpha(t)\cdot f(t)dt = \int_a^b \alpha(t)\cdot d_t\left[\int_a^t f(s)ds\right].$$

PROOF. By Proposition 4.15 the first integral in (2) exists and is a continuous function of f:

$$\left\|\int_a^b \alpha(t)\cdot f(t)dt\right\| \leq \|\alpha\|_B(b-a)\|f\|.$$

On the other hand since the function g is continuous, where $g(t) = \int_a^t f(s)ds$, it follows from Theorem 4.6 that there exists $\int_a^b d\alpha(t)\cdot g(t)$ and using integration by parts we have

$$\left\|\int_a^b \alpha(t)\cdot dg(t)\right\| = \left\|\alpha(b)\cdot g(b) - \int_a^b d\alpha(t)\cdot g(t)\right\| \leq$$

$$\leq \|\alpha\|_B\|g\| + SB[\alpha]\,\|g\| \leq 2SB[\alpha](b-a)\|f\|.$$

Hence the integral of the second member of (2) exists and is a continuous function of f. Therefore in order to prove (2) it is enough to prove it for $f = \chi_{]a,c]}y$ where $c \in [a,b]$ and $y \in F$ since the set of these functions is total in $G([a,b],F)$ by a) of Theorem 3.1. But for $f = \chi_{]a,c]}y$ (2) is trivial.

REMARK 9. One can prove that (2) is still valid if $\alpha \in R([a,b],E_B)$ and $f \in D([a,b],F)$, see [H-DS], Theorem 6.8.

APPENDIX 1

In this appendix we will prove a theorem that implies the existence of the interior integral for LCBT. This result is not obvious at all since if (E,F,G) is a LCBT, G is not necessarily complete but only sequentially complete while the ordered set $\mathbb{D}$ has no countable cofinal subset.

THEOREM 4.17. *Let* (E,F,G) *be a LCBT; for any countable subset* A *of* $[a,b]$ *we denote by* $G_A([a,b],F)$ *the subspace of elements of* $G([a,b],F)$ *that have no discontinuities outside* A. *Let* $d_n \in \mathbb{D}$, $n \in \mathbb{N}$, *be such that*

a) $\bigcup_{n\in\mathbb{N}} d_n \supset A$ *and* $d_n \cap A \subset d_{n+1} \cap A$;

b) $\Delta d_n \longrightarrow 0$.

Then for any $\alpha \in SB([a,b],E)$ *and any* $f \in G_A([a,b],F)$ *we have:*

1) There exists $\lim_n \sum_{i=1}^{|d_n|} [\alpha(t_i^n)-\alpha(t_{i-1}^n)]\cdot f(\xi_i^\bullet)$.

2) There exists $\int_a^b \cdot d\alpha(t)\cdot f(t) = \lim_n \sum_{i=1}^{|d_n|} [\alpha(t_i^n)-\alpha(t_{i-1}^n)]\cdot f(\xi_i^\bullet)$

PROOF. A: If $f \in G_A([a,b],F)$, by c) of Theorem 3.1 for $\varepsilon > 0$ there exists $d_\varepsilon \in \mathbb{D}$ such that $\omega^\bullet_{d_\varepsilon}(f) < \varepsilon$ and therefore we have $F_\varepsilon \subset d_\varepsilon$ where

$$F_\varepsilon = \{t \in \,]a,b] \mid \|f(t)-f(t-)\| > \varepsilon\} \cup$$
$$\cup \{t \in [a,b[\;\mid\; \|f(t+)-f(t)\| > \varepsilon\} \cup \{t \in \,]a,b[\;\mid\; \|f(t+)-f(t-)\| > \varepsilon\}.$$

We define $\delta_\varepsilon = \inf\{|t'-t''| \mid t',t'' \in F_\varepsilon,\ t' \neq t''\}$; we have

(*) $d \in \mathbb{D}$ with $d \supset F_\varepsilon$ and $\Delta d < \delta_\varepsilon$ implies $\omega_d^\bullet(f) < 4\varepsilon$.

Indeed: any interval $]t_{i-1},t_i[$ of d that contains no point $t_j^\varepsilon \in d_\varepsilon$ is contained in some interval $]t_{k-1}^\varepsilon,t_k^\varepsilon[$ of d_ε and therefore $\omega_{]t_{i-1},t_i[}(f) \leq \omega_{]t_{k-1}^\varepsilon,t_k^\varepsilon[}(f) < \varepsilon$. And any interval $]t_{i-1},t_i[$ of d that contains some point $t_j^\varepsilon \in d_\varepsilon$ contains no other point of d_ε (since $\Delta d < \delta_\varepsilon$) and $t_j^\varepsilon \notin F_\varepsilon$; hence

$$\omega_{]t_{i-1},t_i[}(f) \leq \omega_{]t_{i-1},t_i^\varepsilon[}(f) + \|f(t_j^\varepsilon)-f(t_j^\varepsilon-)\| +$$
$$+ \|f(t_j^\varepsilon)-f(t_j^\varepsilon)\| + \omega_{]t_j^\varepsilon,t_i[}(f) < 4\varepsilon.$$

B: We will now prove that the sequence

$$\sum_{i=1}^{|d_n|} [\alpha(t_i^n)-\alpha(t_{i-1}^n)]\cdot f(\xi_i^\bullet), \quad n \in \mathbb{N},$$

is a Cauchy sequence and is therefore convergent since G is a SSCLCS. It is enough to show that for any $q \in \Gamma_G$ the sequence is a Cauchy sequence: given $\varepsilon > 0$ by a) and b) we can take n such that $d_n \supset F_\varepsilon$ and $\Delta d_n < \delta_\varepsilon$. We will prove that for $r,s \geq n$ we have $q[\sigma_{d_r,\xi^\bullet} - \sigma_{d_s,\eta^\bullet}] < 8\varepsilon SB_q[\alpha]$ (hence we have a q-Cauchy sequence); for this purpose it is enough to show that if $d = d_r$ and $\bar{d} = d_r \vee d_s$ we have

$$q[\sigma_{\bar{d},\bar{\xi}^\bullet} - \sigma_{d,\xi^\bullet}] = q\left[\sum_{j=1}^{|\bar{d}|} [\alpha(\bar{t}_j)-\alpha(\bar{t}_{j-1})]\cdot[f(\bar{\xi}_j^\bullet)-f(\xi_{i(j)}^\bullet)]\right] \leq SB_q|\alpha|\cdot 4\varepsilon$$

(where $i(j)$ denotes that index i such that

$$]t_{i-1},t_i[\;\supset\;]\bar{t}_{j-1},\bar{t}_j[)$$

but this follows from the definition of $SB_q[\alpha]$ and from (*).

C. In order to prove that there exists

$$\int_a^b \cdot d\alpha(t)\cdot f(t) = \lim_{d\in\mathbb{D}} \sigma_{d,\xi}\cdot$$

and that we have

$$\int_a^b \cdot d\alpha(t)\cdot f(t) = \lim_n \sigma_{d_n,\xi}\cdot$$

(i.e., 2)) it is enough to show that for any $\varepsilon > 0$ and any $q \in \Gamma_G$ there exists $d_\varepsilon \in \mathbb{D}$ and $d = d_n$ such that for every $\bar{d} \geqslant d_\varepsilon$ we have

$$(**) \qquad q\left[\sigma_{\bar{d},\bar{\xi}}\cdot - \sigma_{d,\xi}\cdot\right] < SB_q\left[\alpha\right]\cdot 4\varepsilon.$$

For this purpose it is enough to take n such that $d_n \supset F_\varepsilon$ and $\Delta d_n < \delta_\varepsilon$; then, as in B we have (**) if $\bar{d} \geqslant d = d_n$.

COROLLARY 4.18. *Let* (E,F,G) *be a LCBT;*

for any $\alpha \in SB(\left[a,b\right],E)$ *and any* $f \in G(\left[a,b\right],F)$

there exists $\int_a^b \cdot d\alpha(t)\cdot f(t)$.

PROOF. The result follows from the preceding theorem if we take as A the set of all points where f is discontinuous (Cf. b) of Corollary 3.2).

APPENDIX 2

THEOREM 4.19. *Given a topological BT* (E,F,G) *and* $\alpha: \left[a,b\right] \longrightarrow E$ *such that for every* $f \in \mathcal{G}(\left[a,b\right],F)$ *there exists* $\int_a^b d\alpha(t)\cdot f(t)$ *then* $\alpha \in SB(\left[a,b\right],E)$.

PROOF. See [H-IME], Theorem I.1.11.

In this appendix we extend Theorem 4.19 to the interior integral.

THEOREM 4.20. *Given a BT* (E,F,G) *and* $\alpha: \left[a,b\right] \longrightarrow E$ *with* $\alpha(a) = 0$, *such that for any* $f \in G(\left[a,b\right],F)$ *there exists* $\int_a^b \cdot d\alpha(t)\cdot f(t)$ *then* $\alpha \in SB_0(\left[a,b\right],E)$.

PROOF. A: Let us first prove that α takes its values in E_B (Cf. §0,C); it is obvious that if $x \in E$, $x \notin E_B$ then there exists $y_n \in F$, $n \in \mathbb{N}$, such that $y_n \longrightarrow 0$ but $\|x \cdot y_n\| \longrightarrow \infty$, hence $x \cdot y_n$ does not converge. If there is a $t \in]a,b]$ such that $\alpha(t) \notin E_B$ we define

$$c = \mathit{sup}\{t \in [a,b] \mid \alpha(s) \in E_B \text{ for all } s \in [a,t]\}.$$

We may have $c = a$ or even $c = b$ (in this case $\alpha(b) \notin E_B$ but $\alpha(t) \in E_B$ if $t < b$).

CASE 1. If $\alpha(c) \in E_B$ there exists a sequence $s_n \downarrow c$ with $\alpha(s_n) \notin E_B$ and a sequence $y_n \xrightarrow{F} 0$ such that

$$\|\alpha(s_n) \cdot y_n\| \longrightarrow \infty,$$

hence $\alpha(s_n) \cdot y_n$ does not converge. In this case we define $f(s_{n+1}) = y_n$, $n \in \mathbb{N}$, and $f(s) = 0$ if $s \neq s_n$, $n = 1,2,\ldots$. Obviously we have $f \in G([a,b],F)$ but

$$\int_a^b \cdot d\alpha(t) \cdot f(t)$$

does not exist since for any $d \in \mathbb{D}$ there is a $d' \geqslant d$ such that $t'_{k-1} = c$ and $t'_k = s_n$; if we take $\xi'^{\bullet}_i = \eta'^{\bullet}_i$ for $i \neq k$, $\xi'^{\bullet}_k = s_{n+1}$ and $\eta'^{\bullet}_k$ such that $f(\eta'^{\bullet}_k) = 0$ then

$$\|\sigma_{d',\xi'^{\bullet}} - \sigma_{d',\eta'^{\bullet}}\| = \|[\alpha(s_n) - \alpha(c)] \cdot y_n\|$$

that does not become arbitrarily small since $\alpha(c)y_n \longrightarrow 0$ but $\alpha(s_n)y_n$ does not converge, hence

$$\int_a^b \cdot d\alpha(t) \cdot f(t)$$

does not exist.

CASE 2. If $\alpha(c) \notin E_B$ we take $s_n \uparrow c$ (hence $s_n \in E_B$) and $y_n \xrightarrow{F} 0$ such that $\alpha(s_n) \cdot y_n \longrightarrow 0$ and $\alpha(c)y_n$ does not converge. We define $f(s_{n+1}) = y_n$, $n \in \mathbb{N}$, and $f(s) = 0$ if $s \neq s_{n+1}$, $n \in \mathbb{N}$. We have $f \in G([a,b],F)$ but then $\int_a^c \cdot d\alpha(t) \cdot f(t)$ does not exist since for any $d \in \mathbb{D}_{[a,c]}$ there is a $\bar{d} \geqslant d$ such that $\bar{t}_{|\bar{d}|-1} = s_n$ and $\bar{t}_{|\bar{d}|} = c$ and if we take $\bar{\xi}^{\bullet}_i = \bar{\eta}^{\bullet}_i$ if $i < |\bar{d}|$ and $\bar{\xi}^{\bullet}_{|\bar{d}|} = s_{n+1}$ and $\bar{\eta}^{\bullet}_{|\bar{d}|}$ such that $f(\bar{\eta}^{\bullet}_{|\bar{d}|}) = 0$ we have

$$\|\sigma_{\bar{d},\xi^{\bullet}} - \sigma_{\bar{d},\eta^{\bullet}}\| = \|[\alpha(c) - \alpha(s_n)]y\|$$

that, as in Case 1, does not become arbitrarily small.

B: Next let us prove that $\alpha: [a,b] \longrightarrow E_B$ is bounded. If α is not bounded there exists a monotonic sequence t_n, for instance $t_n \uparrow c$, such that $\|\alpha(t_n)\|_B > 2^{2^n}$, since

$$\|\alpha(t_n)-\alpha(t_{n-1})\|_B \longrightarrow \infty,$$

and there exists a sequence $y_n \xrightarrow{F} 0$ such that

$$[\alpha(t_n)-\alpha(t_{n-1})]\cdot y_n$$

is not convergent. We define $f(t) = y_n$ if $t_{n-1} \leqslant t < t_n$, $n \in \mathbb{N}$, and $f(t) = 0$ at all other points; obviously $f \in G([a,b],Y)$. Let us show that $\int_a^c \cdot d\alpha(t)\cdot f(t)$ does not exist: give $\varepsilon > 0$ there exists $n \in \mathbb{N}$ such that for the division d_n: $a = t_o < t_1 < \ldots < t_n < c$ we have

$$\left\| \int_a^c \cdot d\alpha(t)\cdot f(t) - \sum_{i=1}^{|d_n|} [\alpha(t_i)-\alpha(t_{i-1})]\cdot y_i - [\alpha(c)-\alpha(t_n)]\cdot y_{n+p} \right\| \leqq \varepsilon$$

for all $p \geqslant 1$, because $f(t) = y_i$ if $t \in]t_{i-1}, t_i[$, $i \in \mathbb{N}$. Hence

$$\left\| \int_a^c \cdot d\alpha(t)\cdot f(t) \right\| \geqslant \left\| \sum_{i=1}^{n} [\alpha(t_i)-\alpha(t_{i-1})] y_i \right\| - \|[\alpha(c)-\alpha(t_i)]\cdot y_{n+p}\| - \varepsilon$$

which becomes arbitrarily big with n because

$$\|\alpha(c)-\alpha(t_i)\|\cdot y_{n+p}$$

becomes arbitrarily small with p increasing since $y_{n+p} \longrightarrow 0$.

C: Hence we proved that $\alpha: [a,b] \longrightarrow E_B$ and that α is bounded. But (E_B, F, G) is a topological BT and therefore by Theorem 1.2 for any $f \in \mathcal{C}([a,b],F)$ there exists

$$\int_a^b d\alpha(t)\cdot f(t) = \int_a^b \cdot d\alpha(t)\cdot f(t),$$

hence by Theorem 4.19 we have $\alpha \in SB_o([a,b],E_B)$; the result follows since by Theorem 4.3 we have $\alpha \in SB_o([a,b],E)$.

APPENDIX 3

In this appendix we give a modified integration by parts formula for the interior integral.

Given a BT (E,F,G) we say that a function $\alpha: [a,b] \longrightarrow E$ is *weakly regulated*, and we write $\alpha \in G^{\sigma}([a,b],E)$, if for every $y \in F$ the function

$$\alpha \cdot y: t \in [a,b] \longmapsto \alpha(t) \cdot y \in G$$

is regulated. Definition:

$$G^{\sigma}SB([a,b],E) = G^{\sigma}([a,b],E) \cap SB([a,b],E).$$

THEOREM 4.21. *Given a BT* (E,F,G), $\alpha \in G^{\sigma}SB([a,b],E)$ *and* $f \in G([a,b],F)$, *there exists*

$$\int_a^b \cdot\alpha(t)\cdot df(t) = \lim_{d \in \mathbb{D}} \sum_{i=1}^{|d|} \alpha(\xi_i^{\bullet}) \cdot [f(t_i) - f(t_{i-1})]$$

and we have

$$\int_a^b \cdot\alpha(t)\cdot df(t) = \alpha(b)f(b) - \alpha(a)f(a) - \int_a^b \cdot d\alpha(t)\cdot f(t) +$$

$$(\alpha)$$

$$+ \sum_{a \leqslant t \leqslant b} \{[\alpha(t+)-\alpha(t)][f(t+)-f(t)] - [\alpha(t)-\alpha(t-)][f(t)-f(t-)]\}$$

where $h(a-) = h(a)$ *and* $h(b+) = h(b)$, *for* $h = \alpha, f$, *and* $\alpha(t+)y = \lim_{h \downarrow 0} \alpha(t+h)y$, etc..

PROOF. A: Let us first prove that the second member of (α) is well defined, i.e., that the series is summable. By a) of Corollary 3.2 the set

$$F_{\varepsilon} = \{t \in [a,b] \mid \|f(t+)-f(t)\| > \varepsilon\}$$

is finite; given any finite subset $F' \subset [a,b[\cap \complement F_{\varepsilon}$, for $0 < h < \inf\{|t'-t''| \mid t',t'' \in F',\ t' \neq t''\}$ we have

$$\|\sum_{t \in F'} [\alpha(t+h)-\alpha(t)][f(t+)-f(t)]\| \leqslant SB[\alpha]\varepsilon,$$

hence

$$\| \sum_{t\in F'} [\alpha(t+)-\alpha(t)]\,[f(t+)-f(t)] \| \leq SB[\alpha]\varepsilon .$$

Therefore by the Cauchy criterium there exists

$$\sum_{a\leq t\leq b} [\alpha(t+)-\alpha(t)]\,[f(t+)-f(t)] .$$

For the other series the proof is analogous.

B: In order to prove now that

$$\int_a^b \cdot\alpha(t)\cdot df(t)$$

exists and that we have (α) it is enough to show that for any $\varepsilon > 0$ there exists $d_\varepsilon \in \mathbb{D}$ such that for $d_\varepsilon \leq d$ we have

$$(\beta)\quad \| \sum_{i=1}^{|d|} \alpha(\xi_i^\bullet)[f(t_i)-f(t_{i-1})] - [\alpha(b)f(b)-\alpha(a)f(a)] + \sum_{i=1}^{|d|} [\alpha(t_i)-\alpha(t_{i-1})]\cdot f(\xi_i^\bullet) - \sum_{i=1}^{|d|} \{ [\alpha(t_{i-1}+)-\alpha(t_{i-1})]\,[f(t_{i-1}+) - f(t_{i-1})] - [\alpha(t_i)-\alpha(t_i-)]\,[f(t_i)-f(t_i-)] \} \| \leq \varepsilon .$$

The sum inside $\| \ \|$ is equal to

$$(\gamma)\quad \sum_{i=1}^{|d|} [\alpha(t_i)-\alpha(t_{i-1})]\,[f(\xi_i^\bullet)-f(t_{i-1})] - \sum_{i=1}^{|d|} [\alpha(t_i-)-\alpha(\xi_i^\bullet)]\,[f(t_i)-f(t_i-)] - \sum_{i=1}^{|d|} [\alpha(t_i)-\alpha(\xi_i^\bullet)]\,[f(t_i-)-f(t_{i-1}+)] + \sum_{i=1}^{|d|} [\alpha(\xi_i^\bullet)-\alpha(t_{i-1}+)]\,[f(t_{i-1}+)-f(t_{i-1})] .$$

The norms of the first and third sums in (γ) are $\leq SB[\alpha]\omega_d^\bullet(f)$ hence if d' is such that

$$\omega_{d'}^\bullet(f) \leq \frac{\varepsilon}{4SB[\alpha]}$$

they are $\leq \frac{\varepsilon}{4}$ for all $d \geq d'$.

Let us now consider the second sum in (γ): by a) of Corollary 3.2 the set

$$T_{\varepsilon} = \{t \in \left]a,b\right] \mid \|f(t)-f(t-)\| > \frac{\varepsilon}{8SB[\alpha]}\}$$

is finite; let k_{ε} be the number of its elements and let $d'' \in \mathbb{D}$ be such that $\omega^{\bullet}_{d''}(\alpha \cdot y) \leqslant \frac{\varepsilon}{8k_{\varepsilon}}$ for every $y = f(t)-f(t-)$ where $t \in T_{\varepsilon}$; then we have for $d \geqslant d''$:

$$\|\sum_{i=1}^{|d|} [\alpha(t_i-)-\alpha(\xi_i)][f(t_i)-f(t_i-)]\| \leqslant \|\sum_{t_i \in T_{\varepsilon}} \ldots\| + \|\sum_{t_i \notin T_{\varepsilon}} \ldots\| \leqslant$$

$$\leqslant k_{\varepsilon} \frac{\varepsilon}{8k_{\varepsilon}} + SB[\alpha] \frac{\varepsilon}{8SB[\alpha]} = \frac{\varepsilon}{4} .$$

In an analogous way there exists $d''' \in \mathbb{D}$ such that for $d \geqslant d'''$ the norm of the last sum in (γ) is $\leqslant \frac{\varepsilon}{4}$ hence for $d \geqslant d' \vee d'' \vee d'''$ we have (β). Q.E.D.

Reciprocally

THEOREM 4.22. *Given a BT* (E,F,G) *and a bounded function* $\alpha: [a,b] \longrightarrow E_B$ *such that there exists*

$$\int_a^b \bullet\alpha(t)\cdot df(t)$$

for every $f \in G([a,b],F)$ *then* $\alpha \in G^{\sigma}SB([a,b],E)$.

PROOF. By the symmetrical of Theorem 1.2 applied to the topological BT (E_B,F,G) for every $f \in \mathcal{C}([a,b],F)$ there exists

$$\int_a^b \alpha(t)\cdot df(t) = \lim_{\Delta d \to 0} \sum_{i=1}^{|d|} \alpha(\xi_i)\cdot[f(t_i)-f(t_{i-1})]$$

and

$$\int_a^b \alpha(t)\cdot df(t) = \int_a^b \bullet\alpha(t)\cdot df(t).$$

Hence using integration by parts we see that $\int_a^b d\alpha(t)\cdot f(t)$ exists for every $f \in \mathcal{C}([a,b],F)$; by Theorem 4.19 we have then $\alpha \in SB([a,b],E)$.

In order to prove that $\alpha \in G^{\sigma}([a,b],E)$ for any $\tau \in]a,b]$ and any $y \in F$ we take $f = \chi_{]\tau,b]}y \in G([a,b],F)$; by hypothesis there exists $\int_a^b \cdot\alpha(t)\cdot df(t)$ and

$$\int_a^b \cdot\alpha(t)\cdot df(t) = \lim_{\xi^\bullet \uparrow \tau} \alpha(\xi^\bullet)y = \alpha(\tau-)y.$$

If we take $\tau \in [a,b[$ and $f = \chi_{[\tau,b[}y$ we have analogously that there exists

$$\alpha(\tau+)y = \int_a^b \cdot\alpha(t)\cdot df(t).$$

EXAMPLE. One can show that if Y is reflexive or weakly sequentially complete, all functions of $SV([a,b],L(X,Y))$ are regulated.

§5 - *Representation theorems and the theorem of Helly*

A - In Theorem 4.12 we saw that the functions of bounded B-variation define naturally linear continuous operators. The next theorems shows us an important situation where all linear continuous operators are represented by functions of bounded semivariation.

THEOREM 5.1. *Let* X *and* Y *be Banach spaces; the mapping*

$$\alpha \in SV_o([a,b],L(X,Y)) \longmapsto F_\alpha \in L[G_-([a,b]),X\ ,Y]$$

is an isometry (i.e. $\|F_\alpha\| = SV[\alpha]$ *) of the first Banach space onto the second where for* $f \in G_-([a,b],X)$ *we define* $F_\alpha(f) = \int_a^b \cdot d\alpha(t)\cdot f(t)$; *we have* $\alpha(t)x = F_\alpha[\chi_{]a,t]}x]$.

PROOF. Let us denote by Φ the mapping $\alpha \longmapsto F_\alpha$.

a) By Theorem 4.12 the mapping is well defined and is obviously linear and continuous ($\|F_\alpha\| \leq SV[\alpha]$).

b) Φ is one to one: if $\alpha \neq 0$ there exist $\tau \in]a,b]$ and $x \in X$ such that $\alpha(\tau)x \neq 0$; we take

$$f = \chi_{]a,\tau]}x \in G_-([a,b],X)$$

and we have $F_\alpha(f) \neq 0$, i.e. $F_\alpha \neq 0$ since

$$F_\alpha(f) = \int_a^b \cdot d\alpha(t)\chi_{]a,\tau]}(t)x = \alpha(\tau)x.$$

c) Φ is onto: given $F \in L[G_-([a,b],X),Y]$ by a) we know that if there exists an $\alpha \in SV_o([a,b],L(X,Y))$ such that $F=F_\alpha$ then we have $\alpha(\tau)x = F[\chi_{]a,\tau]}x]$ for all $\tau \in]a,b]$ and $x \in X$; let us take this as a definition; we must prove

$$\text{(i) } SV[\alpha] \leq \|F\| \qquad \text{(ii) } F_\alpha = F.$$

i)
$$SV_d[\alpha] = \sup_{\|x_i\| \leq 1} \|\sum_{i=1}^{|d|} [\alpha(t_i)-\alpha(t_{i-1})]x_i\| =$$

$$= \sup_{\|x_i\| \leq 1} \|F\left[\sum_{i=1}^{|d|} \chi_{]t_{i-1},t_i]}x_i\right]\| \leq \|F\|.$$

ii) We have $F, F_\alpha \in L[G_-([a,b],X),Y]$; in order to show that $F = F_\alpha$ it is enough to prove that they take the same value on the elements of the form $\chi_{]a,\tau]}x$ since these elements form a total set in $G_-([a,b],X)$ (by a) of Theorem 3.1); we have

$$F_\alpha[\chi_{]a,\tau]}x] = \int_a^b \cdot d\alpha(t)\cdot\chi_{]a,\tau]}(t)x = \alpha(\tau)x = F[\chi_{]a,\tau]}x].$$

COROLLARY 5.2. *For every* $\alpha \in SV([a,b],L(X,Y))$ *we have*

$$SV[\alpha] = \sup\{\|\int_a^b \cdot d\alpha(t)\cdot f(t)\| \mid f \in G_-([a,b],X),\ \|f\| \leq 1\}.$$

REMARK 1. If we take $Y = \mathbb{C}$, by Remark 3 of §4 we have

$$G_-([a,b],X)' \cong BV_o([a,b],X').$$

REMARK 2. If we take $X = \mathbb{C}$, by Remark 6 of §4 we have

$$L[G_-([a,b]),Y] \cong BW_o([a,b],Y).$$

EXAMPLES

1. Take $Y = X$, $t_o \in]a,b]$ and $F(f) \equiv f(t_o)$; then for the corresponding element $\alpha \in SV_o([a,b],L(X))$ we have

$$\alpha(t)x = F[\chi_{]a,t]}x] = \chi_{]a,t]}(t_o)x = \chi_{[t_o,b]}(t)x$$

hence $\alpha = \chi_{[t_o,b]}I_X$.

2. Take $Y = X$, $t_o \in [a,b[$ and $F(f) \equiv f(t_o+)$; then we have

$$\alpha(t)x = F[\chi_{]a,t]}x] = \chi_{]a,t]}(t_o+)x = \chi_{]t_o,b]}(t)x$$

i.e., $\alpha = \chi_{]t_o,b]}I_X$.

3. Take $Y = G_-([a,b],X)$ and $F(f) \equiv f$; then for the corresponding element $\alpha \in SV_o([a,b],L(X,G_-([a,b],X)))$ we have

$$\alpha(t)x = F[\chi_{]a,t]}x] = \chi_{]a,t]}x \in Y = G_-([a,b],X)$$

and for $\sigma \in [a,b]$ we have

$$[\alpha(t)x](\sigma) = \chi_{]a,t]}(\sigma)x = \chi_{[\sigma,b]}(t)x.$$

Since $\int_a^b \cdot d\alpha(t)\cdot f(t) = f$ for every $f \in G_-([a,b],X)$, for $\sigma \in [a,b]$ we have

$$f(\sigma) = \int_a^b \cdot d\chi_{[\sigma,b]}(t)\cdot f(t).$$

4. Take $Y = \mathcal{C}([a,b],X)$ and $F(f)(\sigma) = \int_a^\sigma f(s)ds$. Then we have $\alpha \in SV_o([a,b],L(X,\mathcal{C}([a,b],X)))$ and

$$[\alpha(t)x](\sigma) = F[\chi_{]a,t]}x](\sigma) = \int_a^\sigma \chi_{]a,t]}(s)x\,ds = [\sigma\wedge t-a]x.$$

5. Take $Y = X$ and $F(f) = \int_a^b f(\tau)d\tau$; we have $\alpha \in SV_o([a,b],L(X))$ and

$$\alpha(t)x = F[\chi_{]a,t]}x] = \int_a^b \chi_{]a,t]}(\tau)x\,d\tau = (t-a)x,$$

hence $\alpha(t) = (t-a)I_X$.

6. Z is a Banach space, $X = G([a,b],Z)$, $Y = Z$ and for $f \in G_-([a,b],G([a,b],Z))$ we define $F(f)(\sigma) = f(\sigma)(\sigma)$,

where $\sigma \in [a,b]$. Then $\alpha \in SV_o([a,b],L[G([a,b],Z),Z])$ and for $g \in G([a,b],Z)$ and $\sigma \in]a,b]$ we have

$$[\alpha(t)g](\sigma) = F[\chi_{]a,t]}g](\sigma) = [\chi_{]a,t]}(\sigma)g](\sigma) = \chi_{[\sigma,b]}(t)g(\sigma)$$

and $[\alpha(t)g](a) = 0$.

7. Take $Y = c_o([a,b],X)$ and $F(f) = f_+ - f$, i.e., for every $\sigma \in [a,b[$, $F(f)(\sigma) = f(\sigma+)-f(\sigma)$ and $F(f)(b) = -f(b)$. Then $\alpha \in SV_o([a,b],L(X,c_o([a,b],X)))$ and for $\sigma \in [a,b[$ we have

$$[\alpha(t)x](\sigma) = F(\chi_{]a,t]}x)(\sigma) = \chi_{]a,t]}(\sigma+)x - \chi_{]a,t]}(\sigma)x =$$

$$= \chi_{]\sigma,b]}(t)x - \chi_{[\sigma,b]}(t)x = -\chi_{\{\sigma\}}(t)x$$

and

$$[\alpha(t)x]b = F[\chi_{]a,t]}x](b) = -\chi_{]a,t]}(b)x = -\chi_{\{b\}}(t)x.$$

8. Take $U \in R([a,b],L(X,Y))$ and $F(f) = \int_a^b U(t)\cdot f(t)dt$ for $f \in G_-([a,b],X)$. Then $\alpha \in SV_o([a,b],L(X,Y))$ and

$$\alpha(t)x = F[\chi_{]a,t]}x] = \int_a^b U(\tau)\chi_{]a,t]}(\tau)xd\tau =$$

$$= \int_a^t U(\tau)xd\tau = \left[\int_a^t U(\tau)d\tau\right]x$$

i.e.

$$\alpha(t) = \int_a^t U(\tau)d\tau.$$

9. Take $A \in \mathcal{C}([c,d]\times[a,b],L(X,Z))$, $Y = \mathcal{C}([a,b],Z)$ and for $f \in G([a,b],X)$ we define

$$F(f)(t) = \int_a^b A(t,\sigma)\cdot f(\sigma)d\sigma$$

where $t \in [c,d]$. Then $F(f) \in Y = \mathcal{C}([c,d],Z)$,

$$A \in SV_o([a,b],L[X,\mathcal{C}([c,d],Z)])$$

and for $s \in [a,b]$ and $t \in [c,d]$ we have

$$[\alpha(s)x](t) = F[\chi_{]a,s]}x](t) = \int_a^b A(t,\sigma)\chi_{]a,s]}(\sigma)x\,d\sigma = \int_a^s A(t,\sigma)x\,d\sigma.$$

B - Let X be a normed space and Y a Banach space. Given a function $u:]a,b] \longrightarrow L(X,Y)$ for every $d \in \mathbb{D}$ we define

$$s_d[u] = \sup\{\|\sum_{i=0}^{|d|} u(i)x_i\| \mid x_i \in X, \|x_i\| \leq 1\}$$

and $s[u] = \sup\{s_d[u] \mid d \in \mathbb{D}\}$. We write $u \in s(]a,b],L(X,Y))$ if $s[u] < \infty$.

THEOREM 5.3. $s(]a,b],L(X,Y))$ *is a Banach space when endowed with the norm* $u \longmapsto s[u]$.

PROOF. One can give a direct proof of Theorem 5.3 but the result also follows from Theorem 5.5 bellow.

REMARK 3. In the definitions above we do not use any structure of $]a,b]$; hence $]a,b]$ may be replaced by any set I (and we replace $d \in \mathbb{D}$ by the finite subsets F of I).

EXAMPLE 1. If $Y = \mathbf{C}$ we get

$$s(I,L(X,\mathbf{C})) = \ell_1(I,X') = \{x' \in X'^I \mid \|x'\|_1 < \infty\}$$

(where $\|x'\|_1 = \sum_{i \in I} \|x'_i\|$) i.e., the space of X'-valued absolutely summable series with indices in I.

EXAMPLE 2. If $X = \mathbf{C}$ one can show that

$$s(I,L(\mathbf{C},Y)) = \sum(I,Y) = \{y \in Y^I \mid \|y\|_\Sigma < \infty\}$$

(where $\|y\|_\Sigma = \sup_{F \subset I} \|\sum_{i \in F} y_i\|$) i.e., the space of Y-valued summable series with indices in I.

THEOREM 5.4. *Let* X *be a normed space,* Y *a Banach space and* $u \in s(I,L(X,Y))$; *we have*

a) For every $x \in c_0(I,X)$ *there exists* $F_u(x) = \sum_{i \in I} u(i)x_i \in Y$;

b) $\|F_u(x)\| \leq s[u]\,\|x\|$;

c) $F_u \in L[c_0(I,X),Y]$ *and* $\|F_u\| \leq s[u]$.

PROOF. a) In order to show that the series $\sum_{i\in I} u(i)x_i$ is summable, by the Cauchy criterium it is enough to prove that for every $\varepsilon > 0$ there exists a finite subset $F_\varepsilon \subset I$ such that for any finite subset $F' \subset I$ with $F' \cap F_\varepsilon = \emptyset$ we have

$$\| \sum_{i\in F'} u(i)x_i \| \leq \varepsilon.$$

This is obvious if $s[u] = 0$; if $s[u] \neq 0$, since $x \in c_o(I,X)$, given $\varepsilon / s[u] > 0$ the set

$$F_\varepsilon = \{ i \in I \mid \|x_i\| \geq \frac{\varepsilon}{s[u]} \}$$

is finite, and for $F' \cap F_\varepsilon = \emptyset$ we have

$$\| \sum_{i\in F'} u(i)x_i \| \leq s[u] \frac{\varepsilon}{s[u]} = \varepsilon.$$

b) It is immediate that F_u is linear and that

$$\|F_u(x)\| \leq s[u]\, \|x\|,$$

hence c).

The next theorem completes the preceding one.

THEOREM 5.5. *Let* X *be a normed space and* Y *a Banach space; the mapping*

$$u \in s(I,L(X,Y)) \longmapsto F_u \in L[c_o(I,X),Y]$$

is an isometry (i.e. $\|F_u\| = s[u]$*) of the first Banach space onto the second, where for* $x \in c_o(I,X)$ *we define*

$$F_u[x] = \sum_{i\in I} u(i)x_i ;$$

for $i \in I$ *and* $x_o \in X$ *we have* $u(i)x_o = F_u(e_i x_o)$ *where* e_i *is the element of* $c_o(I)$ *that takes the value* 1 *at* i *and is zero at all other elements of* I*).*

PROOF. Let us denote by Φ the mapping $u \longmapsto F_u$.

a) By Theorem 5.4 F_u is well defined and $\|F_u\| \leq s[u]$.

b) The mapping Φ is injective i.e. $u \neq 0$ implies $F_u \neq 0$; indeed, if $u \neq 0$ there exist $i \in I$ and $x_o \in X$ such that $u(i)x_o \neq 0$; then we have $F_u(e_i x_o) = u(i)x_o \neq 0$.

c) The mapping Φ is surjective: given $F \in L[c_o(I,X),Y]$

we want to show that there exists $u \in s(I,L(X,Y))$ such that $F = F_u$ and $\|F\| = s[u]$. For every $i \in I$ and $x_o \in X$ we define $u(i)x_o = F(e_i x_o)$; $u(i) \in L(X,Y)$ since

$$\|u(i)x_o\| = \|F(e_i x_o)\| \leq \|F\| \|e_i x_o\| = \|F\| \|x_o\|.$$

If J is a finite subset of I we have

$$s_J[u] = \sup_{\|x_i\| \leq 1} \|\sum_{i \in J} u(i)x_i\| =$$

$$= \sup_{\|x_i\| \leq 1} \|F\left[\sum_{i \in J} c_i x_i\right]\| \leq \|F\|,$$

hence $s[u] \leq \|F\|$. $F = F_u$ because both operators are continuous and they are equal on the elements $e_i x_o$, $i \in I$, $x_o \in X$, which form a total subset of $c_o(I,X)$.

THEOREM 5.6. *Let* X *and* Y *be Banach spaces; the mapping* $(\alpha,u) \longmapsto F = F_\alpha + F_u$ *from* $SV_o(\left[a,b\right],L(X,Y)) \times s(\left[a,b\right],L(X,Y))$ *to* $L[G(\left[a,b\right],X),Y]$ $(\simeq L[G_-(\left[a,b\right],X),Y] \times L[c_o(\left[a,b\right],X),Y])$ *is a bicontinuous isomorphism of the first Banach space onto the second, where for every* $f \in G(\left[a,b\right],X)$ *we define*

$$F_\alpha[f] = \int_a^b \cdot d\alpha(t) \cdot f(t)$$

and

$$F_u(f) = \sum_{a \leq t \leq b} u(t) \cdot [f(t) - f(t-)] \qquad (f(a-)=0);$$

we have $\alpha(t)x = F[X_{]a,t]}x]$ *and* $u(t)x = F[X_{\{t\}}x]$ *for every* $t \in \left[a,b\right]$ *and* $x \in X$.

PROOF. By Theorem 3.12 the mapping

$$f \in G(\left[a,b\right],X) \longmapsto (I_-f,\ f - I_-f) \in G_-(\left[a,b\right],X) \times c_o(\left[a,b\right],X)$$

is a bicontinuous isomorphism of the first Banach space onto the second. Hence for any Banach space Y we have the natural mapping $F \longmapsto (F_1,F_2)$ from $L[G(\left[a,b\right],X),Y]$ to $L[G_-(\left[a,b\right],X),Y] \times L[c_o(\left[a,b\right],X),Y]$ where $F_1(f) = F(f_-)$ and $F_2(f) = F(f - I_-f)$ (hence $F_1(f - I_-f) = 0$ since $(f - I_-f)_- = 0$, and, $F_2(f_-) = 0$ since $f_- - I_-f = 0$) which is also a bicontinuous isomorphism of the first Banach space onto the second; so the result follows from the Theorems 5.1 and 5.5.

REMARK 4. In the numerical case (i.e. $X = Y = \mathbb{R}$) this theorem is due to Kaltenborn [K].

C - The theorem of Helly of this item is fundamental in this work.

THEOREM 5.7. *Let* X *and* Y *be Banach spaces and* $\alpha_n \in SV_o([a,b],L(X,Y))$, $n \in \mathbb{N}$, *such that for every* $f \in G_-([a,b],X)$ *there exists*

$$F(f) = \lim_{n\to\infty} \int_a^b \cdot d\alpha_n(t)\cdot f(t),$$

then

a) There exists $M > 0$ *such that* $SV[\alpha_n] \leq M$ *for all* $n \in \mathbb{N}$.

b) There exists $\alpha \in SV_o([a,b],L(X,Y))$ *such that*

$$F(f) = \int_a^b \cdot d\alpha(t)\cdot f(t)$$

for every $f \in G([a,b],X)$ *and we have* $\alpha_n(t)\cdot x \longrightarrow \alpha(t)\cdot x$ *for every* $t \in [a,b]$ *and* $x \in X$.

PROOF. We define $F_n(f) = \int_a^b \cdot d\alpha_n(t)\cdot f(t)$; by d) of Theorem 4.12 we have $F_n \in L[G_-([a,b],X),Y]$, hence by the theorem of Banach-Steinhauss there exists $M > 0$ such that $\|F_n\| \leq M$ for all $n \in \mathbb{N}$ (and therefore $SV[\alpha_n] \leq M$ by Theorem 5.1) and $F \in L[G_-([a,b],X),Y]$. By Theorem 5.1 there exists

$$\alpha \in SV_o([a,b],L(X,Y))$$

such that

$$F(f) = \int_a^b \cdot d\alpha(t)\cdot f(t)$$

for every $f \in G_-([a,b],X)$. If we take then $f = \chi_{]a,\tau]}x$ we have

$$\alpha_n(\tau)x = \int_a^b \cdot d\alpha_n(t)\cdot f(t) \longrightarrow F(f) = \int_a^b \cdot d\alpha(t)\chi_{]a,\tau]}(t)x = \alpha(\tau)x$$

and this completes the proof of b).

In what follows we give a reciprocal of Theorem 5.7.

THEOREM 5.8. *THE THEOREM OF HELLY - Given a BT* (E,F,G) *and a sequence* $\alpha_n \in SB([a,b],E)$ *with* $SB[\alpha_n] \leq M$ *for every* $n \in \mathbb{N}$ *and such that there exists* $\alpha: [a,b] \longrightarrow E$ *with* $\alpha_n(t)y \longrightarrow \alpha(t)y$ *for every* $t \in [a,b]$ *and all* $y \in F$, *then*

1) $\alpha \in SB([a,b],E)$ *and* $SB[\alpha] \leq M$.

2) For every $f \in G([a,b],F)$ *we have*

$$\int_a^b \cdot d\alpha_n(t)\cdot f(t) \longrightarrow \int_a^b \cdot d\alpha(t)\cdot f(t).$$

In the numerical case (i.e., $E = F = G = \mathbb{R}$ - hence the α_n are functions of bounded variation) this theorem was proved by Helly for the usual Riemann-Stieltjes integral. We will obtain Theorem 5.8 as a particular case of the

THEOREM 5.9. *Let* (E,F,G) *be a BT,* $\mathfrak{F}$ *a filter on a set* L *and for every* $\lambda \in L$ *let be* $\alpha_\lambda \in SB([a,b],E)$ *such that*

a) there exist $L_0 \in \mathfrak{F}$ *and* $M > 0$ *such that* $SB[\alpha_\lambda] \leq M$ *for all* $\lambda \in L_0$;

b) there exists $\alpha: [a,b] \longrightarrow E$ *such that*

$$\lim \alpha_\lambda(t)\cdot y = \alpha(t)\cdot y$$

for all $t \in [a,b]$ *and all* $y \in F$.

Then we have

1) $\alpha \in SB([a,b],E)$ *and* $SB[\alpha] \leq M$;

2) $\lim_{\mathfrak{F}} \int_a^b \cdot d\alpha_\lambda(t)\cdot f(t) = \int_a^b \cdot d\alpha(t)\cdot f(t)$ *for all* $f \in G([a,b],F)$.

PROOF. For $d \in \mathbf{D}$ and $y_i \in F$ with $\|y_i\| \leq 1$, $i = 1,2,\ldots,|d|$, we have

$$\left\| \sum_{i=1}^{|d|} [\alpha(t_i)-\alpha(t_{i-1})]\cdot y_i \right\| \leq$$

$$\leq \left\| \sum_{i=1}^{|d|} [\alpha_\lambda(t_i)-\alpha_\lambda(t_{i-1})]\cdot y_i \right\| +$$

$$+ \left\| \sum_{i=1}^{|d|} \{ [\alpha_\lambda(t_i)-\alpha(t_i)]\cdot y_i - [\alpha_\lambda(t_{i-1})-\alpha(t_{i-1})]\cdot y_i \} \right\| .$$

By a) the first summand is $\leq M$ if $\lambda \in L_o$. By b) for every $i = 1,2,\ldots,|d|$ there exists $L_i \in \mathfrak{F}$ such that for $\lambda \in L_i$ we have

$$\| [\alpha_\lambda(t_i) - \alpha(t_i)] y_{\bar{i}} \| < \frac{\varepsilon}{2|d|} ,$$

where $\bar{i} = i,\ i-1$. Hence for $\lambda \in L_o \cap L_1 \cap \ldots \cap L_{|d|}$ we have

$$\| \sum_{i=1}^{|d|} [\alpha(t_i) - \alpha(t_{i-1})] \cdot y_i \| \leq M + \varepsilon$$

i.e. 1).

2) By d) of Theorem 4.12 we have

$$\| F_{\alpha_\lambda} \| \leq SB[\alpha_\lambda] \quad \text{and} \quad \| F_\alpha \| \leq SB[\alpha],$$

hence, $\|F_\alpha\|$, $\|F_{\alpha_\lambda}\| \leq M$ for $\lambda \in L_o$; by b) we have

$$\lim_{\mathfrak{F}} F_{\alpha_\lambda}[\chi_{]a,\tau]} y] = \lim_{\mathfrak{F}} \int_a^b \cdot d\alpha_\lambda(t) \cdot \chi_{]a,\tau]}(t) y =$$

$$= \lim_{\mathfrak{F}} \alpha_\lambda(\tau).y = \alpha(\tau) \cdot y = \int_a^b \cdot d\alpha(t) \cdot \chi_{]a,\tau]}(t) y = F_\alpha[\chi_{]a,\tau]} y] .$$

This implies that $\lim_{\mathfrak{F}} F_{\alpha_\lambda}[f] = F_\alpha[f]$ for every $f \in E([a,b],F)$ and since $\|F_{\alpha_\lambda}\| \leq M$ for $\lambda \in L_o$ we have $\lim_{\mathfrak{F}} F_{\alpha_\lambda}(f) = F_\alpha(f)$ por all $f \in G([a,b],F)$ i.e. 2); indeed: by a) of Theorem 3.1 there exists $f_\varepsilon \in E([a,b],F)$ such that $\|f - f_\varepsilon\| \leq \frac{\varepsilon}{3M}$, hence

$$\|F_\alpha(f) - F_{\alpha_\lambda}(f)\| \leq \|F_\alpha(f - f_\varepsilon)\| + \|F_\alpha(f_\varepsilon) - F_{\alpha_\lambda}(f_\varepsilon)\| + \|F_{\alpha_\lambda}(f - f_\varepsilon)\| \leq$$

$$\leq \|F_\alpha\| \|f - f_\varepsilon\| + \|F_\alpha(f_\varepsilon) - F_{\alpha_\lambda}(f_\varepsilon)\| + \|F_{\alpha_\lambda}\| \|f - f_\varepsilon\|;$$

the first summand is $\leq M \frac{\varepsilon}{3M} = \frac{\varepsilon}{3}$ and the same is true for the third one if $\lambda \in L_o$; since we just proved that for $f_\varepsilon \in E([a,b],F)$ we have $\lim_{\mathfrak{F}} F_{\alpha_\lambda}(f_\varepsilon) = F_\alpha(f_\varepsilon)$, there exists $L_\varepsilon \in \mathfrak{F}$ such that for $\lambda \in L_\varepsilon$ the second summand too is $< \frac{\varepsilon}{3}$, hence $\|F_\alpha(f) - F_{\alpha_\lambda}(f)\| \leq \varepsilon$ for $\lambda \in L_o \cap L_\varepsilon$.

REMARK 5. We will use the extension above with L a topological space and $\mathfrak{F}$ the system of neighborhoods of a point of L.

We give now some examples that show that in general the theorem of Helly cannot be improved.

Ex.1 - There exist $\alpha_n \in BV([0,1])$ with $V[\alpha_n] \leq 1$ and $\alpha_n(t) \longrightarrow \alpha(t)$ (hence $V[\alpha] \leq 1$) and there exists $f\colon [0,1] \longrightarrow \mathbb{R}$ bounded such that

$$\int_0^1 \cdot f(t)d\alpha_n(t) \quad \text{exists but} \quad \int_0^1 \cdot f(t)d\alpha(t)$$

does not exist (hence f is not regulated): take $\alpha_n = \chi_{]\frac{1}{n},1]}$ $\alpha = \chi_{]0,1]}$ and $f(t) = \operatorname{sen}\frac{\pi}{t}$.

Ex.2 - There exist $\alpha_n \in BV([0,1])$ with $V[\alpha_n] \leq 2$ and $\alpha_n(t) \longrightarrow 0$ and there exists $f\colon [0,1] \longrightarrow \mathbb{R}$ bounded such that $\int_0^1 \cdot f(t)d\alpha_n(t) \not\longrightarrow 0$ (hence f is not regulated): take $\alpha_n = \chi_{\{1/2^n\}}$, $f = \chi_A$ where $A = \bigcup_{n=1}^{\infty}\left[\frac{1}{2^n}, \frac{1}{2^n} + \frac{1}{2^{n+2}}\right]$.

We have $\int_0^1 \cdot f(t)d\alpha_n(t) = -1$.

Ex.3 - If the sequence $\alpha_n \in \mathcal{C}BV([a,b])$ is such that $\|\alpha_n\| \longrightarrow 0$ but $V[\alpha_n] \longrightarrow \infty$ then there exists $f \in \mathcal{C}([a,b])$ such that $\int_a^b f(t)d\alpha_n(t)$ is not convergent.

PROOF. Define $F_n(f) = \int_a^b f(t)d\alpha_n(t)$. If $F_n(f)$ is convergent for every $f \in \mathcal{C}([a,b])$ then, by the theorem of Banach-Steinhaus, there exists $M > 0$ such that $\|F_n\| \leq M$ for all $n \in \mathbb{N}$. Since α_n is a continuous function we have $\|F_n\| = V[\alpha_n]$ (Cf. I.2.13 of [H-IME]) in contradiction to the hypothesis that $V[\alpha_n] \longrightarrow \infty$.

REMARK 6. By an argument of cathegory it is easy to prove that $\int_a^b f(t)d\alpha_n(t)$ does not converge for "almost" all continuous functions f (i.e. for a dense G_δ of $\mathcal{C}([a,b])$) but it is very difficult to give an explicit example of a continuous function f such that

$$\int_a^b f(t)\,d\alpha_n(t)$$

does not converge, because if only $f \in \mathcal{C}BV([a,b])$ we have already $\int_a^b f(t)\,d\alpha_n(t) \longrightarrow 0$ as one can see using integration by parts.

D - Let X and Y be Banach spaces; Theorem 5.1 shows that $SV_o([a,b], L(X,Y))$ is a Banach space when endowed with the norm $\alpha \longmapsto SV[\alpha]$. Theorem 5.7 and 5.9 suggest still another notion of convergence on $SV_o([a,b], L(X,Y))$.

We say that a filter $\mathfrak{F}$ on $SV_o([a,b], L(X,Y))$ *σ-converges to* $\alpha_o \in SV_o([a,b], L(X,Y))$, and we write $\alpha \xrightarrow[\mathfrak{F}]{\sigma} \alpha_o$ or simply $\alpha \xrightarrow{\sigma} \alpha_o$, if the following conditions are satisfied

$\sigma 1$ - There exist $H \in \mathfrak{F}$ and $M > 0$ such that $SV[\alpha] \leq M$ for all $\alpha \in H$.

$\sigma 2$ - $\lim_{\mathfrak{F}} \alpha(t)x = \alpha_o(t)x$ for all $t \in [a,b]$ and $x \in X$.

We denote by $SV_o^\sigma([a,b], L(X,Y))$, the space

$$SV_o([a,b], L(X,Y))$$

endowed with this notion of convergence.

REMARK 6. Obviously the σ-convergence can be defined on $SB([a,b], E)$ for any BT (E,F,G).

REMARK 7. By Theorem 5.7 we see that the definition above is equivalent to saying that there exists an $H \in \mathfrak{F}$ that is bounded in $SV_o([a,b], L(X,Y))$ and that

$$\lim_{\mathfrak{F}} \int_a^b \cdot d\alpha(t) \cdot f(t) = \int_a^b \cdot d\alpha_o(t) \cdot f(t)$$

for every $f \in G([a,b], X)$.

We will now give a representation theorem for the elements of $L[G_-([a,b], X), G([c,d], Y)]$.

THEOREM 5.10. *Let* X *and* Y *be Banach spaces; we have*

$$L[G_-([a,b], X), G([c,d], Y)] = G([c,d], SV_o^\sigma([a,b], L(X,Y))).$$

More precisely, the mapping

$\mathcal{A}\in G([c,d],SV_o^\sigma([a,b],L(X,Y))) \longmapsto F_{\mathcal{A}}\in L[G_-([a,b],X),G([c,d],Y)]$

is an isometry (i.e. $\|F_{\mathcal{A}}\| = \|\mathcal{A}\|$ *with* $\|\mathcal{A}\| = \sup_{c\leq t\leq d} SV[\mathcal{A}(t)]$*) of the first Banach space onto the second, where for every* $f\in G_-([a,b],X)$ *we define*

$$F_{\mathcal{A}}(f)(t) = \int_a^b \cdot d_\sigma \mathcal{A}(t)(\sigma)\cdot f(\sigma),$$

$t\in[c,d]$; *we have* $\mathcal{A}(t)(\sigma)x = F_{\mathcal{A}}[\chi_{]a,\sigma]}x](t)$ *for* $t\in[c,d]$, $\sigma\in[a,b]$, $x\in X$.

PROOF. Let us first observe that $F_{\mathcal{A}}(f)(t)$ is well defined since $\mathcal{A}(t)\in SV_o([a,b],L(X,Y))$ and $f\in G([a,b],X)$. The function $F_{\mathcal{A}}(f)$ is regulated since by the definition of the σ-convergence on $SV_o([a,b],L(X,Y))$ and Remark 7, $t_n\downarrow t\in[a,b[$ implies that $\int_a^b \cdot d_\sigma\mathcal{A}(t_n)(\sigma)\cdot f(\sigma)$ is convergent, i.e. $F_{\mathcal{A}}(f)(t_n)$ is convergent; the same applies if we consider $t_n\uparrow t$ $]a,b]$.

Let us now denote by Φ the mapping $\mathcal{A}\longmapsto F_{\mathcal{A}}$; Φ is obviously linear. Φ is injective since if we take $\mathcal{A}\neq 0$ then there exists a $t_o\in[c,d]$ such that $\mathcal{A}(t_o)\neq 0$, hence there exist $\sigma\in]a,b]$ and $x\in X$ such that $\mathcal{A}(t_o)(\sigma)x\neq 0$, if we take then $f=\chi_{]a,\sigma]}x$, $F_{\mathcal{A}}(f)\neq 0$ since

$$(\alpha)\qquad F_{\mathcal{A}}[\chi_{]a,\sigma]}x](t_o) = \int_a^b \cdot d_s\mathcal{A}(t_o)(s)\chi_{]a,\sigma]}(s)x = \mathcal{A}(t_o)(\sigma)x.$$

In order to prove that Φ is surjective we have to show that for every $F\in L[G_-([a,b],X),G([c,d],Y)]$ there exists an $\mathcal{A}\in G([c,d],SV_o([a,b],L(X,Y)))$ such that $F=F_{\mathcal{A}}$. By (α) we see that if there exists such an $\mathcal{A}$ we have

$$\mathcal{A}(t)(\sigma)x = F[\chi_{]a,\sigma]}x](t)$$

for $t\in[c,d]$, $\sigma\in[a,b]$ and $x\in X$; we take this as the definition of $\mathcal{A}$ and we will prove that

(i) $\mathcal{A}\in G([c,d],SV_o^\sigma([a,b],L(X,Y)))$ and

(ii) $F=F_{\mathcal{A}}$.

We will also show that $\|F_{\mathcal{A}}\| = \|\mathcal{A}\|$.

(i') $\mathcal{A}(t)(\sigma)\in L(X,Y)$ since

$$\|\mathcal{A}(t)(\sigma)x\| = \|F[\chi_{]a,\sigma]}x](t)\| \leq \|F[\chi_{]a,\sigma[}x\| \leq$$
$$\leq \|F\|\|\chi_{]a,\sigma]}x\| \leq \|F\|\,\|x\|$$

and since $\mathcal{A}(t)(\sigma)$ is obviously linear

(i") $\mathcal{A}(t) \in SV_o([a,b],L(X,Y))$; indeed for $d \in \mathbb{D}$ and $x_i \in X$, $\|x_i\| \leq 1$, $i = 1,2,\ldots,|d|$, we have

$$\|\sum_{i=1}^{|d|}[\mathcal{A}(t)(s_i)-\mathcal{A}(t)(s_{i-1})]x_i = \|F[\sum_{i=1}^{|d|}\chi_{]s_{i-1},s_i]}x](t)\| \leq$$

$$\leq \|F[\sum_{i=1}^{|d|}\chi_{]s_{i-1},s_i]}x]\| \leq \|F\|\,\|\sum_{i=1}^{|d|}\chi_{]s_{i-1},s_i]}x_i\| \leq \|F\|$$

i.e.

$$(\beta) \qquad SV[\mathcal{A}(t)] \leq \|F\| \quad \text{for every} \quad t \in [c,d].$$

(i"') Let us prove that $\mathcal{A}$ is regulated, i.e., for instances, that $t_n \downarrow t \in [c,d[$ implies that $\mathcal{A}(t_n)$ is σ-convergent in $SV_o([a,b],L(X,Y))$: by (β) we have

$$SV[\mathcal{A}(t_n)] \leq \|F\|$$

for every n, i.e. the condition $\sigma 1$ is satisfied; we have also $\sigma 2$ i.e. the sequence $\mathcal{A}(t_n)(s)x$ is convergent for every $s \in [a,b]$ and $x \in X$ since by definition we have

$$\mathcal{A}(t_n)(s)x = F[\chi_{]a,s]}x](t_n)$$

and $F[\chi_{]a,s]}x] \in G([c,d],X)$.

(ii) $F = F_{\mathcal{A}}$ since both are linear continuous operators from $G\_([a,b],X)$ into $G([c,d],Y)$ and they take the same value on the elements of the form $\chi_{]a,\sigma]}x$, $\sigma \in [a,b]$, $x \in X$, i.e. on a total subset of $G\_([a,b],X)$.

By (β) we have $\|\mathcal{A}\| \leq \|F\|$; we also have $\|F\| \leq \|\mathcal{A}\|$ since

$$\|F\| = \sup\{\|F(f)\| \mid f \in G\_([a,b],X),\ \|f\| \leq 1\}$$

and $\|F(f)\| = \sup_{c \leq t \leq d} \|F(f)(t)\|$ and

$$\|F(f)(t)\| = \|\int_a^b \cdot d_\sigma \mathcal{A}(t)(\sigma)\cdot f(\sigma)\| \leq SV[\mathcal{A}(t)]\,\|f\|.$$

REMARK 8. From now on we write $A(t,\sigma) = \mathcal{A}(t)(\sigma)$; in the proof of (i"') we saw that the condition that

$$\mathcal{A} : [c,d] \longrightarrow SV_o^{\sigma}([a,b],L(X,Y))$$

is regulated is equivalent to say that for every $s \in [a,b]$ the function A_s is weakly regulated (see the Appendix 3 of §4, Chapter I). Or still, $A: [c,d]\times[a,b] \longrightarrow L(X,Y)$ is characterized by the following properties:

(SV^u) A is uniformly of bounded semivariation as a function of the second variable (i.e., for every $t \in [c,d]$ we have $A^t \in SV_o([a,b],L(X,Y))$ and $\sup_{c\leq t\leq d} SV[A^t] < \infty$).

(G^{σ}) A is weakly regulated as a function of the first variable (i.e., for every $s \in [a,b]$ we have

$$A_s \in G^{\sigma}([c,d],L(X,Y))).$$

A is a bounded function since

$$\|A(t,s)\| \leq \|A(t,a)\| + SV[A^t] \leq \|A_a\| + \sup_{c\leq t\leq d} SV[A^t],$$

$\|A_a\|$ being finite (A_a is weakly regulated, hence for every $x \in X$ we have $\sup_{c\leq t\leq d} \|A_a(t)x\| < \infty$ and the principle of uniform boundedness implies that $\|A_a\| = \sup_{c\leq t\leq d} \|A_a(t)\| < \infty$).

From now on we write also F_A instead of $F_{\mathcal{A}}$ and A_F is the element that corresponds to F.

EXAMPLES. Using Theorem 5.10 it is easy to prove

1 - $F \in L[G_-([a,b]),G([c,d])]$ is such that $f \geq 0$ implies $F(f) \geq 0$ if and only if for every $t \in [c,d]$, $A^t \in BV_o([a,b])$ is monotonic increasing.

2 - $F \in L(G_-([a,b]),G([c,d])]$ is such that f is increasing implies $F(f) \geq 0$ if and only if $A_b \equiv 0$ and $A^t \leq 0$ for every $t \in [c,d]$.

3 - $F \in L[G_-([a,b]),G([c,d])]$ is such that f is increasing implies $F(f)$ is increasing if and only if A_b is a constant function and A_s is decreasing for every $s \in [a,b]$.

4 - $F \in L[G_-([a,b]), G([c,d])]$ is such that $f \geqslant 0$ implies that $F(f)$ is increasing if and only if for any

$$c \leqslant t_1 \leqslant t_2 \leqslant d \quad \text{and} \quad a \leqslant s_1 \leqslant s_2 \leqslant b$$

we have

$$A(t_2,s_2) - A(t_2,s_1) \geqslant A(t_1,s_2) - A(t_1,s_1).$$

In an analogous way as Theorem 5.10 on proves the

THEOREM 5.11. *Let* X *and* Y *be Banach spaces and* K *a compact space; we have*

$$L[G_-([a,b],X), \mathscr{C}(K,Y)] \simeq \mathscr{C}[K, SV_0^\sigma([a,b], L(X,Y))].$$

More precisely, the mapping

$$\mathscr{A} \in \mathscr{C}[K, SV_0^\sigma([a,b], L(X,Y))] \longmapsto F_{\mathscr{A}} \in L[G_-([a,b],X), \mathscr{C}(K,Y)]$$

is an isometry (i.e. $\|F_{\mathscr{A}}\| = \|\mathscr{A}\|$ *with* $\|\mathscr{A}\| = \sup_{t\in K} SV[\mathscr{A}(t)]$) *of the first Banach space onto the second where for* $f \in G_-([a,b],X)$ *we define*

$$F_{\mathscr{A}}(f)(t) = \int_a^b \cdot d_s\mathscr{A}(t)(s)\cdot f(s),$$

$t \in K$; *we have* $\mathscr{A}(t)(s)x = F_{\mathscr{A}}[\chi_{]a,s]}x](t)$, $t \in K$, $s \in [a,b]$, $x \in X$.

REMARK 9. In this case, in an obvious way, apply analogous considerations as those made in the preceding remark.

REMARK 10. In an analogous way one can give representation theorems for the spaces of linear continuous mappings of $c_0([a,b],X)$ into $G([c,d],Y)$ or $\mathscr{C}(K,Y)$ working with $s([a,b],L(X,Y))$ endowed with an obvious σ-convergence.

§6 - *Representation theorems for open intervals*

A - In this item we extend the results of §§4 and 5 to SSCLCS.

THEOREM 6.1. *Let* (E,F,G) *be a LBCT,* $\alpha \in SB(]a,b[,E)$ *and* $f \in G(]a,b[,F)$.

a) There exists $F_\alpha(f) = \int_a^b \cdot d\alpha(t)\cdot f(t) \in G$.

b) $F_\alpha(f)$ *depends only on* f_- *or on the class of* f *in* $\tilde{G}(]a,b[,F)$.

c) For every $q \in \Gamma_G$ *we have* $q[F_\alpha(f)] \leq SB_q[\alpha]\ \|f\|$.

d) $F_\alpha \in L[G(]a,b[,F),G]$ *and* $q[F_\alpha] \leq SB_q[\alpha]$.

e) For every $(d,\xi^\bullet) \in \mathcal{D}^\bullet$ *and every* $q \in \Gamma_G$ *we have*

$$q\left[\int_a^b \cdot d\alpha(t)\cdot f(t) - \sigma_{d,\xi^\bullet}(f;\alpha)\right] \leq SB_q[\alpha]\,\omega_d^\bullet(f).$$

The proof follows the steps of the proof of Theorem 4.12. We recall that for G SSCLCS, $SB(]a,b[,E)$ was defined in the item B of §4 and that the existence of

$$\int_a^b \cdot d\alpha(t)\cdot f(t)$$

was proved in Corollary 4.18.

THEOREM 6.2. *Let* X *be a Banach space and* Y *a SSCLCS, the mapping*

$$\alpha \in SV_0(]a,b[,L(X,Y)) \longmapsto F_\alpha \in L[G_-(]a,b[,X),Y]$$

is a linear bicontinuous isomorphism of the first SSCLCS onto the second where for $f \in G_-(]a,b[,X)$ *we define*

$$F_\alpha(f) = \int_a^b \cdot d\alpha(t)\cdot f(t);$$

we have $\alpha(t)x = F_\alpha[\chi_{]a,t]}x]$.

The proof follows the steps of the proof of Theorem 5.1. We recall that $SV_0(]a,b[,L(X,Y))$ is endowed with the set of seminorms $\alpha \longmapsto SV_q[\alpha]$, $q \in \Gamma_Y$, and that $L[G_-(]a,b[,X),Y]$ is endowed with the set of seminorms $F \longmapsto q[F]$, $q \in \Gamma_Y$, where $q[F] = \sup\{q[F(f)] \mid f \in G_-(]a,b[,X),\ \|f\| \leq 1\}$ (see §0, D, LCSS 5).

REMARK 1. With the obvious adaptations we have the analogous of the Theorems 5.5 and 5.6.

The Theorem of Helly extends too:

THEOREM 6.3. *Let* (E,F,G) *be a LCBT and* $\mathfrak{F}$ *a filter on a set* L *and for every* $\lambda \in L$ *let* $\alpha_\lambda \in SB([a,b],E)$ *be such that*

a) For every $q \in \Gamma_G$ *there exist* $L_q \in \mathfrak{F}$ *and* $M_q > 0$ *such that* $SB_q[\alpha_\lambda] \leq M_q$ *for every* $\lambda \in L_q$.

b) There exists $\alpha: [a,b] \longrightarrow E$ *such that*

$$\lim_{\mathfrak{F}} \alpha_\lambda(t)\cdot y = \alpha(t)\cdot y$$

for all $t \in [a,b]$ *and all* $y \in F$.

Then we have

1) $\alpha \in SB([a,b],E)$ *and* $SB_q[\alpha] \leq M_q$ *for every* $q \in \Gamma_G$.

2) $\lim\limits_{\mathfrak{F}} \int_a^b \cdot d\alpha_\lambda(t)\cdot f(t) = \int_a^b \cdot d\alpha(t)\cdot f(t)$ *for every* $f \in G([a,b],F)$.

The proof follows the steps of the proof of Theorem 5.9.

If X is a Banach space and Y a SSCLCS we define the σ-convergence on $SV_o([a,b],L(X,Y))$ in an analogous way as was done in D of §5; the condition $\sigma 1$ becomes: for every $q \in \Gamma_Y$ there exist $H_q \in \mathfrak{F}$ and $M_q > 0$ such that $SV_q[\alpha] \leq M_q$ for all $\alpha \in H_q$. Then we have

THEOREM 6.4. *Let* X *be a Banach space and* Y *a SSCLCS; we have*

$$L[G_-([a,b],X),G([c,d],Y)] \simeq G([c,d],SV_o^\sigma([a,b],L(X,Y)))$$

More precisely; the mapping

$$\mathcal{A} \in G([c,d],SV_o^\sigma([a,b],L(X,Y))) \longmapsto F_{\mathcal{A}} \in L[G_-([a,b],X),G([c,d],Y)]$$

is a linear bicontinuous isomorphism (i.e. $q[F_{\mathcal{A}}] = q[\mathcal{A}]$ *for every* $q \in \Gamma_Y$ *with* $q[\mathcal{A}] = \sup\limits_{c\leq t\leq d} SV_q[\mathcal{A}(t)]$*) of the first SSCLCS onto the second, where for* $f \in G([a,b],X)$ *we define*

$$F_{\mathcal{A}}(f)(t) = \int_a^b \cdot d_\sigma \mathcal{A}(t)(\sigma)\cdot f(\sigma),$$

$t \in [c,d]$; *we have* $\mathcal{A}(t)(\sigma)x = F_{\mathcal{A}}[\chi_{]a,\sigma]}x](t)$ *for* $t \in [c,d]$, $x \in X$.

REMARK 2. In a similar way we have the analogous of Theorem 5.11 and of the representation theorem mentioned in remark 10 of §5.

B - In this item we extend the previous results to open intervals.

Let $(E,F,G)_B$ be a BT; we say that $\alpha:]a,b[\longrightarrow E$ is a (normalized) *function of bounded* B-*variation and compact support*, and we write $\alpha \in SB_{oo}(]a,b[,E)$ if α has the following properties

1) There exist $[\bar{a},\bar{b}] \subset]a,b[$ and $c \in E$ such that $\alpha(t) =$ for $t < \bar{a}$ and $\alpha(t) = c$ for $t > \bar{b}$.

2) $\alpha \in SB([\bar{a},\bar{b}],E)$.

The smallest closed interval $[\bar{a},\bar{b}]$ with property 1) is called the *support* of α.

Let $(E,F,G)_B$ be a LCBT; we say that $\alpha:]a,b[\longrightarrow E$ is a (normalized) function of bounded B-variation and allmost compact support, and we write $\alpha \in SB_{oo}(]a,b[,E)$, if α satisfies the following properties

1) For every $q \in \Gamma_G$ there exist $[a_q,b_q] \subset]a,b[$ and $c_q \in E$ such that for every $y \in F$ we have $q[\alpha(t)y] = 0$ if $t < a_q$ and $q[\alpha(t)\cdot y - c_q \cdot y] = 0$ if $t > b_q$.

2) $\alpha \in SB_q([a_q,b_q],E)$.

The smallest interval $[a_q,b_q]$ with the property of 1) is called the q-*support of* α.

In the case of the LCBT $(L(X,Y),X,Y)$ these definitions particularize in an obvious way.

Let F be a Banach space; we say that a function $f:]a,b[\longrightarrow F$ is *regulated*, and we write $f \in G(]a,b[,F)$, if f has only discontinuities of the first kind; this amounts to say that for every $[c,d] \subset]a,b[$ we have

$$f|_{[c,d]} \in G([c,d],F).$$

We define $f_-(t) = f(t-)$ for $t \in]a,b[$. $G(]a,b[,F)$ is a Frechet space when endowed with the family of seminorms $f \longmapsto \|f\|_{[c,d]}$, $[c,d] \subset]a,b[$.

THEOREM 6.5. *Let* (E,F,G) *be a LCBT,* $\alpha \in SB_{oo}(]a,b[,E)$ *and* $f \in G(]a,b[,F)$. .

a) There exists

$$F_\alpha(f) = \int_a^b \cdot d\alpha(t) \cdot f(t) \overset{def.}{=\!=} \lim_n \int_{a_n}^{b_n} \cdot d\alpha(t) \cdot f(t)$$

where $a_n \downarrow a$, $b_n \uparrow b$.

b) $F_\alpha(f)$ *depends only on* f_-.

c) For every $q \in \Gamma_G$ *we have*

$$q[F_\alpha(f)] \leqslant SB_{q,[a_q,b_q]}[\alpha] \|f_-\|_{[a_q,b_q]}$$

d) $F_\alpha \in L[G(]a,b[,F),G]$.

PROOF. a') For every n there exists $\int_{a_n}^{b_n} \cdot d\alpha(t) \cdot f(t)$; indeed: for any $q \in \Gamma_G$ we have $\alpha \in SB_q([a_n,b_n],E)$ if

$$[a_n,b_n] \supset [a_q,b_q]$$

and a fortiori for a smaller interval; hence by Theorem 6.1 the integral exists.

a") There exists $\lim_n \int_{a_n}^{b_n} \cdot d\alpha(t) \cdot f(t)$; indeed: since G is a SSCLCS it is enough to prove that the sequence

$$\int_{a_n}^{b_n} \cdot d\alpha(t) \cdot f(t)$$

is a Cauchy sequence and this follows from the fact that for every $q \in \Gamma_G$ we have

$$q\left[\int_{a_n}^{b_n} \cdot d\alpha(t) \cdot f(t) - \int_{a_q}^{b_q} \cdot d\alpha(t) \cdot f(t)\right] = 0$$

if $[a_n,b_n] \supset [a_q,b_q]$ (since then $SB_{q,[a_n,a_q]}[\alpha] = 0$ and $SB_{q,[b_q,b_n]}[\alpha] = 0$).

b) Follows from the definition of $F_\alpha(f)$ and from b) of Thereom 6.1.

d) We have to prove that for every $q \in \Gamma_G$ there exist $\| \|_{[c,d]} \in \Gamma_{G([a,b],F)}$ and $c > 0$ such that

$$q[F_\alpha(f)] \leqslant c\|f\|_{[c,d]}$$

for every $f \in G(]a,b[,F)$: we take $[c,d] = [a_q,b_q]$, then we have

$$q[F_\alpha(f)] = q\Big[\int_a^b \cdot d\alpha(t)\cdot f(t)\Big] = q\Big[\int_{a_q}^{b_q} \cdot d\alpha(t)\cdot f(t)\Big] \leqslant$$

$$\leqslant SB_{q,[a_q,b_q]}[f]\cdot \|f\|_{[a_q,b_q]}$$

hence we proved also c).

THEOREM 6.6. *Let* X *be a Banach space and* Y *a SSCLCS; the mapping*

$$\alpha \in SV_{oo}(]a,b[,L(X,Y)) \longmapsto F_\alpha \in L[G_-(]a,b[,X),Y]$$

is an injective linear application of the first vector space onto the second, where for $f \in G_-(]a,b[,X)$ *we define*

$$F_\alpha(f) = \int_a^b \cdot d\alpha(t)\cdot f(t);$$

we have $\alpha(t)x = F_\alpha[\chi_{]a,t]}x]$.

PROOF. By Theorem 6.5 $F_\alpha(f)$ is well defined and

$$F_\alpha \in L[G_-(]a,b[,X),Y].$$

Let us denote by Φ the mapping $\alpha \longmapsto F_\alpha$; Φ is obviously linear.

a) Φ is injective, i.e. $\alpha \neq 0$ implies $F_\alpha \neq 0$; indeed: if $\alpha \neq 0$ there exist $t \in]a,b[$ and $x \in X$ such that $\alpha(t)x \neq 0$; hence if we take $f = \chi_{]a,t]}x \in G_-(]a,b[,X)$ we have $F_\alpha(f) \neq 0$ since

$$(*) \qquad F_\alpha(\chi_{]a,t]}x) = \alpha(t)x$$

because for every $q \in \Gamma_Y$ we have

$$q[F_\alpha(\chi_{]a,t]}x)-\alpha(t)x] = q\Big[\int_a^b \cdot d\alpha(\tau)\chi_{]a,t]}(\tau)x-\alpha(t)x\Big] =$$

$$= q\Big[\lim_n \int_{a_n}^{b_n} \cdot d\alpha(\tau)\chi_{]a,t]}(\tau)x - \alpha(t)x\Big] =$$

$$= q\left[\lim_n (\alpha(t \wedge b_n)x - \alpha(a_n)x) - \alpha(t)x\right] = 0$$

since $q[\alpha(a_n)x] = 0$ for $a_n < a_q$.

b) In order to prove that Φ is surjective we have to show that for every $F \in L[G_-(]a,b[,X),Y]$ there is an $\alpha \in SV_{oo}(]a,b[,L(X,Y))$ such that $F = F_\alpha$. By (*) we know that if there exists such an α we have $\alpha(t)x = F[\chi_{]a,t]}x]$ for all $t \in]a,b[$ and all $x \in X$; let us take this as the definition of α.

i) $\alpha(t) \in L(X,Y)$; indeed, for every $q \in \Gamma_Y$ we have

$$q[\alpha(t)x] = q[F(\chi_{]a,t]}x] \leq q[F] \|\chi_{]a,t]}x\| \leq q[F] \|x\|.$$

ii) For every $q \in \Gamma_Y$ there is an $[a_q,b_q] \subset]a,b[$ such that for all $x \in X$ we have $q[\alpha(t)x] = 0$ if $t < a_q$ and $q[\alpha(t)x - \alpha(b_q)x] = 0$ if $t > b_q$; indeed, since F is continuous, for every $q \in \Gamma_Y$ there exist

$$\| \ \|_{[a_q,b_q]} \in \Gamma_{G_-(]a,b[,X)}$$

and $c_q > 0$ such that $q[F(f)] \leq c_q \|f\|_{[a_q,b_q]}$ for all $f \in G_-(]a,b[,X)$; if we take $f = \chi_{]a,t]}x$ we have

$$q[\alpha(t)x] = q[F(\chi_{]a,t]}x] \leq c_q \|\chi_{]a,t]}x\|_{[a_q,b_q]} = 0$$

for $t < a_q$ and

$$q[\alpha(t)x - \alpha(b_q)x] = q[F(\chi_{]b_q,t]}x)] \leq c_q \|\chi_{]b_q,t]}x\|_{[a_q,b_q]} = 0$$

for $t > b_q$.

(iii) $\alpha \in SV_q([a_q,b_q],L(X,Y))$; indeed: For $d \in \mathbb{D}_{[a_q,b_q]}$ and $x_i \in X$, $\|x_i\| \leq 1$, $i = 1,2,\ldots,|d|$ we have

$$q\left[\sum_{i=1}^{|d|} [\alpha(t_i) - \alpha(t_{i-1})]x_i\right] = q\left[F(\sum_{i=1}^{|d|} \chi_{]t_{i-1},t_i]}x_i)\right] \leq$$

$$\leq c_q \left\|\sum_{i=1}^{|d|} \chi_{]t_{i-1},t_i]}x_i\right\|_{[a_q,b_q]} \leq c_q.$$

Hence by (i), (ii) and (iii) we have

$$\alpha \in SV_{oo}(]a,b[,L(X,Y)).$$

(iv) $F_\alpha = F$ because both are linear continuous operators from $G_-(]a,b[,X)$ into Y that by (*) take the same value on the elements of the form $\chi_{]a,t]}x$ and these elements form a total subset of $G_-(]a,b[,X)$.

Let X be a Banach space and $x:]a,b[\longrightarrow X$; we write $x \in c_o^{loc}(]a,b[,X)$ if for every $[c,d] \subset]a,b[$ we have $x|_{[c,d]} \in c_o([c,d],X)$

REMARK 3. The analogous of Theorem 3.12 is true if we replace $G([a,b],X)$, $G_-([a,b],X)$, $c_o([a,b],X)$ respectively by $G(]a,b[,X)$, $G_-(]a,b[,X)$, $c_o^{loc}(]a,b[,X)$.

Let X be a Banach space and Y a SSCLCS; given $u:]a,b[\longrightarrow L(X,Y)$ we write $u \in s_{oo}(]a,b[,L(X,Y))$ if the following properties are satisfied:

1) For every $q \in \Gamma_Y$ there exists $[a_q,b_q]$ such that for every $x \in X$ we have $q[u(t)x] = 0$ if $t \notin [a_q,b_q]$.

2) $s_q[u] < \infty$.

THEOREM 6.7. *Let* X *be a Banach space and* Y *a SSCLCS; the mapping*

$$u \in s_{oo}(]a,b[,L(X,Y)) \longmapsto F_u \in L[c_o^{loc}(]a,b[,X),Y]$$

is an injective linear application of the first vector space onto the second, where for $x \in c_o^{loc}(]a,b[,X)$ *we define*

$$F_u[x] = \sum_{a<t<b} u(t)x_t \ ;$$

we have $u(t)x_o = F_u[\chi_{\{t\}}x_o]$ *for every* $t \in]a,b[$ *and* $x_o \in X$.

The proof follows the steps of the Theorem 6.6 (see also the Theorems 5.5 and 5.4).

In an analogous way as from the Theorems 5.1 and 5.5 follows the Theorem 5.6, from the Theorems 6.6 and 6.7 follows the

THEOREM 6.8. *Let* X *be a Banach space and* Y *a SSCLCS; the mapping*

$$(\alpha,u)\in SV_{oo}(]a,b[,L(X,Y))\times s_{oo}(]a,b[,L(X,Y))\longrightarrow$$
$$F=F_\alpha+F_u\in L[G(]a,b[,X),Y]$$

($\simeq L[G_-(]a,b[,X),Y]\times L[c_o^{loc}(]a,b[,X),Y]$) *is an injective linear application of the first vector space onto the second, where for every* $f\in G(]a,b[,X)$ *we define*

$$F_\alpha(f)=\int_a^b \cdot d\alpha(t)\cdot f(t) \quad \textit{and} \quad F_u(f)=\sum_{a<t<b} u(t)[f(t)-f(t-)];$$

we have $\alpha(t)x=F[\chi_{]a,t]}x]$ *and* $u(t)x=F[\chi_{\{t\}}x]$ *for every* $t\in]a,b[$ *and* $x\in X$.

EXAMPLES

1. Take $Y=G(]a,b[,X)$ and $F(f)=f$; then for the corresponding elements $\alpha\in SV_{oo}(]a,b[,L(X,G(]a,b[,X)))$ and $u\in s_{oo}(]a,b[,L(X,G(]a,b[,X)))$ we have

$$\alpha(t)x=F[\chi_{]a,t]}x]=\chi_{]a,t]}x\in Y=G(]a,b[,X),$$
$$u(t)x=F[\chi_{\{t\}}x]=\chi_{\{t\}}x$$

and for $\sigma\in]a,b[$ we have

$$[\alpha(t)x](\sigma)=\chi_{]a,t]}(\sigma)x=\chi_{[\sigma,b[}(t)x,$$
$$[u(t)x](\sigma)=\chi_{\{t\}}(\sigma)x=\chi_{\{\sigma\}}(t)x.$$

Since $F(f)=F_\alpha(f)+F_u(f)$ for every $f\in G(]a,b[,X)$, for $\sigma\in]a,b[$ we have

$$f(\sigma)=\int_a^b \cdot d\chi_{[\sigma,b[}(t)\cdot f(t)+\sum_{a<t<b}\chi_{\{\sigma\}}(t)[f(t)-f(t-)]=$$
$$=f(\sigma-)+[f(\sigma)-f(\sigma-)].$$

2. Take $Y=G(\mathbb{R},X)$, $p>0$ and $F\in L[G(\mathbb{R},X)]$ defined by $F(f)(t)=f(t+p)-f(t)$ for $f\in G(\mathbb{R},X)$. For $t\in\mathbb{R}$ and $x\in X$ we have $\alpha(t)x=F[\chi_{]a,t]}x]\in G(\mathbb{R},X)$ and

$u(t)x=F[\chi_{\{t\}}x]\in G(\mathbb{R},X)$ hence for $\sigma\in\mathbb{R}$

we have

$$[\alpha(t)x](\sigma) = \chi_{]a,t]}(\sigma+p)x - \chi_{]a,t]}(\sigma)x = \chi_{[\sigma,\sigma+p[}(t)x$$

$$[u(t)x](\sigma) = \chi_{\{t\}}(\sigma+p)x - \chi_{\{t\}}(\sigma)x = [\chi_{\{\sigma+p\}}(t)-\chi_{\{\alpha\}}(t)]x$$

The Theorem of Helly extends too:

THEOREM 6.9. *Let* (E,F,G) *be a LCBT and* $\mathcal{F}$ *a filter on* $SB_{oo}(]a,b[,E)$ *and* $\alpha_o:]a,b[\longrightarrow E$ *such that*

$\sigma 1)$ *For every* $q \in \Gamma_G$ *there exist* $H_q \in \mathcal{F}$ *and* $M_q > 0$ *such that all* $\alpha \in H_q$ *have their* q-*support contained in the same interval* $[a_q,b_q] \subset]a,b[$ *with* $SB_{q,[a_q,b_q]}[\alpha] \leq M_q$.

$\sigma 2)$ $\lim_{\mathcal{F}} \alpha(t)y = \alpha_o(t)y$ *for all* $t \in]a,b[$ *and* $y \in F$.

Then we have

1) $\alpha_o \in SB_{oo}(]a,b[,E)$ *and for every* $q \in \Gamma_G$ *the* q-*support of* α_o *is contained in* $[a_q,b_q]$ *with*

$$SB_{q,[a_q,b_q]}[\alpha_o] \leq M_q.$$

2) $\int_a^b \cdot d\alpha(t)\cdot f(t) \xrightarrow[\mathcal{F}]{} \int_a^b \cdot d\alpha_o(t)\cdot f(t)$ *for every* $f \in G(]a,b[,F)$.

The proof follows the steps of Theorem 5.9. The theorem sugests the following definition

Let X be a Banach space and Y a SSCLCS; we say that a filter $\mathcal{F}$ on $SV_{oo}(]a,b[,L(X,Y))$ *σ-converges* to $\alpha_o \in SV_{oo}(]a,b[,L(X,Y))$, and we write $\alpha \xrightarrow[\mathcal{F}]{\sigma} \alpha_o$, if the properties $\sigma 1)$ and $\sigma 2)$ are satisfied.

The following theorem has a proof analogous to that of Theorem 5.10

THEOREM 6.10. *Let* X *be a Banach space and* Y *a SSCLCS; we have*

$$L[G\_(]a,b[,X),G(]c,d[,Y)] \simeq G[]c,d[,SV^{\sigma}_{oo}(]a,b[,L(X,Y))]$$

more precisely

$$\mathcal{A} \in G(]c,d[,SV^{\sigma}_{oo}(]a,b[,L(X,Y))) \longmapsto F_{\mathcal{A}} \in L[G\_(]a,b[,X),G(]c,d[,Y)]$$

is an injective linear application of the first vector space onto the second, where for $f \in G\_(]a,b[,X)$ *we define*

$$F_{\mathcal{A}}(f)(t) = \int_a^b \cdot d_\sigma \mathcal{A}(t)(\sigma)\cdot f(\sigma);$$

we have $\mathcal{A}(t)(\sigma)x = F_{\mathcal{A}}[X_{]a,\sigma]}x](t)$.

REMARK 4. We define $A(t,\sigma) = \mathcal{A}(t)(\sigma)$; it is easy to see that then $A:]c,d[\times]a,b[\longrightarrow L(X,Y)$ is characterized by the following properties:

(SV^u) - A is locally uniformly of bounded semivariation in the second variable (i.e. for any

$$[\bar{c},\bar{d}]\times[\bar{a},\bar{b}] \subset]c,d[\times]a,b[$$

we have $A^t \in SV([\bar{a},\bar{b}],L(X,Y))$ for all $t\in[\bar{c},\bar{d}]$ and for every $q\in\Gamma_Y$ we have $\sup_{\bar{c}\leq t\leq\bar{d}} SV_{q,[\bar{a},\bar{b}]}[A^t] < \infty$).

(G^σ) - A is weakly regulated as a function of the first variable (i.e. for every $s\in]a,b[$ and $x\in X$ the function $t\in]c,d[\longmapsto A(t,s)x\in Y$ is regulated, that is, has only discontinuities of the first kind).

REMARK 5. Still apply the comments of Remark 2.

REMARK 6. In Chapter III we will apply Theorem 6.10 with Y=X.

APPENDIX

Let X and Y be Banach spaces, $1<p<\infty$ and $p' = \frac{p}{p-1}$ (i.e. $\frac{1}{p}+\frac{1}{p'} = 1$). For $f\in G([a,b],X)$ we define

$$\|f\|_p = \left(\int_a^b \|f(t)\|^p\right)^{1/p}$$

and it is immediate that the mapping $f\in G_-([a,b],X) \longmapsto \|f\|_p$ is a norm. We denote by $G^-_{L_p}([a,b],X)$ the space $G_-([a,b],X)$ endowed with this norm; this space is not complete (its completion is the space $L_p([a,b],X)$ of the equivalence classes of functions that are p-integrable in the sense of Bochner-Lebesgue).

In this appendix we extend the main results of §§4,5 and 6 to the spaces $G^-_{L_p}([a,b],X)$.

For $\alpha: [a,b] \longrightarrow L(X,Y)$ we define

$$SV_{p'}[\alpha] = \inf\{c \mid \|\sum_{i=1}^{|d|}[\alpha(t_i)-\alpha(t_{i-1})]x_i\| \leq$$

$$\leq c\left[\sum_{i=1}^{|d|}\|x_i\|^p(t_i-t_{i-1})\right]^{\frac{1}{p}} \quad \text{for all} \quad d\in \mathbb{D},\ x_i\in X\}$$

$$SV_0^{p'}(\left[a,b\right],L(X,Y))=\{\alpha:\ \left[a,b\right] \longrightarrow L(X,Y) \mid \alpha(a)=0 \text{ and } SV_{p'}[\alpha] < \infty\}$$

THEOREM 6.11. *For* $\alpha\in SV_0^{p'}(\left[a,b\right],L(X,Y))$ *and* $f\in G(\left[a,b\right],X)$ *we have*

a) $\alpha\in \mathcal{C}SV_0(\left[a,b\right],L(X,Y))$ *and* $SV[\alpha] \leq (b-a)^{\frac{1}{p}}SV_{p'}[\alpha]$.

b) There exists $F_\alpha(f) = \int_a^b d\alpha(t)\cdot f(t)$.

c) $\|F_\alpha(f)\| \leq SV_{p'}[\alpha]\,\|f\|_p$.

d) $F_\alpha\in L[G_{L_p}^-(\left[a,b\right],X),Y]$ *and* $\|F_\alpha\| \leq SV_{p'}[\alpha]$.

PROOF. a) For $d\in \mathbb{D}$ and $x_i\in X$ with $\|x_i\| \leq 1$, $i=1,2,\dots,|d|$ we have

$$\|\sum_{i=1}^{|d|}[\alpha(t_i)-\alpha(t_{i-1})]\cdot x_i\| \leq SV_{p'}[\alpha]\left[\sum_{i=1}^{|d|}\|x_i\|^p(t_i-t_{i-1})\right]^{\frac{1}{p}} \leq$$

$$\leq SV_{p'}[\alpha]\left[\sum_{i=1}^{|d|}(t_i-t_{i-1})\right]^{\frac{1}{p}} = (b-a)^{\frac{1}{p}}SV_{p'}[\alpha].$$

The continuity of α follows from

$$\|\alpha(t)-\alpha(s)\| \leq |t-s|^{\frac{1}{p}}\, SV_{p'}[\alpha].$$

b) Follows from Theorems 4.12 and 1.2.

c) For $(d,\xi)\in \mathcal{D}$ we have

$$\|\sum_{i=1}^{|d|}[\alpha(t_i)-\alpha(t_{i-1})]f(\xi_i)\| \leq SV_{p'}[\alpha]\left[\sum_{i=1}^{|d|}\|f(\xi_i)\|^p(t_i-t_{i-1})\right]^{\frac{1}{p}}$$

hence the result follows from

$$\|f\|_p = \left[\int_a^b\|f(t)\|^p dt\right]^{\frac{1}{p}} = \lim_{\Delta d\to 0}\left[\sum_{i=1}^{|d|}\|f(\xi_i)\|^p(t_i-t_{i-1})\right]^{\frac{1}{p}}.$$

d) It follows from c).

THEOREM 6.12. *The mapping*

$$\alpha \in SV_0^{p'}(]a,b[,L(X,Y)) \longmapsto F_\alpha \in L[G_{L_p}^-(]a,b[,X),Y].$$

is an isometry (i.e. $\|F_\alpha\| = SV_{p'}[\alpha]$*) of the first Banach space onto the second, where for* $f \in G(]a,b[,X)$ *we define*

$$F_\alpha(f) = \int_a^b d\alpha(t)\cdot f(t);$$

we have $\alpha(t)x = F_\alpha[\chi_{]a,t[}x]$.

PROOF. a) Let us denote by Φ the mapping $\alpha \longmapsto F_\alpha$; by Theorem 6.11 $F_\alpha(f)$ is well defined and we have

$$F_\alpha \in L[G_{L_p}^-(]a,b[,X),Y]$$

with $\|F_\alpha\| \leqslant SV[\alpha]$; hence Φ is well defined. In the usual way one proves that Φ is injective (see Theorem 5.1).

b) In order to show that Φ is surjective we prove that every $F \in L[G_{L_p}^-(]a,b[,X),Y]$ there is an $\alpha \in SV_0^{p'}(]a,b[,L(X,Y))$ such that $F=F_\alpha$; we define $\alpha(t)x = F[\chi_{]a,t[}x]$.

(i) $\alpha(t) \in L(X,Y)$ since

$$\|\alpha(t)x\| = \|F[\chi_{]a,t[}]\| \leqslant \|F\|\,\|\chi_{]a,t[}x\|_p = \|F\|(t-a)^{\frac{1}{p}}\|x\|$$

(ii) $\alpha \in SV_0^{p'}(]a,b[,L(X,Y))$: for $d \in \mathbb{D}$ and $x_i \in X$, $i = 1,2,\dots,|d|$ we have

$$\Big\|\sum_{i=1}^{|d|}[\alpha(t_i)-\alpha(t_{i-1})]x_i\Big\| = \Big\|F\Big[\sum_{i=1}^{|d|}\chi_{]t_{i-1},t_i[}x_i\Big]\Big\| \leqslant$$

$$\leqslant \|F\|\,\Big\|\sum_{i=1}^{|d|}\chi_{]t_{i-1},t_i[}x_i\Big\|_p = \|F\|\Big[\sum_{i=1}^{|d|}\|x_i\|^p(t_i-t_{i-1})\Big]^{\frac{1}{p}}$$

hence $SV_{p'}[\alpha] \leqslant \|F\|$.

(iii) $F_\alpha = F$ since both are linear continuous and take the same value on the elements $\chi_{]a,t[}x$, $t \in]a,b[$, $x \in X$, which form a total set in $G_{L_p}^-(]a,b[,X)$.

Let us show that the theorem above extends a similar

theorem of Bochner and Taylor [B-T] given for $Y = \mathbb{C}$ (Theorem 6.14 bellow:

If Z is a Banach space in [B-T] is given the following definition

$$V^{p'}([a,b],Z) = \{\alpha: [a,b] \longrightarrow Z \mid V_{p'}[\alpha] =$$

$$= \sup_{d\in\mathbb{D}}\left[\sum_{i=1}^{|d|} \frac{\|\alpha(t_i)-\alpha(t_{i-1})\|^{p'}}{|t_i-t_{i-1}|^{p'-1}}\right]^{\frac{1}{p'}} < \infty\}$$

$$V_0^{p'}([a,b],Z) = \{\alpha\in V^{p'}([a,b],Z) \mid \alpha(a) = 0\}.$$

THEOREM 6.13. $V_0^{p'}([a,b],X') = SV_0^{p'}([a,b],L(X,\mathbb{C}))$ *and* $V_{p'}[\alpha] = SV_{p'}[\alpha]$.

PROOF. It is enough to show that $V_{p'}[\alpha] = SV_{p'}[\alpha]$. We have

$$\|\sum_{i=1}^{|d|}<\alpha(t_i)-\alpha(t_{i-1}),x_i>\| = \|\sum_{i=1}^{|d|}<\frac{\alpha(t_i)-\alpha(t_{i-1})}{|t_i-t_{i-1}|^{1/p}}, x_i|t_i-t_{i-1}|^{\frac{1}{p}}>\| \leq$$

$$\leq \left[\sum_{i=1}^{|d|} \frac{\|\alpha(t_i)-\alpha(t_{i-1})\|^{p'}}{|t_i-t_{i-1}|^{p'-1}}\right]^{\frac{1}{p'}} \left[\sum_{i=1}^{|d|}\|x_i\|^{p}(t_i-t_{i-1})\right]^{\frac{1}{p}}$$

by the Hölder inequality; hence $SV_{p'}[\alpha] \leq V_{p'}[\alpha]$.

Reciprocally, we recall that for $x_1',\dots,x'_{|d|}\in X'$ we have

$$\left[\sum_{i=1}^{|d|}\|x_i'\|^{p'}\right]^{\frac{1}{p'}} = \sup\{|\sum_{i=1}^{|d|}<x_i',x_i>| \mid x_i\in X, \left[\sum_{i=1}^{|d|}\|x_i\|^{p}\right]^{\frac{1}{p}}\leq 1\}$$

hence

$$\sup\left[\sum_{i=1}^{|d|} \frac{\|\alpha(t_i)-\alpha(t_{i-1})\|^{p'}}{|t_i-t_{i-1}|^{p'-1}}\right]^{\frac{1}{p'}} =$$

$$=\sup\{|\sum_{i=1}^{|d|}<\frac{\alpha(t_i)-\alpha(t_{i-1})}{|t_i-t_{i-1}|^{1/p}}, x_i|t_i-t_{i-1}|^{\frac{1}{p}}> \mid |\sum_{i=1}^{|d|}\|x_i\|^{p}(t_i-t_{i-1})\leq 1, x_i\in X$$

$$= \sup\{|\sum_{i=1}^{|d|} <\alpha(t_i)-\alpha(t_{i-1}), x_i>| \mid \sum_{i=1}^{|d|} \|x_i\|^p (t_i - t_{i-1}) \leqslant 1,\ x_i \in X\} \leqslant SV_{p'}[\alpha]$$

hence $V_{p'}[\alpha] \leqslant SV_{p'}[\alpha]$.

Theorems 6.12 and 6.13 imply

THEOREM 6.14. $G^-_{L_p}([a,b],X)' \simeq V_0^{p'}([a,b],X')$.

For the spaces $SV_0^p([a,b],L(X,Y))$ the analogous of the Theorem of Helly is true:

THEOREM 6.15. *Let* $\mathcal{F}$ *be a filter on* $SV_0^{p'}([a,b],L(X,Y))$ *and* $\alpha_0 : [a,b] \longrightarrow L(X,Y)$ *such that*

σ1) There exists $H \in \mathcal{F}$ *and* $M > 0$ *with* $SV_{p'}[\alpha] \leqslant M$ *for* $\alpha \in H$.

σ2) $\lim_{\mathcal{F}} \alpha(t)x = \alpha_0(t)x$ *for all* $t \in [a,b]$ *and all* $x \in X$.

Then we have

a) $\alpha_0 \in SV_0^{p'}([a,b],L(X,Y))$ *and* $SV_{p'}[\alpha_0] \leqslant M$.

b) $\lim_{\mathcal{F}} \int_a^b d\alpha(t)\cdot f(t) = \int_a^b d\alpha_0(t)\cdot f(t)$ *for all* $f \in G([a,b],X)$.

The proof follows the steps of the proof of Theorem 5.9.

We say that a filter $\mathcal{F}$ on $SV_0^{p'}([a,b],L(X,Y))$ σ-<u>converges</u> to $\alpha_0 \in SV_0^{p'}([a,b],L(X,Y))$, and we write $\alpha \xrightarrow[\mathcal{F}]{\sigma} \alpha_0$, if the properties σ1) and σ2) are satisfied. $SV_0^{p',\sigma}([a,b],L(X,Y))$ denotes the space $SV_0^{p'}([a,b],L(X,Y))$ endowed with this convergence. We have

THEOREM 6.16. *Let* X *and* Y *be Banach spaces; we have*

$$L[G^-_{L_p}([a,b],X), G([c,d],Y)] \simeq G([c,d], SV_0^{p',\sigma}([a,b],L(X,Y)))$$

more precisely, the mapping

$$\mathcal{A} \in G([c,d], SV_0^{p',\sigma}([a,b],L(X,Y))) \longmapsto F_{\mathcal{A}} \in L[G^-_{L_p}([a,b],X), G([c,d],Y)]$$

is an isometry (i.e. $\|F_{\mathcal{A}}\| = \|\mathcal{A}\|$ *with* $\|\mathcal{A}\| = \sup_{c\leqslant t\leqslant d} SV_{p'}[\mathcal{A}(t)]$)

of the first Banach space onto the second, where for every $f \in G_-(]a,b],X)$ *we define* $F_{\mathcal{A}}(f)(t) = \int_a^b d_\sigma \mathcal{A}(t)(\sigma) f(\sigma)$, $t \in [c,d]$; *we have* $\mathcal{A}(t)(\sigma)x = F_{\mathcal{A}}[X_{]a,\sigma]}x](t)$ *for* $t \in [c,d]$, $\sigma \in]a,b]$, $x \in X$.

The proof follows the steps of the proof of Theorem 5.10.

REMARK 7. In an analogous way as was done in Remark 8 we define $A: [c,d] \times]a,b] \longrightarrow L(X)$ by $A(t,\sigma) = \mathcal{A}(t)(\sigma)$; A is characterized by the following properties:

$(SV^u_{p'})$ - A is uniformly of bounded p'-semivariation as a function of the second variable, i.e., for every $t \in [c,d]$ we have $A^t \in SV_0^{p'}(]a,b],L(X,Y))$ with $\sup_{c \leq t \leq d} SV_{p'}[A^t] < \infty$.

(G^σ) - A is weakly regulated as a function of the first variable.

REMARK 8. In an analogous way one gives representation theorems for $L[G^-_{L_p}(]a,b],X),\mathcal{G}(K,Y)]$ where K is a compact space, for $L[G^-_{L_p}(]a,b],X),G([c,d],Y)]$, for $L[G^{-loc}_{L_p}(]a,b[,X),G(]c,d[,Y)]$ etc.

CHAPTER II

The Analysis of Regulated Functions

§1 - *The theorem of Bray and the formula of Dirichlet*

A - Let X be a normed space and Y a Banach space; given a function

$$h: [c,d] \times [a,b] \longrightarrow L(X,Y)$$

we write $h \in G^u([c,d]\times[a,b],\ L(X,Y))$ if h is regulated as a function of the first variable (i.e., $h_s \in G([c,d],L(X,Y))$ for every $s \in [a,b]$) and h is uniformly of bounded semivariation in the second variable (i.e., for every $t \in [c,d]$ we have $h^t \in SV([a,b],\ L(X,Y))$ and $\sup_{c\leq t\leq d} SV[h^t] < \infty$); hence h is bounded (see Remark 8 of §5 of Chapter I).

THEOREM 1.1. The theorem of Bray - *Let* X *be a normed space and* Y, Z *Banach spaces. Given* $\alpha \in SV([c,d],\ L(Y,Z))$, $h \in G^u([c,d]\times[a,b],\ L(X,Y))$ *and* $g \in G([a,b],X)$ [*or* $g \in G([a,b],\ L(X))$] *we have*

$$(1) \qquad \int_a^b \cdot d_s \Big[\int_c^d \cdot d\alpha(t)\cdot h(t,s)\Big]\cdot g(s) = \int_c^d \cdot d\alpha(t)\Big[\int_a^b \cdot d_s h(t,s)\cdot g(s)\Big]$$

$$(2) \qquad \Big\|\int_c^d \cdot d\alpha(t)\Big[\int_a^b \cdot d_s h(t,s)\cdot g(s)\Big]\Big\| \leq SV[\alpha] \sup_{c\leq t\leq d} SV[h^t]\,\|g\|.$$

In order to prove the theorem of Bray we need two lemmas.

LEMMA 1.2. *With the hypothesis of Theorem 1.1, for every* $s \in [a,b]$ *we define* $\bar{h}(s) = \int_c^d \cdot d\alpha(t)\cdot h(t,s)$; *then we have* $\bar{h} \in SV([a,b],L(X,Z))$ *and*

$$(3) \qquad SV[\bar{h}] \leq SV[\alpha] \sup_{c\leq t\leq d} SV[h^t].$$

PROOF. By Theorem I.4.12 $\bar{h}(s)$ is well defined since

$$\alpha \in SV([c,d],L(Y,Z)) \quad \text{and} \quad h_s \in G([c,d],Y).$$

For $d \in \mathbf{D}_{[a,b]}$ and $x_i \in X$ with $\|x_i\| \le 1$, $i = 1,2,\ldots,|d|$ we have

$$\left\|\sum_{i=1}^{|d|}[\bar{h}(s_i)-\bar{h}(s_{i-1})]x_i\right\| = \left\|\int_c^d \cdot d\alpha(t)\cdot \sum_{i=1}^{|d|}[h(t,s_i)-h(t,s_{i-1})]x_i\right\| \le$$

$$\le SV[\alpha] \sup_{c\le t\le d} \left\|\sum_{i=1}^{|d|}[h^t(s_i)-h^t(s_{i-1})]x_i\right\| \le SV[\alpha] \sup_{c\le t\le d} SV[h^t] .$$

QED

LEMMA 1.3. *With the hypothesis of Theorem 1.1, for every* $t \in [c,d]$ *we define* $\bar{g}(t) = \int_a^b \cdot d_s h(t,s)\cdot g(s)$; *then we have* $\bar{g} \in G([c,d],Y)$ [*or* $g \in G([c,d],L(X,Y))$] *and*

$$\|\bar{g}\| \le \sup_{c\le t\le d} SV[h^t]\,\|g\|. \tag{4}$$

PROOF. By Theorem I.4.12 $\bar{g}(t)$ is well defined since $h^t \in SV([a,b],L(X,Y))$ and $g \in G([a,b],X)$ [or $g \in G([a,b],L(X))$; cf. Theorem I.4.4]. In order to prove that $\bar{g}$ is regulated we will show that if $t_n \downarrow t \in [c,d[$ there exists

$$\bar{g}(t+) = \lim_n \bar{g}(t_n);$$

for increasing sequences we have an analogous result. By the hypothesis made on h in Theorem 1.1, for every $s \in [c,d]$ there exists $h(t+,s) = \lim_n h(t_n,s)$ and there exists M such that $SV\left(h^{t_n}\right) \le M$ for every n; hence by the Theorem of Helly (I.5.8) we have $SV[h^{t+}] \le M$ and for every $g \in G([a,b],X)$ $[g \in G([a,b],L(X))]$

$$\bar{g}(t_n) = \int_a^b \cdot d_s h^{t_n}(s)\cdot g(s) \longrightarrow \int_a^b \cdot d_s h^{t+}(s)\cdot g(s) = \bar{g}(t+).$$

(4) follows from c) of Theorem I.4.12.

PROOF OF THEOREM 1.1. We will prove that both members of (1) are well defined and are linear continuous functions of g [a) and b) bellow]. Afterwards [c) bellow] it will be enough to prove (1) if $g = \chi_{|a,\sigma|}x$ [or $g = \chi_{|a,\sigma|}u$] where $\sigma \in [a,b]$ and $x \in X$ $[u \in L(X)]$ since the set of these functions is total in $G([a,b],X)$ $[G([a,b],L(X))]$.

a) From Lemma 1.2 it follows that the first member of (1) is well defined and depends continuously on g since

$$\|\int_a^b \cdot d_s \, [\int_c^d \cdot d\alpha(t)h(t,s)]g(s)\| = \|\int_a^b \cdot d\bar{h}(s)\cdot g(s)\| \leq SV[\bar{h}]\|g\|.$$

b) From Lemma 1.3 it follows that the second member of (1) is well defined and depends continuously on g because we have

$$(2) \qquad \|\int_c^d \cdot d\alpha(t)[\int_a^b \cdot d_s h(t,s)\cdot g(s)]\| \leq SV[\alpha]\|\bar{g}\| \leq$$

$$\leq SV[\alpha] \sup_{c\leq t\leq d} SV[h^t]\,\|g\|.$$

c) Let us calculate both sides of (1) for $g = \chi_{|a,\sigma|}x$:

$$\int_a^b \cdot d_s[\int_c^d \cdot d\alpha(t)g(t,s)]\chi_{|a,\sigma|}(s)x = \int_c^d \cdot d\alpha(t)h(t,\sigma) - \int_c^d \cdot d\alpha(t)\cdot h(t,a)x$$

$$\int_c^d \cdot d\alpha(t)[\int_a^b \cdot d_s h(t,s)\cdot \chi_{|a,\sigma|}(s)x] = \int_c^d \cdot d\alpha(t)\cdot[h(t,\sigma)x-h(t,a)x];$$

both second members are obviously equal.

REMARK 1. If in Theorem 1.1 we replace the hypothesis "regulated" for h and g by "continuous" we may replace $\int\cdot$ by $\int$ and in the numerical case (i.e. $X = Y = Z = \mathbb{R}$) the corresponding theorem was proved by Bray [B].

COROLLARY 1.4. *With the hypothesis of Theorem 1.1 we take* $(c,d) = (a,b)$ *and for* $s\in (a,b)$ *we define*

$$\tilde{h}(s) = \int_a^s \cdot d\alpha(t)\cdot h(t,s).$$

We have $\tilde{h}\in SV((a,b),L(X,Z))$ *and*

$$(5) \qquad SV[\tilde{h}] \leq SV[\alpha]\,[\|h\|_\Delta + \sup_{a\leq t\leq b} SV[h^t]]$$

where $\|h\|_\Delta = \sup_{a\leq t\leq b} \|h(t,t)\|$.

PROOF. We define $h_o(t,s) = Y(s-t)h(t,s)$; h_o has the same properties as h in Theorem 1.1 and

$$SV[h_o^t] \leq \|h(t,t)\| + SV_{]t,b]}[h^t] .$$

The result follows from Lemma 1.2 since $\tilde{h} = \tilde{h}_o$.

REMARK 2. $\tilde{h}$ may be not regulated even when α or h is continuous (see however Theorem 1.13).

B - The formula of Dirichlet.

LEMMA 1.5. *Let* (E,F,G) *be a BT,* $h\in SB([a,b],E)$ *and* $g\in G([a,b],F)$.

a) For every $c\in]a,b]$ *we have*

$$\int_a^b \cdot d[\chi_{[c,b]}(t)h(t)]\cdot g(t) = \int_c^b \cdot dh(t)\cdot g(t) + h(c)\cdot g(c-).$$

b) For every $c\in [a,b[$ *we have*

$$\int_a^b \cdot d[\chi_{[a,c]}(t)h(t)]\cdot g(t) = \int_a^c \cdot dh(t)\cdot g(t) - h(c)\cdot g(c+).$$

PROOF. It follows immediately from the definition of $\int_a^b \cdot$

THEOREM 1.6. *With the hypothesis of Theorem 1.1 we take* $[c,d] = [a,b]$. *We have*

$$(6) \qquad \int_a^b \cdot d_s[\int_a^s \cdot d\alpha(t)h(t,s)]\cdot g(s) =$$

$$= \int_a^b \cdot d\alpha(t)[\int_t^b \cdot d_s h(t,s)\cdot g(s) + h(t,t)\cdot g(t-)] .$$

$$(6') \qquad \int_a^b \cdot d_s[\int_s^b \cdot d\alpha(t)h(t,s)]\cdot g(s) =$$

$$= \int_a^b \cdot d\alpha(t)[\int_a^t \cdot d_s h(t,s)\cdot g(s) - h(t,t)\cdot g(t+)] .$$

$$(7) \qquad \|\int_a^b \cdot d_s[\int_a^b \cdot d\alpha(t)h(t,s)]\cdot g(s)\| \leq$$

$$\leq SV_{[a,b]}[\alpha]\left[\|h\|_\Delta + \sup_{a\leq t\leq b} SV_{[t,b]}[h^t]\right] \|g\| .$$

For $a \leq \bar{a} < \bar{b} \leq b$ *we have*

$$\left\|\int_{\bar{a}}^{\bar{b}} \cdot d_s\left[\int_{s_0}^{s} \cdot d\alpha(t)\cdot h(t,s)\right]\cdot g(s)\right\| \leq$$

(8) $$\leq SV_{[\bar{a},\bar{b}]}[\alpha]\left[\|h\|_\Delta + \sup_{\bar{a}\leq t\leq \bar{b}} SV_{[t,\bar{b}]}[h^t]\right]\|g\|_{[\bar{a},\bar{b}]} +$$

$$+ SV_{\{s_0,\bar{a}\}}[\alpha] \sup_{t\in\{s_0,\bar{a}\}} SV_{[\bar{a},\bar{b}]}[h^t] \|g\|_{[\bar{a},\bar{b}]} .$$

(9) $$\leq SV_{[a,b]}[\alpha]\left[\|h\|_\Delta + 2 \sup_{a\leq t\leq b} SV_{[\bar{a},\bar{b}]}[h^t]\right] \|g\|_{[\bar{a},\bar{b}]} .$$

PROOF. We define $h_0(t,s) = Y(s-t)h(t,s)$. h_0 has the same properties of h in Theorem 1.1. Hence we replace h by h_0 in (1) and apply a) of Lemma 1.5 in order to obtain (6). We get (6') in an analogous way. (7) follows immediately from (6) if we apply (2). If we write

$$\int_{\bar{a}}^{\bar{b}} \cdot d_s\int_{s_0}^{s} \cdot = \int_{\bar{a}}^{\bar{b}} \cdot d_s\int_{\bar{a}}^{s} \cdot - \int_{\bar{a}}^{\bar{b}} \cdot d_s\int_{\bar{a}}^{s_0} \cdot$$

and apply respectively (7) and (2) to these two integrals we obtain (8). (9) is a majoration of (8).

COROLLARY 1.7. *If* $\tilde{h}(s) = \int_{s_0}^{s} \cdot d\alpha(t)\cdot h(t,s)$ *then* $\tilde{h} \in SV([a,b],L(X,Z))$ *and for every* $[\bar{a},\bar{b}]\subset[a,b]$ *we have*

(8') $$SV_{[\bar{a},\bar{b}]}[\tilde{h}] \leq SV_{[\bar{a},\bar{b}]}[\alpha]\left[\|h\|_{\bar{\Delta}} + \sup_{\bar{a}\leq t\leq \bar{b}} SV_{[t,\bar{b}]}[h^t]\right] +$$

$$+ SV_{\{s_0,\bar{a}\}}[\alpha] \sup_{t\in\{s_0,\bar{a}\}} SV_{[\bar{a},\bar{b}]}[h^t] .$$

(9') $$SV_{[\bar{a},\bar{b}]}[\tilde{h}] \leq SV_{[a,b]}[\alpha]\left[\|h\|_\Delta + 2 \sup_{a\leq t\leq b} SV_{[\bar{a},\bar{b}]}[h^t]\right] .$$

If $s_0 = a$ *we have*

(7') $\quad SV_{\left[a,b\right]}[\tilde{h}] \leq SV_{\left[a,b\right]}[\alpha]\left[\|h\|_{\Delta} + \sup_{a\leq t\leq b} SV_{\left[t,b\right]}[h^t]\right]$.

PROOF. The proofs follow immediately from the Corollary 1.4 and from (8), (9) and (7), respectively, if we recall that by I.5.2 we have

$$SV_{\left[\bar{a},\bar{b}\right]}[\tilde{h}] = \sup\{\|\int_{\bar{a}}^{\bar{b}} d\tilde{h}(s)\cdot g(s)\| \mid g\in G(\left[a,b\right],X),\ \|g\|\leq 1\}.$$

COROLLARY 1.8. *a) If* $\tilde{g}^1(t) = \int_a^t \cdot d_s h(t,s)\cdot g(s) - h(t,t)g(t+)$ *we have*

$\tilde{g}^1 \in G(\left[a,b\right],Y)$ $\quad [$or $\tilde{g}^1 \in G(\left[a,b\right],L(X,Y))]$.

b) *If* $\tilde{g}^2(t) = \int_t^b d_s h(t,s)\cdot g(s) + h(t,t)\cdot g(t-)$ *we have*

$\tilde{g}^2 \in G(\left[a,b\right],Y)$ $\quad [$or $\tilde{g}^2 \in G(\left[a,b\right],L(X,Y))]$.

PROOF. We take $\tau \in \left[a,b\right[$ and $\beta = \chi_{\left[a,\tau\right[} I_Y \in SV(\left[a,b\right],L(Y))$. Then by (6') there exists

$$\int_a^b \cdot d\beta(t)\cdot\tilde{g}^1(t) = \int_a^b \cdot d_s\left[\int_s^b \cdot d\beta(t)h(t,s)\right]g(s),$$

but

$$\int_a^b \cdot d\beta(t)\cdot\tilde{g}^1(t) = \int_a^b \cdot d\chi_{\left[a,\tau\right[}(t)\tilde{g}^1(t) = -\tilde{g}^1(\tau+).$$

In an analogous way one proves the existence of $\tilde{g}^1(\tau-)$, $\tilde{g}^2(\tau+)$ and $\tilde{g}^2(\tau-)$.

REMARK 3. The summands of $\tilde{g}^1$ and $\tilde{g}^2$ are not necessarily regulated functions since h^t is not regulated in general.

PROPOSITION 1.9. **The formula of substituition** - *If*

$$\alpha \in SV(\left[a,b\right],L(Y,Z)), \quad h \in G(\left[a,b\right],L(X,Y))$$

and $g \in G(\left[a,b\right],X)$ $[$ *or* $g \in G(\left[a,b\right],L(X))]$ *we have*

(10) $$\int_a^b \cdot d_s\left[\int_a^s \cdot d\alpha(t)h(t)\right]\cdot g(s) = \int_a^b \cdot d\alpha(t)\cdot h(t)g(t).$$

PROOF. The result follows from (6) if we take there

$$h(t,s) \equiv h(t).$$

THEOREM 1.10. The formula of Dirichlet - *With the hypothesis of Theorem 1.1 we take* $[c,d] = [a,b]$ *and* g *continuous; then we have*

$$(11)\qquad \int_a^b \left[\int_a^s \cdot d\alpha(t)\cdot h(t,s)\right] dg(s) = \int_a^b \cdot d\alpha(t)\left[\int_t^b h(t,s)dg(s)\right].$$

PROOF. Since g is continuous, by (1) and by I.1.2 we have

$$\int_a^b d_s\left[\int_a^b \cdot d\alpha(t)h(t,s)\right] g(s) = \int_a^b \cdot d\alpha(t)\left[\int_a^b d_s h(t,s)\cdot g(s)\right]$$

and using integration by parts in $\int_a^b d_s$ in both integrals we obtain

$$\int_a^b \left[\int_a^b \cdot d\alpha(t)\cdot h(t,s)\right] dg(s) = \int_a^b \cdot d\alpha(t)\left[\int_a^b h(t,s)\cdot dg(s)\right].$$

If we take $h_o(t,s) = Y(s-t)h(t,s)$ then h_o has the same properties as h in Theorem 1.1; hence, we may replace h by h_o in the last equality and we get (11).

REMARK 4. Theorem 1.10 may also be proved by using (6) and integration by parts.

COROLLARY 1.11. *With the hypothesis of Theorem 1.10 we define*

$$\hat{g}(t) = \int_t^b h(t,s)dg(s)$$

then $\hat{g}$ *is regulated.*

PROOF. It follows from b) of Corollary 1.8 using integration by parts in the integral that appears in the definition of $\tilde{g}^2$.

REMARK 5. If the function g is only regulated, $\int_t^b \cdot h(t,s)dg(s)$ may not exist (see Theorem 4.22 of Chapter I).

COROLLARY 1.12. *With the hypothesis of Theorem 1.1 we take* $[c,d] = [a,b]$*; then we have*

$$(12)\qquad \int_a^b \left[\int_a^s \cdot d\alpha(t)h(t,s)\right] g(s)ds = \int_a^b \cdot d\alpha(t)\left[\int_t^b h(t,s)g(s)ds\right].$$

PROOF. We define $k(t) = \int_a^t g(s)ds$. By Corollary 1.4 and I.4.16 the first integral in (12) is equal to

$$\int_a^b \left[\int_a^s \cdot d\alpha(t)h(t,s)\right] dk(s).$$

Again by I.4.16 the second integral in (12) is equal to

$$\int_a^b \cdot d\alpha(t) \left[\int_t^b h(t,s)dk(s)\right].$$

Hence the result follows from Theorem 1.10 since k is continuous.

THEOREM 1.13. *With the hypothesis of Theorem 1.1 we take* $[c,d] = [a,b]$; *we further suppose that*

a) $\lim_{\delta \downarrow 0} SV_{[t-\delta,t+\delta]}[\alpha] = 0$ *for every* $t \in [a,b]$.

b) $\lim_{\delta \downarrow 0} \sup_{a \leq t \leq b} SV_{[s-\delta,s+\delta]}[h^t] = 0$ *for every* $s \in [a,b]$.

Then $\tilde{h}$ *is continuous, where* $\tilde{h}(s) = \int_a^s d\alpha(t)h(t,s)$, *and*

$$(13) \quad \int_a^b \left[\int_a^s d\alpha(t)h(t,s)\right] dg(s) = \int_a^b d\alpha(t) \left[\int_t^b h(t,s)dg(s)\right].$$

PROOF. By I.5.2 we have

$$\|\tilde{h}(s_1)-\tilde{h}(s_2)\| \leq SV_{[s_1,s_2]}[\tilde{h}] =$$

$$= \sup\{\|\int_{s_1}^{s_2} d_s\left[\int_a^s d\alpha(t)h(t,s)\right] f(s)\| \mid f \in G([s_1,s_2],X), \|f\| \leq 1\}.$$

By (8) (with $\bar{a} = s_1$ and $\bar{b} = s_2$) and from a) and b) follows that $\tilde{h}$ is continuous. Let us now prove (13): Since $\tilde{h}$, α and h^t, $t \in [a,b]$, are continuous functions (6) becomes

$$\int_a^b d_s \left[\int_a^s d\alpha(t)\cdot h(t,s)\right] g(s) = \int_a^b d\alpha(t)\left[h(t,t)g(t-) + \right.$$

$$\left. + \int_t^b d_s h(t,s)\cdot g(s)\right].$$

Using integration by parts in both integrals $\int d_s$ we obtain (13).

COROLLARY 1.14. *With the same hypothesis as in Theorem 1.13 we define*

$$\tilde{g}(t) = \int_a^t d_s h(t,s)\cdot g(s) \quad \textit{and} \quad \hat{g}(t) = \int_a^t h(t,s)\cdot dg(s).$$

We have

a) $\tilde{g}$ *is regulated;* $\tilde{g}$ *is continuous if* h *is continuous.*

(14) $$\tilde{g}(t+) = \int_a^t d_s h(t+,s)\cdot g(s) \qquad a \leqslant t < b$$

(14') $$\tilde{g}(t-) = \int_a^t d_s h(t-,s)\cdot g(s) \qquad a < t \leqslant b.$$

b) $\hat{g}$ *is regulated;* $\hat{g}$ *is continuous if* g *and* h *are continuous;*

(15) $$\hat{g}(t+) = \int_a^t h(t+,s)dg(s)+h(t+,s)[g(t+)-g(t)], \quad a \leqslant t < b$$

(15') $$\hat{g}(t-) = \int_a^t h(t-,s)dg(s)-h(t-,s)[g(t)-g(t-)], \quad a < t \leqslant b.$$

PROOF. a) $\tilde{g}(t+\varepsilon) = \int_a^{t+\varepsilon} d_s h(t+\varepsilon,s)\cdot g(s) =$

$$= \int_a^t d_s [h(t+\varepsilon,s) - h(t+,s)]\cdot g(s) + \int_t^{t+\varepsilon} d_s h(t+\varepsilon,s)\cdot g(s) +$$

$$+ \int_a^t d_s h(t+,s)\cdot g(s).$$

The frrst and the second integrals go to zero when $\varepsilon \downarrow 0$, respectively by the Theorem of Helly (I.5.8) and by the hypothesis b) of Theorem 1.13; hence (14). In an analogous way one proves (14'). (14) and (14') show that $\tilde{g}$ is continuous if h is continuous.

b) Using integration by parts we have

$$\tilde{g}(t) = h(t,t)g(t) - h(t,a)g(a) - \hat{g}(t),$$

hence

(α) $$\tilde{g}(t+) = h(t+,t)\cdot g(t+) - h(t+,a)\cdot g(a) - \hat{g}(t+).$$

Using again integration by parts, the expression for $\tilde{g}(t+)$ becomes

$$(\beta) \qquad \tilde{g}(t+) = \int_a^t d_s h(t+,s)g(s) = h(t+,t)g(t) - h(t+,a)g(a) - \\ - \int_a^t h(t+,s)dg(s)$$

and if we compare (α) and (β) we obtain (15). In an analogous way we obtain (15'). (15) and (15') show that $\hat{g}$ is continuous if g and h are continuous.

COROLLARY 1.15. *With the same hypothesis as in Theorem 1.13 the function* $h_\Delta: t\in [a,b] \longmapsto h(t,t)\in L(X,Y)$ *is regulated.*

PROOF. We take $g = I_X\in G([a,b],L(X))$; hence, with the notations of Corollary 1.8.a) and 1.14 we have $h_\Delta = \tilde{g} - \tilde{g}^1$ hence the result since $\tilde{g}$ and $\tilde{g}^1$ are regulated.

REMARK 6. One can, obviously, give an elementary direct proof of Corollary 1.15 or, more generally, one can prove directly that the restriction of h to any segment of $[a,b]\times[a,b]$ (i.e., the function $t \longmapsto h(t_o+t\cos\theta, s_o+t\sin\theta)$) is regulated.

REMARK 7. It is easy to see that all the results of this § are still valid if we replace the hypothesis $g\in G([a,b],L(X))$ by $g\in G([a,b],L(W,X))$ where W is a normed space.

REMARK 8. It is not difficult to see that all the results of this § are still valid if Z is a SSCLCS (working with the seminorms $q\in\Gamma_Z$ and the corresponding semivariations).

REMARK 9. More generally the results of this § are valid if instead of $L(W,X)$ (or $L(X)$ or X) and $L(X,Y)$ and $L(Y,Z)$ we consider systems of spaces with bilinear mappings related in an associative way (see [H-DS]).

REMARK 10. For $g: [a,b] \longrightarrow X$ then, with obvious adaptations, all results of this § but corollaries 1.8, 1.11 and 1.15 are still valid if we suppose only that h is weakly regulated as a function of the first variable (and satisfies (SV^u)); in this case, for instance, in Lemma 1.2 (and in Theorem 1.1 etc.) the integral

$$\int_c^d \cdot d\alpha(t)\cdot h(t,s)$$

is defined in the weak sense, i.e., for every $x \in X$ there exists

$$\bar{h}(t)x = \int_c^d \cdot d\alpha(t) \cdot h(t,s),$$

etc.

For $g: [a,b] \longrightarrow L(X)$ [or $g: [a,b] \longrightarrow L(W,X)$] all the results of this § are still valid if we replace everywhere the property "regulated" by "weakly regulated".

§2 - *Extension to open intervals*

A - Let X be a normed space and Y a Banach space; given a function

$$h:]c,d[\times]a,b[\longrightarrow L(X,Y)$$

we write $h \in G^u(]c,d[\times]a,b[, L(X,Y))$ if for every $[\bar{c},\bar{d}] \times [\bar{a},\bar{b}] \subset]c,d[\times]a,b[$ we have

$$h \in G^u([\bar{c},\bar{d}] \times [\bar{a},\bar{b}], L(X,Y)).$$

The proofs of Theorem 2.1 to Corollary 2.5 that follow are analogous to the proofs of the corresponding results of §1.

THEOREM 2.1. *Let* X *be a normed space,* Y *a Banach space and* Z *a SSCLCS. Given* $\alpha \in SV_{oo}(]c,d[, L(Y,Z))$, $g \in G(]a,b[,X)$ [*or* $g \in G(]a,b[, L(X))$] *and* $h \in G^u(]c,d[\times]a,b[, L(X,Y))$ *that satisfies*

(00) *for every* $[\bar{c},\bar{d}] \subset]c,d[$ *there exists* $[\bar{a},\bar{b}] \subset]a,b[$ *such that for* $t \in [\bar{c},\bar{d}]$ *we have* $h(t,s) = 0$ *if* $s < \bar{a}$ *and* $h(t,s) = L(t,\bar{b})$ *if* $s > \bar{b}$

then we have

$$(1) \qquad \int_a^b \cdot d_s\left[\int_c^d \cdot d\alpha(t) \cdot h(t,s)\right] \cdot g(s) = \int_c^d \cdot d\alpha(t)\left[\int_a^b \cdot d_s h(t,s) \cdot g(s)\right];$$

given $q \in \Gamma_Z$ *and* $[\bar{c},\bar{d}]$ *containing the* q-*support of* α, *if* $[\bar{a},\bar{b}]$ *correspond to* $[\bar{c},\bar{d}]$ *by (00) then*

(2) $$q\left[\int_c^d \cdot d\alpha(t)\left[\int_a^b \cdot d_s h(t,s)\cdot g(s)\right]\right] \leqslant SV_q[\alpha] \sup_{\bar{c}\leqslant t\leqslant \bar{d}} SV[h^t]\cdot \|g\|_{(\bar{a},\bar{b})}\cdot$$

LEMMA 2.2. *With the hypothesis and notations of Theorem 2.1, for every* $s \in \,]a,b[$ *we define*

$$\bar{h}(s) = \int_c^d \cdot d\alpha(t)\cdot h(t,s);$$

then we have $\bar{g} \in G([c,d],Y)$ *or* $[\bar{g} \in G([c,d],L(X,Y))]$ *and*

(4) $$\|\bar{g}\|_{(\bar{c},\bar{d})} \leqslant \sup_{\bar{c}\leqslant t\leqslant \bar{d}} SV[h^t]\, \|g\|_{(\bar{a},\bar{b})}\cdot$$

COROLLARY 2.4. *With the hypothesis of Theorem 2.1 we take* g *continuous; then we have*

(5) $$\int_a^b \left[\int_c^d \cdot d\alpha(t)\cdot h(t,s)\right] dg(s) = \int_c^d \cdot d\alpha(t)\left[\int_a^b h(t,s)\,dg(s)\right].$$

PROOF. Since g is continuous we may replace $\int_a^b \cdot d_s$ in (1) by $\int_a^b d_s$; the result follows using integration by parts.

REMARK 1. The preceding results are still valid if we replace $]a,b[$ by a closed interval $[a,b]$. In this case it is enough to suppose that $h \in G^u([\bar{c},\bar{d}] \times [a,b], L(X,Y))$, i.e., that for every $[\bar{c},\bar{d}] \subset \,]c,d[$ we have $h \in G^u([\bar{c},\bar{d}] \times [a,b], L(X,Y))$.

COROLLARY 2.5. *With the hypothesis of Theorem 2.1 we take* $]c,d[\,=\,]a,b[$ *and for every* $s \in \,]a,b[$ *we define*

$$\tilde{h}(s) = \int_a^s \cdot d\alpha(t)\cdot h(t,s).$$

We have $\tilde{h} \in SV_{oo}(]a,b[, L(X,Z))$; *given* $q \in \Gamma_Z$ *and* (a_q,b_q) *containing the* q-*support of* α, *if* $(\bar{a}_q,\bar{b}_q)$ *corresponds to* (a_q,b_q) *by (00) (with* $\bar{a}_q \leqslant a_q$ *and* $\bar{b}_q \geqslant b_q$*) then*

$$(6) \qquad SV_q[\tilde{h}] \leqslant SV_q[\alpha]\left[\|h_\Delta\|\left(\bar{a}_q,\bar{b}_q\right) + \sup_{\bar{a}_q\leqslant t\leqslant \bar{b}_q} SV[h^t]\right]$$

where

$$\|h_\Delta\|\left(\bar{a}_q,\bar{b}_q\right) = \sup_{\bar{a}_q\leqslant t\leqslant \bar{b}_q} \|h(t,t)\|.$$

B - *The formula of Dirichlet*

THEOREM 2.6. *With the hypothesis of Theorem 2.1 we take* $]c,d[\ = \ ]a,b[$ *and* g *continuous; then we have*

$$(7) \qquad \int_a^b \left[\int_a^s \cdot d\alpha(t)\cdot h(t,s)\right] dg(s) = \int_a^b \cdot d\alpha(t)\left[\int_t^b h(t,s)dg(s)\right].$$

PROOF. If we take $h_o(t,s) = Y(s-t)h(t,s)$ then h_o has the same properties as h in Theorem 2.1. Hence we may replace h by h_o in Corollary 2.5 and we get (7).

THEOREM 2.7. *Given* X, Y *and* Z *as in Theorem 2.1,* $\alpha \in SV_{oo}(]a,b[,\ L(Y,Z))$, $h\in G^u(]a,b[\times]a,b[,\ L(X,Y))$ *and* $g\in \mathcal{C}(]a,b[,X)$ [*or* $g\in \mathcal{C}(]a,b[,\ L(X))$] *for every* $s\in\ ]a,b[$ *we have*

$$(8) \qquad \int_a^s \left[\int_a^\sigma \cdot d\alpha(t)\cdot h(t,\sigma)\right] dg(\sigma) = \int_a^s d\alpha(t)\left[\int_t^s h(t,\sigma)dg(\sigma)\right].$$

PROOF. If we take

$$h_o(t,\sigma) = \chi_{]a,s]\times]a,s]}(t,\sigma)Y(\sigma-t)h(t,\sigma)$$

then h_o satisfies the same properties as h in Theorem 2.6. Hence we may replace h by h_o in (7) and we get (8).

REMARK 2. The extension of the other results of §1 to the case of open intervals and Z a SSCLCS is now obvious.

CHAPTER III

Volterra Stieltjes-Integral Equations with Linear Constraints

Let X be a Banach space and Y a SSCLCS; in this chapter we consider systems of the form

$$(K) \qquad y(t) - y(t_o) + \int_{t_o}^{t} d_\sigma K(t,\sigma) \cdot y(\sigma) = f(t) - f(t_o)$$

$$(F) \qquad F[y] = c$$

where $y, f \in G(]a,b[,X)$, $F \in L[G(]a,b[,X),Y]$ and

$$K: \;]a,b[\times]a,b[\longrightarrow L(X)$$

is a continuous function which satisfies the property (SV^{uo}) defined on §1.

In §1 we show that there is a resolvent associated to K; for this purpose K need not be continuous but only regulated as a function of the first variable; by Remark 10 of §1 of Chapter II the results of this § may even be extended to the case where K is only weakly regulated as a function of the first variable.

In §2 the results of §1 are applied to the case of a Stieltjes Integro-Differential Equation and new properties of the resolvent are found.

In §3 we study the system (K), (F) and find its Green function.

REMARK 1. We will see along this chapter that the extension of the results to the case of closed intervals $[c,d]$ is automatic and in §1 we go the other way around.

REMARK 2. In order that (K) makes a sense it is obviously sufficient for K to be defined only on the set

$$\Gamma = \{(t,\sigma) \in]a,b[\times]a,b[\mid t \leqslant \sigma \leqslant t_o \text{ or } t_o \leqslant \sigma \leqslant t\}$$

and the same applies to the resolvent R when we consider the equation (ρ) of §1. In order to simplify the notations we extend K from Γ to $]a,b[\times]a,b[$ or even to $]a,b[\times\mathbb{R}$ by defining

$$K(t,\sigma)=\begin{cases}K(t,t) & \text{if } \sigma\geqslant t\geqslant t_0\\ K(t,t_0) & \text{if } \sigma\leqslant t_0\leqslant t\end{cases}\qquad K(t,\sigma)=\begin{cases}K(t,t) & \text{if } \sigma\leqslant t\leqslant t_0\\ K(t,t_0) & \text{if } \sigma\geqslant t_0\geqslant t\end{cases}$$

If in Γ K is regulated as a function of the first variable and satisfies (SV^{uo}) as a function of the second variable (see definition bellow or Theorem 1.13 of Chapter II: (SV^{uo}) ≡ b)) it is obvious that the extended function still satisfies (SV^{uo}) and it follows immediately from II.1.15 that it is also regulated as a function of the first variable; this would not be true if we had only (SV^{u}); more precisely, if $K_\Delta: t\in]a,b[\longmapsto K(t,t)\in L(X)$ were not regulated.

REMARK 3. Equations of the type (K) occur quite naturally; indeed:

a) For differential and integral equations it is natural to work not with functions but with equivalence classes of functions: two functions y_1 and y_2 are equivalent if we have

$$\int_s^t [y_1(\sigma)-y_2(\sigma)]\,d\sigma = 0$$

for all s and t; i.e., instead of working, for instance, with $G(]a,b[,X)$ we consider the quotient space $\tilde{G}(]a,b[,X)$ (see Chapter I, §3) or the space $G\_(]a,b[,X)$ isometric to it (I.3.13).

Therefore, as a generalization of linear integral operators it is natural to consider operators

$$\ell\in L[G\_(]a,b[,X),G(]c,d[,Y)];$$

then, by I.6.10 there exists a kernel

$$K\in G(]c,d[,SV^{\sigma}_{oo}(]a,b[,L(X,Y)))$$

such that for every $f\in G\_(]a,b[,X)$ we have

$$\ell(f)(t) = \int_a^b \cdot d_\sigma K(t,\sigma)\cdot f(\sigma),$$

where $K(t,\sigma)x = \ell[\chi_{]a,\sigma]}x](t)$, $t\in]a,b[$, $\sigma\in]c,d[$, $x\in X$.

b) If we want further the operator ℓ to have properties similar to those of Volterra integral operators, i.e., that $]c,d[=]a,b[$, $Y = X$ and that there exists a point $t_o\in]a,b[$ such that for every $t\in]a,b[$, $\ell(f)|\{t_o,t\}$ depends only on $f|\{t_o,t\} = \chi_{\{t_o,t\}}f$ then the operator ℓ takes the form

$$k(f)(t) = \int_a^b d_\sigma K(t,\sigma)\chi_{\{t_o,t\}}(\sigma)f(\sigma) = \int_{t_o}^t d_\sigma K(t,\sigma)\cdot f(\sigma).$$

Now however in general k(f) is not anymore a regulated function unless we impose further restrictions on the kernel K.

Furthermore, we also want K to have a resolvent and for this purpose it is necessary for K to be regulated as a function of the first variable and for the function

$$K_\Delta:\ t\in]a,b[\longmapsto K(t,t)\in L(X)$$

to be regulated; indeed: in order to consider the resolvent equation we have to work with integrals of the form $\int_{t_o}^t d_\sigma K(t,\sigma)\circ U(\sigma)$ where $U\in G(]a,b[,L(X))$; since this integral do not change if we replace $K(t,\sigma)$ by $K(t,\sigma)-K(t,t_o)$ we suppose for a moment that $K(t,t_o) = 0$. Then for $\tau\geqslant t_o$ we take $U = \chi_{]a,\tau]}I_X\in G(]a,b[,L(X))$; we get

$$k[\chi_{]a,\tau]}I_X](t) = \int_{t_o}^t d_\sigma K(t,\sigma)\chi_{]a,\tau]}(\sigma) = \begin{cases} K(t,t) & \text{if} \quad t\leqslant\tau \\ K(t,\tau) & \text{if} \quad t\geqslant\tau \end{cases}$$

In an analogous way for $\tau\leqslant t_o$ we take $U = \chi_{[\tau,b[}I_X$ and we get

$$k[\chi_{[\tau,b[}I_X](t) = \begin{cases} K(t,t) & \text{if} \quad t\geqslant\tau \\ K(t,\sigma) & \text{if} \quad t\leqslant\tau \end{cases}$$

Hence, since τ is arbitrary we see that if $k(U)$ is regulated for every U then K is regulated as a function of the first variable and K_Δ is regulated too.

Also in order that (K) has a resolvent it is necessary for the equation

$$\text{(i)} \qquad y(t) - x + \int_{t_o}^{t} d_\sigma K(t,\sigma)y(\sigma) = f(t) - f(t_o)$$

to have a unique solution. However if K satisfies the necessary conditions we just found and is locally uniformly of bounded semivariation and satisfies even (SV^o), (i) does not have a unique solution (see the Example after 1.3).

However the condition $K \in G^{uo}$ defined in §1 will assure that all this necessary conditions are satisfied and that K has a resolvent.

§1 - *The resolvent of a Volterra Stieltjes-integral equation*

A - Let X be a Banach space, $]a,b[$ and open interval of $\mathbb{R}$, not necessarily bounded, and $t_o \in]a,b[$. We consider the Volterra Stieltjes-integral equation

$$\text{(K)} \qquad y(t)-y(t_o) + \int_{t_o}^{t} d_\sigma K(t,\sigma)y(\sigma) = f(t)-f(t_o) \qquad t \in]a,b[$$

where $y,f \in G(]a,b[,X)$ and $K:]a,b[\times]a,b[\longrightarrow L(X)$ satisfies the properties

(G) - K is regulated as a function of the first variable.

(SV^{uo}) - For every $[c,d] \subset]a,b[$ and every $\varepsilon > 0$ there exists a $\delta > 0$ such that for all $s,t \in [c,d]$ we have

$$SV_{[s-\delta,s+\delta]}[K^t] \leq \varepsilon.$$

(SV^{uo}) expresses that in every

$$[c,d]\times[c,d] \subset]a,b[\times]a,b[$$

the semivariation of K on an interval of the second variable goes uniformly to 0 with the length of the interval, i.e.

$\lim_{\delta\downarrow 0} SV^{\delta}_{[c,d]}[K] = 0$ where

$$SV^{\delta}_{[c,d]}[K] = \sup\{SV_{[s-\delta,s+\delta]}[K^t] \mid s,t \in [c,d]\}.$$

It is easy to see that

1.1. *The property* $(SV^{u\sigma})$ *implies the properties* (SV^u) *and* (SV^{σ}):

(SV^u) - *For every* $[c,d] \subset]a,b[$ *there exists* $M > 0$ *such that* $\sup_{c\leq t\leq d} SV_{[c,d]}[K^t] \leq M$.

(SV^{σ}) - *For every* $s,t \in]a,b[$ *we have*

$$\lim_{\delta\downarrow 0} SV_{[s-\delta,s+\delta]}[K^t] = 0.$$

We recall that (SV^u) says that locally K is uniformly of bounded semivariation as a function of the second variable.

Since $\|K(t,s_1)-K(t,s_2)\| \leq SV_{[s_1,s_2]}[K^t]$ we have

1.2. *If* K *has the property* (SV^{o}) *then for every* $t\in]a,b[$ K^t *is a continuous function.*

Since $K^t \in SV([t_o,t],L(X))$ the integral in (K) is well defined and by II.1.14a) we have

1.3. *Let* K *satisfy* (G) *and* (SV^{uo}), *then*

a) *The function* $t \in]a,b[\longmapsto \int_{t_o}^{t} d_{\sigma}K(t,\sigma)\cdot y(\sigma) \in X$ *is regulated.*

b) *If* K *is continuous the function*

$$t \in]a,b[\longmapsto \int_{t_o}^{t} d_{\sigma}K(t,\sigma)\cdot y(\sigma) \in X$$

is continuous and a solution y *of* (K) *is continuous if and only if* f *is continuous.*

We will prove that when K has the properties (G) and (SV^{uo}) then for every $x \in X$ (K) has only one solution such that $y(t_o) = x$ (Theorem 1.6). If however K satisfies only the properties (G), (SV^u) and (SV^{σ}) this is no longer true, as is shown by the

EXAMPLE. We take $]a,b[=]-1,1[$, $t_o = 0$, $X = \mathbb{R}$. We take $K(0,s) = 0$ and for $t > 0$ we define

$$K(t,\sigma) = (1 - \frac{1}{t}\sigma)\chi_{[0,t]}(\sigma)$$

and for $t < 0$ we take $K(-t,\sigma) = K(t,\sigma)$. Then for $f = 0$ and $y(t_o) = 0$ the equation

$$y(t) + \int_{t_o}^{t} d_\sigma K(t,\sigma)y(\sigma) = 0$$

has two solutions, $y \equiv 0$ and $y(t) = \mathit{sg}\ t$ (= 1 if $t > 0$, = 0 if $t = 0$, = -1 if $t < 1$).

In this § we want to prove that for $f \in G(]a,b[,X)$ and $x \in X$ there is one and only one $y \in G(]a,b[,X)$ solution of (K) and such that $y(t_o) = x$. Obviously it is sufficient to prove the same result for any closed interval $[c,d] \subset]a,b[$ that contains t_o since if y is the solution in $[c,d]$ and $\bar{y}$ the solution in $[\bar{c},\bar{d}] \supset [c,d]$ by the unicity of the solution in $[c,d]$ we have $\bar{y}|_{[c,d]} = y$, hence we can use the solutions on the intervals $[c,d] \subset]a,b[$ to get the solution in $]a,b[$. The same reasoning applies obviously to equations (R^*), (R_*) and others considered bellow.

FROM NOW ON WE WILL CONSIDER A FIXED INTERVAL $[c,d] \subset]a,b[$ CONTAINING t_o

We denote by $G([c,d]\times[c,d],L(X))$, or simply by G, the set of all bounded functions $U: [c,d]\times[c,d] \longrightarrow L(X)$ that satisfy (G), i.e., are regulated as functions of the first variable, that is, $U_s \in G([c,d],L(X))$ for every $s \in [c,d]$. G is a Banach space when endowed with the norm

$$U \in G \longmapsto \|U\| = \mathit{sup}\{\|U(t,s)\| \mid s,t \in [c,d]\}.$$

We denote by G^u the vector subspace of G formed by the functions that satisfy (SV^u). G^u is endowed with the norm $|||U||| = \|U\| + SV^u[U]$ where we recall that

$$SV^u[U] = SV^u_{[c,d]}[U] = \mathit{sup}_{c \leq t \leq d}\ SV_{[c,d]}[U^t].$$

THEOREM 1.4. $G^u_{||| \ |||}$ *is a Banach space.*

PROOF. Let $U_n \in G^u$, $n \in \mathbb{N}$, be a Cauchy sequence. Then U_n is uniformly convergent to a function $U \in G$ and for every $\varepsilon > 0$ there exists n_ε such that for $n,m \geq n_\varepsilon$ we have

$SV[U_n^t - U_m^t] \leq \varepsilon$ for every $t \in [c,d]$ and this implies immediately

$SV[U_n^t - U^t] \leq \varepsilon$ for every $t \in [c,d]$ and $n > n_\varepsilon$. Hence $U \in G^u$ and U is the limit of the sequence U_n in the norm of G^u.

G^{uo} denotes the subspace of G^u formed by the functions that satisfy the property (SV^{uo}). We will show (Proposition 1.14) that G^{uo} is a closed subspace of G^u.

REMARK 4. If $K \in G^{uo}$, for every $t \in [c,d]$ we have obviously

$$\int_{t_o}^{t} d_\sigma [K(t,\sigma) - K(t,t)] \cdot y(\sigma) = \int_{t_o}^{t} d_\sigma K(t,\sigma) \cdot y(\sigma)$$

hence the equation (K) does not change if eventually we replace K by $K - K_\Delta$, i.e. $K(t,\sigma)$ by $K(t,\sigma) - K(t,t)$, that is, we suppose that K is normalized: $K(t,t) = 0$. Furthermore, since $K \in G^{uo}$, by II.1.15 K_Δ is regulated and this implies immediately that $K - K_\Delta \in G^{uo}$; nothing of the kind would be true if we had only $K \in G^u$.

B - We give now 4 important examples of an equation (K).

EXAMPLE A - We consider the Stieltjes integro-differential equation

$$(L') \qquad y' + A' \cdot y = f'$$

where (L') is an abridged way of writing that we have

$$(L) \qquad y(t) - y(s) + \int_s^t dA(\sigma) \cdot y(\sigma) = f(t) - f(s)$$

for all $s,t \in]a,b[$. We suppose that $y, f \in G(]a,b[,X)$ and

$$A \in \mathcal{C}SV^{loc}(]a,b[,L(X))$$

(i.e. A is a continuous function and for every $[c,d] \subset]a,b[$ we have $A \in SV([c,d],L(X))$). In this case the condition (SV^{uo}) becomes simply

(SV°) $\lim_{\delta \downarrow 0} SV_{]s-\delta, s+\delta[}[A] = 0$ for every $s \in]a,b[$.

The equation (L) is equivalent to

$$y(t)-y(t_o) + \int_{t_o}^{t} dA(\sigma)\cdot y(\sigma) = f(t)-f(t_o) \quad \text{for every} \quad t \in]a,b[$$

since it is obtained as the difference of its values for t and s; hence (L) is a particular instance of (K).

We recall that (L) or (L') contain as a particular case the ordinary linear differential equations; (L) will allow discontinuous solutions (for f discontinuous).

EXAMPLE B - We consider the Volterra integral equation

$$\text{(V)} \qquad y(t) - y(t_o) + \int_{t_o}^{t} B(t,\sigma)\, y(\sigma) = f(t) - f(t_o).$$

If we define

$$K(t,\sigma) = \int_{t_o}^{\sigma} B(t,s)ds$$

the equation (V) takes the form (K); here we suppose that for every $t \in]a,b[$ the function B^t is Darboux integrable (or Bochner-Lebesgue integrable). In order for K to be regulated as a function of the first variable it is sufficient that for every $t \in]a,b[$ there exist functions B^{t+} and B^{t-} such that for every $s \in]a,b[$ we have

$$\lim_{\varepsilon \downarrow 0} \left\| \int_{t_o}^{s} [B(t+\varepsilon,\sigma)-B^{t+}(\sigma)]d\sigma \right\| = 0$$

and

$$\lim_{\varepsilon \downarrow 0} \left\| \int_{t_o}^{s} [B(t-\varepsilon,\sigma)-B^{t-}(\sigma)]d\sigma \right\| = 0.$$

In order that (K) satisfies the property (SV^{uo}) it is sufficient that for every $[c,d] \subset]a,b[$ and every $\varepsilon > 0$ there exists $\delta > 0$ such that for every $s \in [c,d]$ we have

$$\sup_{c \leq t \leq d} \int_{s-\delta}^{s+\delta} \|B(t,\sigma)\| d\sigma < \varepsilon$$

since by I.5.2 we have

$$SV_{[s-\delta,s+\delta]}[K^t] =$$

$$= \sup\{\|\int_{s-\delta}^{s+\delta} d_\sigma K(t,\sigma)\cdot f(\sigma)\| \mid f\in G([s-\delta,s+\delta],\mathbf{X}),\ \|f\|\leqslant 1\} =$$

$$= \sup_{\|f\|\leqslant 1} \|\int_{s-\delta}^{s+\delta} d_\sigma\Big[\int_{t_o}^{\sigma} B(t,\tau)d\tau\Big]\cdot f(\sigma)\| =$$

$$= \sup_{\|f\|\leqslant 1} \|\int_{s-\delta}^{s+\delta} B(t,\sigma)f(\sigma)d\sigma\| \leqslant \int_{s-\delta}^{s+\delta} \|B(t,\sigma)\|d\sigma .$$

These conditions are obviously satisfied if B is a continuous function or, more generally, a locally bounded (measurable) function which as a function of the first variable is regulated (for almost all $s\in\,]a,b[$).

EXAMPLE C. We consider the differential equation

$$A_o(A_1y)' + By = g'$$

where $g\in BV^{loc}(]a,b[,X)$, $B\in G(]a,b[,L(X))$ and A_o, A_1 are such that there exist and are regulated the functions

$$t\in\,]a,b[\ \longmapsto A_i(t)^{-1}\in L(X) \qquad i = 1,2.$$

If we multiply the equation by A_o^{-1} and integrate it we obtain

$$A_1(t)y(t)-A_1(s)y(s) + \int_s^t A_o(\sigma)^{-1}B(\sigma)y(\sigma)d\sigma = \int_s^t \cdot A_o(\sigma)^{-1}\cdot dg(\sigma) \qquad t\in\,]a,b[$$

and this is the meaning that must be given to the original equation. If we make $z(t) = A_1(t)y(t)$ we obtain an equation in the form of the preceding examples:

$$z(t) - z(s) + \int_s^t A(\sigma)z(\sigma)d\sigma = f(t) - f(s)$$

where

$$A(\sigma) = A_o(\sigma)^{-1}B(\sigma)A_1(\sigma)^{-1} \quad\text{and}\quad f(t) = \int_{t_o}^t \cdot A_o(\sigma)^{-1}\cdot dg(\sigma).$$

EXAMPLE D. We will show that a linear delay differential equation may be reduced to a particular case of equation (K). This example is due to José Carlos Fernandes de Oliveira.

a) Let X be a Banach space, $t_1 > t_o$ and $0 < r < t_1 - t_o$ (the delay). Given $y \in G([t_o - r, t_1], X)$ for every $t \in [t_o, t_1]$ we define $y_t \in G([-r, 0], X)$ by $y_t(s) = y(s+t)$, $s \in [-r, 0]$. A linear delay differential equation is an equation of the form

$$\text{(D)} \qquad y'(t) = \mathcal{A}(t, y_t) + g(t) \qquad t \in [t_o, t_1]$$

where $y \in G([t_o - r, t_1], X)$, $g \in G([t_o, t_1], X)$ and

$$\mathcal{A}: [t_o, t_1] \times \tilde{G}([-r, 0], X) \longrightarrow X$$

has the following properties:

1) $\mathcal{A}^t \in L[\tilde{G}([-r, 0], X), X]$ for every $t \in [t_o, t_1]$, i.e., as a function of the second variable $\mathcal{A}$ is linear and continuous.

2) $\mathcal{A}_f \in G([t_o, t_1], X)$ for every $f \in \tilde{G}([-r, 0], X)$, i.e., for every $f \in G([-r, 0], X)$ the function

$$t \in [t_o, t_1] \longmapsto \mathcal{A}(t, f) \in X$$

is regulated. Hence by I.3.13 and I.5.1 we have

$$\mathcal{A}^t \in L[G_-([-r, 0], X), X] \simeq SV_o([-r, 0], L(X)).$$

Let us denote by A^t the element of $SV_o([-r, 0], L(X))$ corresponding to $\mathcal{A}^t$, i.e., for every $f \in G_-([-r, 0], X)$ we have

$$\mathcal{A}(t, f) = \mathcal{A}^t(f) = \int_{-r}^{0} \cdot d_s A^t(s) \cdot f(s).$$

Furthermore if we define $F_{\mathcal{A}}(f)(t) = \mathcal{A}^t(f)$, by the hypothesis above we have $F_{\mathcal{A}} \in L[G([-r, 0], X), G([t_o, t_1], X)]$ hence by Theorem 5.10 of Chapter I and Remark 8 that follows it there exists one and only one function

$$A: [t_o, t_1] \times [-r, 0] \longrightarrow L(X)$$

that has the properties (SV^u) and (G^σ) of the remark we mentioned and is such that for every $f \in G([-r, 0], X)$ we have

$$\mathcal{A}(t, f) = \int_{-r}^{0} \cdot d_s A(t, s) \cdot f(s) \qquad \text{for every } t \in [t_o, t_1].$$

Hence (D) takes the form

$$(\tilde{D}) \qquad y'(t) = \int_{-r}^{0} \cdot d_s A(t,s) \cdot y(s+t) + g(t) \qquad t \in [t_o, t_1]$$

b) But for $y \in G([t_o - r, t_1], X)$ the function $\tilde{y}$ in general is not anymore regulated, where

$$\tilde{y}(t) = \int_{-r}^{0} \cdot d_s A(t,s) \cdot y(s+t), \qquad t \in [t_o, t_1].$$

However if we suppose that $A \in G^{uo}([-r,0] \times [t_o, t_1], L(X))$ then it follows that for every $y \in G([t_o - r, t_1], X)$ the function $\tilde{y}$ is regulated; indeed: we have

$$\tilde{y}(t) = \int_{t-r}^{t} \cdot\ d_s A(t, s-t) \cdot y(s)$$

and by remark 6 of §1 of Chapter II the function B, where $B(t,s) = A(t,s-t)$ (with the extension made according to remark 2) still belongs to G^{uo}, i.e. satisfies the hypothesis of Theorem 1.13 of Chapter II; hence the result follows from a) of II.1.14.

Therefore if $A \in G^{uo}$, every regulated solution y of $(\tilde{D})$ has a regulated derivative y', hence y is continuous (for $t \in [t_o, t_1]$).

c) For (D) or $(\tilde{D})$ the initial value problem consists in giving a function $\phi \in G([-r,0],X)$ and look for a function $y \in G([t_o - r, t_1], X)$ that is a solution of (D) or $(\tilde{D})$ for $t \in [t_o, t_1]$ and such that $y_{t_o} = \phi$.

We will show that this problem may be reduced to a particular case of (K). $(\tilde{D})$ is equivalent to

$$y'(t) = \int_{t-r}^{t} d_s A(t, s-t) \cdot y(s) + g(t) \qquad t \in [t_o, t_1].$$

We recall that we suppose that A has been extended to $[t_o, t_1] \times \mathbb{R}$ taking $A(t,s) = A(t,0)$ if $s > 0$ and $A(t,s) = A(t,-r)$ if $s \leqslant -r$; then we may write

$$y'(t) = \int_{t_o-r}^{t_o} d_sA(t,s-t)\cdot y(s) + \int_{t_o}^{t} d_sA(t,s-t)\cdot y(s) + g(t)$$

For $s\in \left[t_o-r,t_o\right]$ we have $y(s) = \phi(s-t_o)$; if we take

$$\bar{g}(t) = g(t) + \int_{t_o-r}^{t_o} d_sA(t,s-t)\cdot\phi(s-t_o)$$

we obtain

$$y'(t) - \int_{t_o}^{t} d_sA(t,s-t)\cdot y(s) = \bar{g}(t);$$

therefore

$$y(t) - y(t_o) - \int_{t_o}^{t}\left[\int_{t_o}^{\tau} d_sA(\tau,s-\tau)y(s)\right]d\tau = \int_{t_o}^{t}\bar{g}(\tau)d\tau.$$

We recall that $y(t_o) = \phi(0)$ and we take

$$f(t) = \int_{t_o}^{t}\bar{g}(\tau)d\tau;$$

we get

$$y(t) - \phi(0) - \int_{t_o}^{t}\left[\int_{t_o}^{\tau} d_sA(\tau,s-\tau)y(s)\right]d\tau = f(t).$$

As we saw in b) $B(t,s) = A(t,s-t)$ satisfies the hypothesis of Theorem 1.13 of Chapter II and a fortiori of Theorem 1.1 of that chapter hence we may apply (6') of II.1.6 and we obtain

$$y(t)-\phi(0) - \int_{t_o}^{t} d_s\left[\int_{s}^{t} A(\tau,s-\tau)d\tau\right]y(s) - \int_{t_o}^{t}A(\tau,0)y(\tau)d\tau = f(t).$$

If we make $K(t,s) = -\int_{s}^{t}A(\tau,s-\tau)d\tau$ and if we normalize A in such a way that $A(t,0) = 0$ instead of $A(t,-r) = 0$ we finally obtain

$$y(t)-\phi(0) + \int_{t_o}^{t} d_sK(t,s)y(s) = f(t) \qquad t\in \left[t_o,t_1\right]$$

where

$$f(t) = \int_{t_o}^{t}\left[\int_{t_o-r}^{t_o} d_sA(\tau,s-\tau)\phi(s-t_o)+g(\tau)\right]d\tau$$

(and $y(t) = \phi(t-t_o)$ for $t\in\left[t_o-r,t_o\right]$).

C - The main theorem of this § is the following

THEOREM 1.5. *Given* $K\in G^{uo}$ *we have*

I - There exists one and only one element $R\in G$, *the resolvent of* K, *such that*

$$(R^*) \qquad R(t,s) = I_X-\int_s^t d_\sigma K(t,\sigma)\circ R(\sigma,s) \qquad \text{for all} \quad s,t\in\left[c,d\right].$$

II - $R\in G^{uo}$ *and* $R(t,t) = I_X$ *for all* $t\in\left[c,d\right]$.

III - For every $f\in G(\left[c,d\right],X)$ *and* $x\in X$ *the system*

$$(K) \qquad y(t)-y(t_o)+\int_{t_o}^{t} d_\sigma K(t,\sigma)\cdot y(\sigma) = f(t)-f(t_o) \qquad t\in\left[c,d\right]$$

$$y(t_o) = x$$

has one and only one solution $y\in G(\left[c,d\right],X)$; *this solution is given by*

$$(\rho) \qquad y(t) = R(t,t_o)x + \int_{t_o}^{t} R(t,s)df(s) \qquad t\in\left[c,d\right]$$

and depends continuously on x *and* f *(and* K*).*

IV - If K *is normalized (i.e.* $K(t,t) = 0$ *for every* $t\in\left[c,d\right]$*) we have*

$$(R_*) \qquad R(t,s) = I_X + \int_s^t R(t,\sigma)\circ d_\sigma K(\sigma,s) \qquad \text{for all} \quad s,t\in\left[c,d\right].$$

V - The mapping that to every $K\in G^{uo}$ *associates its resolvent* R *is injective and bicontinuous (not linear) from the set of all* $K\in G^{uo}$ *such that* $K(t,t) \equiv 0$ *onto the set of all* $R\in G^{uo}$ *such that* $R(t,t) \equiv I_X$.

REMARK 5. The really difficult part of this theorem is the proof of II; the proof of I is quite simple. However II is necessary in order for the integrals in (ρ) and (R_*) to be defined, to prove that y given by (ρ) satisfies (K) and to prove V.

We will now prove many partial results till we complete the proof of Theorem 1.5.

THEOREM 1.6. *Given* $K \in G^{uo}$, *for every* $f \in G([c,d],X)$ *and every* $x \in X$ *the equation*

$$y(t) - x + \int_{t_o}^{t} d_\sigma K(t,\sigma)\cdot y(\sigma) = f(t) - f(t_o) \qquad t \in [c,d]$$

has at most one solution $y \in G([c,d],X)$ *(the existence is proved in Corollary 1.16).*

PROOF. If y_1 and y_2 are two solutions then $z = y_2 - y_1$ os a solution of

$$z(t) = -\int_{t_o}^{t} d_\sigma K(t,\sigma)\cdot z(\sigma) \qquad t \in [c,d]$$

and we will prove that $z \equiv 0$, hence $y_1 \equiv y_2$. For $t > t_o$ we have

$$\|z(t)\| \leqslant SV_{[t_o,t]}[K^t]\ \|z\|_{[t_o,t]}$$

and if we take $t_1 > t$ we have

$$\|z\|_{[t_o,t_1]} \leqslant \sup_{t_o \leqslant t \leqslant t_1} SV_{[t_o,t_1]}[K^t]\ \|z\|_{[t_o,t_1]}$$

Since K satisfies (SV^{uo}) there exists $t_1 > t_o$ such that

$$\sup_{t_o \leqslant t \leqslant t_1} SV_{[t_o,t_1]}[K^t] < 1$$

hence $z(t) = 0$ for $t \in [t_o,t_1]$. We define

$$t_o' = \sup\{t > t_o \mid z_{[t_o,t]} = 0\}$$

and we have $t_o' = d$ and hence $z|_{[t_o,d]} = 0$; indeed since $z(t) = 0$ for $t \in [t_o,t_o')$ z satisfies

$$z(t) = -\int_{t_o'}^{t} d_\sigma K(t,\sigma)\cdot z(\sigma)$$

and then, as above we prove that there exists $t_1 > t_0'$ such that $z(t) = 0$ for all $t \in [t_0, t_1]$ in contradiction to the definition of t_0'. In an analogous way one proves that $z(t) = 0$ for $c \leqslant t \leqslant t_0$.

COROLLARY 1.7. *Given* $K \in G^{uo}$, *the resolvent* $R \in G$ *that satisfies*

$$(R^*) \qquad R(t,s) = I_X - \int_s^t d_\sigma K(t,\sigma) \circ R(\sigma,s) \qquad \text{for all} \quad s,t \in [c,d]$$

is unique (the existence is proved in Theorem 1.9).

PROOF. For every $s \in [c,d]$ we have $R_s \in G([a,b], L(X))$ and

$$R_s(t) = I_X - \int_s^t d_\sigma K(t,\sigma) \circ R_s(\sigma);$$

the result follows immediately from the Theorem 1.6 if we consider $y(t) = R_s(t)x$ where $x \in X$.

THEOREM 1.8. *Given* $K \in G^{uo}$ *and* $R \in G^{uo}$ *satisfying*

$$(R^*) \qquad R(t,s) = I_X - \int_s^t d_\sigma K(t,\sigma) \circ R(\sigma,s)$$

we have

a) *For every* $f \in G([c,d], X)$ *and* $x \in X$ *the function*

$$(\rho) \qquad y(t) = R(t,t_0)x + \int_{t_0}^t R(t,s)\,df(s)$$

is the solution of

$$(K) \qquad y(t) - y(t_0) + \int_{t_0}^t d_\sigma K(t,\sigma) y(\sigma) = f(t) - f(t_0) \qquad t \in [c,d]$$

such that $y(t_0) = x$.

b) y *may be written as*

$$(\rho') \qquad y(t) = f(t) + R(t,t_0)[x - f(t_0)] - \int_{t_0}^t d_s R(t,s) \cdot f(s) \qquad t \in [c,d]$$

and y *depends continously on* x *and* f.

PROOF. a) It is enough to prove that if $u(t) = R(t,t_0)x$ and $v(t) = \int_{t_0}^t R(t,s)\,df(s)$, $t \in [c,d]$, we have

$$u(t) - x + \int_{t_o}^{t} d_\sigma K(t,\sigma)\cdot u(\sigma) = 0$$

and

$$v(t) + \int_{t_o}^{t} d_\sigma K(t,\sigma)\cdot v(\sigma) = f(t) - f(t_o);$$

the first equality is immediate if we apply (R^*) to x and take $s = t_o$. In order to prove the second one we have to show that

$$\int_{t_o}^{t} R(t,s)\cdot df(s) + \int_{t_o}^{t} d_\sigma K(t,\sigma)\left[\int_{t_o}^{\sigma} R(\sigma,s)df(s)\right] = f(t) - f(t_o).$$

If we replace the expression of R from (R^*) in the first integral we have to prove that

$$\int_{t_o}^{t}\left[I_X - \int_{s}^{t} d_\sigma K(t,\sigma)\circ R(\sigma,s)\right]df(s) +$$

$$+ \int_{t_o}^{t} d_\sigma K(t,\sigma)\left[\int_{t_o}^{\sigma} R(\sigma,s)\cdot df(s)\right] = f(t) - f(t_o)$$

i.e.

$$\int_{t_o}^{t}\left[\int_{s}^{t} d_\sigma K^t(\sigma)\ R(\sigma,s)\right]\cdot df(s) = \int_{t_o}^{t} d_\sigma K^t(\sigma)\left[\int_{t_o}^{\sigma} R(\sigma,s)df(s)\right]$$

and this is the formula of Dirichlet (Theorem 1.13 of Chapter II).

b) (ρ') follows from (ρ) using integration by parts and the continuous dependence is also immediate since (ρ') implies

$$\|y\| \leqslant \|f\| + \|R_{t_o}\|\left(\|x\| + \|f\|\right) + \sup_{c\leqslant t\leqslant d} SV_{[c,d]}\left(R^t\right)\|f\|.$$

THEOREM 1.9. *For every* $K\in G^{uo}$ *there exists one and only one* $R\in G$ *such that*

$$(R^*)\qquad R(t,s) = I_X - \int_{s}^{t} d_\sigma K(t,\sigma)\circ R(\sigma,s)\quad \text{for all}\quad s,t\in[c,d].$$

PROOF. For every $U\in G$ we define $\mathcal{T}U = \mathcal{T}_K U$ by

$$(\mathcal{T}U)(t,s) = I_X - \int_{s}^{t} d_\sigma K(t,\sigma)\circ U(\sigma,s)\quad \text{for all}\quad s,t\in[c,d].$$

By I.4.12 and I.4.4 the integral is well defined since $K^t \in G(]c,d[,L(X))$ and since we have $U_s \in G(]c,d[,L(X))$; by II.1.14.a) we have $(\mathcal{T}U)_s \in G(]c,d[,L(X))$ and since we have $\|(\mathcal{T}U)(t,s)\| \leq 1 + SV_{]s,t[}[K^t]\,\|U\|$ it follows that

$$\|\mathcal{T}U\| \leq 1 + SV^u[K]\,\|U\|,$$

i.e. $\mathcal{T}U \in G$.

Hence an element $R \in G$ that satisfies (R^*) is a fixed point of the transformation $\mathcal{T}$ of G. In order to prove the existence and uniqueness of this fixed point we will introduce a norm in G equivalent to its natural norm and show that with respect to this new norm $\mathcal{T}$ is a contraction.

Let us take $\lambda > 0$; for $U \in G$ we define

$$\|U\|_\lambda = \sup\{\|U(t,s)e^{-\lambda|t-s|}\| \mid s,t \in]c,d[\};$$

it is immediate that we have $\|U\|_\lambda \leq \|U\| \leq e^{\lambda(d-c)}\|U\|_\lambda$, hence the norms $\|\ \|$ and $\|\ \|_\lambda$ on G are equivalent. We will now prove that there exists $\lambda > 0$ such that $\mathcal{T}$ is a contraction; it is enough to prove it for the linear transformation $\mathcal{T}_o$ where

$$(\mathcal{T}_o U)(t,s) = \int_s^t d_\sigma K(t,\sigma)\circ U(\sigma,s), \quad s,t \in]c,d[.$$

Let us find an upper bound for $\|(\mathcal{T}_o U)(t,s)e^{-\lambda|t-s|}\|$; we take $\delta > 0$:

1) For $|t-s| \leq \delta$ we have

$$\|(\mathcal{T}_o U)(t,s)e^{-\lambda|t-s|}\| = \left\|\int_s^t d_\sigma K(t,\sigma)\circ U(\sigma,s)e^{-\lambda|t-s|}\right\| \leq$$

$$\leq \left\|\int_s^t d_\sigma K(t,\sigma)\circ U(\sigma,s)e^{-\lambda|\sigma-s|}\right\| \leq$$

$$\leq SV_{]s,t[}[K^t]\,\|U\|_\lambda \leq SV^\delta[K]\,\|U\|_\lambda.$$

2) For $|t-s| \geq \delta$ let us suppose that $c \leq s \leq t-\delta$; if $t+\delta \leq s \leq d$ the calculations are analogous. We have

$$\|(\mathcal{T}_o U)(t,s)e^{-\lambda|t-s|}\| = \left\|\int_s^t d_\sigma K(t,\sigma)\circ U(\sigma,s)e^{-\lambda|t-s|}\right\| =$$

$$= \left\| \int_s^t d_\sigma K(t,\sigma) \circ U(\sigma,s) e^{-\lambda(\sigma-s)} e^{-\lambda(t-\sigma)} \right\| \leqslant \left\| \int_s^{t-\delta} \right\| + \left\| \int_{t-\delta}^t \right\|$$

and let us find upper bounds for these integrals:

a) $$\left\| \int_s^{t-\delta} d_\sigma K(t,\sigma) \circ U(\sigma,s) e^{-\lambda(\sigma-s)} \cdot e^{-\lambda(t-\sigma)} \right\| \leqslant$$

$$\leqslant SV_{[s,t-\delta]}[K^t] \sup_{s\leqslant\sigma\leqslant t-\delta} \| U(\sigma,s) e^{-\lambda(\sigma-s)} \| e^{-\lambda\delta} \leqslant$$

$$\leqslant SV^u[K] \, \|U\|_\lambda e^{-\lambda\delta}.$$

b) $$\left\| \int_{t-\delta}^t d_\sigma K(t,\sigma) \circ U(\sigma,s) e^{-\lambda(\sigma-s)} e^{-\lambda(t-\sigma)} \right\| \leqslant$$

$$\leqslant SV_{[t-\delta,t]}[K^t] \, \|U\|_\lambda \leqslant SV^\delta[K] \, \|U\|_\lambda.$$

Hence for $|t-s| \geqslant \delta$ we have

$$\| (\mathcal{T}_o U)(t,s) e^{-\lambda(t-s)} \| \leqslant \left[e^{-\lambda\delta} SV^u[K] + SV^\delta[K] \right] \|U\|_\lambda.$$

Hence we have

$$\| \mathcal{T}_o(U) \|_\lambda \leqslant \left[e^{-\lambda\delta} SV^u[K] + SV^\delta[K] \right] \|U\|_\lambda.$$

Since K satisfies (SV^{uo}) we may take $\delta > 0$ such that $SV^\delta[K] < \frac{1}{4}$ and afterwards we take $\lambda > 0$ such that

$$e^{-\lambda\delta} SV^u[K] < \tfrac{1}{4};$$

then $\mathcal{T}_o$ is a contraction of $G_{\| \, \|_\lambda}$.

REMARK 6. In the case of the example (L) we will show in §2 that for all $s,t \in [c,d]$ we have $R(t,s) \in \text{Isom}\, X$ (i.e. $R(t,s)$ is a bicontinuous linear injection from X onto X) and we have even $R(t,s)^{-1} = R(s,t)$. In the general case this is not true; we have always $R(t,t) = I_X \in \text{Isom}\, X$ and if $K\colon [c,d] \times [c,d] \longrightarrow L(X)$ is a continuous function so is R (by Theorem 1.25) hence we have then $R(t,s) \in \text{Isom}\, X$ *for* t *and* s *sufficiently close*. In general however $R(t,s) \in L(X)$ may not be injective.

EXAMPLE. In order to prove that $R(t_1,t_o)$ is not injective it is enough to show that there exists an $x \neq 0$ such that $R(t_1,t_o)x = 0$. If we define $y(t) = R(t,t_o)x$, $t \in [c,d]$, then y satisfies

$$y(t) - x + \int_{t_o}^{t} d_\sigma K(t,\sigma)\cdot y(\sigma) = 0$$

and we have to prove that $y(t_1) = 0$. We take $X = \mathbb{R}$, $x = 1$, $]a,b[=]-\pi,\pi[$, $t_o = 0$ and consider the equation

$$y(t) - 1 + \operatorname{tg}\frac{t}{2}\int_0^t y(\sigma)d\sigma = 0;$$

its solution is the function $y(t) = \cos t$ which has a zero at $t_1 = \frac{\pi}{2}$.

D - We will now begin the proof that the resolvent is in G^{uo}.

PROPOSITION 1.10. *If* $K \in G^{uo}$, *for every* $U \in G^u$ *we have* $\mathcal{T}U \in G^u$ *where* $\mathcal{T}$ *denotes the transformation defined by* K

$$(\mathcal{T}U)(t,s) = I_X - \int_s^t d_\sigma K(t,\sigma)\circ U(\sigma,s) \qquad s,t \in [c,d].$$

PROOF. II.1.14.a) implies that for every $s \in [c,d]$ we have $(\mathcal{T}U)_s \in G([c,d],L(X))$; $\mathcal{T}U$ is bounded since

$$\|(\mathcal{T}U)(t,s)\| \leqslant 1 + \left\|\int_s^t d_\sigma K^t(\sigma)\cdot U_s(\sigma)\right\| \leqslant 1 + SV_{[s,t]}[K^t]\|U\|$$

hence $\|\mathcal{T}U\| \leqslant 1 + SV^u[K]\cdot\|U\|$. From II.1.4 it follows that for every $t \in [c,d]$ we have $(\mathcal{T}U)^t \in SV([c,d],L(X))$. We still have to prove that $\mathcal{T}U$ is uniformly of bounded semivariation as a function of the second variable: by (9') of §1 of Chapter II we have

$$SV_{[c,d]}[(\mathcal{T}U)^t] \leqslant SV_{[c,d]}[K^t]\left[\|U\|+2SV^u[U]\right],$$

hence

$$SV^u[\mathcal{T}U] \leqslant SV^u[K]\cdot\left[\|U\|+2SV^u[U]\right].$$

REMARK 7. The proof above also shows that the affine transformation $\mathcal{T}$ is continuous in G^u.

LEMMA 1.11 - *Let* X *and* Y *be Banach spaces;*

$$\alpha \in SV([a,b], L(X,Y)) \quad \textit{and} \quad \Lambda \in BV([a,b]).$$

We have

$$SV[\Lambda\alpha] \leq SV[\Lambda]\,\|\alpha\| + \|\Lambda\|\,SV[\alpha].$$

PROOF. We recall that $BV([a,b]) = SV([a,b], L(\mathbf{C}))$ with $SV[\Lambda] = V[\Lambda]$. For $d \in \mathbf{D}$ and $x_i \in X$, $i = 1,2,\ldots,|d|$ with $\|x_i\| \leq 1$ we have

$$\|\sum_{i=1}^{|d|} [\Lambda(t_i)\alpha(t_i) - \Lambda(t_{i-1})\alpha(t_{i-1})]x_i\| =$$

$$= \|\sum_{i=1}^{|d|} [\Lambda(t_i)\alpha(t_i) - \Lambda(t_i)\alpha(t_{i-1}) + \Lambda(t_i)\alpha(t_{i-1}) - \Lambda(t_{i-1})\alpha(t_{i-1})]x_i\| \leq$$

$$\leq \|\sum_{i=1}^{|d|} [\alpha(t_i) - \alpha(t_{i-1})]\Lambda(t_i)x_i\| + \|\sum_{i=1}^{|d|} [\Lambda(t_i) - \Lambda(t_{i-1})]\alpha(t_{i-1})x_i\| \leq$$

$$\leq SV[\alpha]\,\|\Lambda\| + SV[\Lambda]\,\|\alpha\|$$

hence the result.

We recall (Theorem 1.9) that the resolvent is a fixed point of the transformation $\mathcal{T}$. If $\mathcal{T}$ were a contraction of G^u we would have proved the existence of the resolvent in G^u. In general however $\mathcal{T}$ is not a contraction with respect to the norm of G^u. But we will show that we can introduce in G^u a norm equivalent to $|||\ |||$ and such that $\mathcal{T}$ is a contraction in this new norm.

DEFINITION. Given $\lambda > 0$ and $\delta > 0$ for every $U \in G^u$ we define

$$|||U|||_{\lambda,\delta} = \|U\|_{\lambda,\delta} + SV_{\lambda,\delta}[U]$$

where

$$\|U\|_{\lambda,\delta} = \sup\{\sup_{|t-s|\leq\delta} \|U(t,s)\|\ ,\ \sup_{|t-s|\geq\delta} \|U(t,s)e^{-\lambda|t-s|}\|\}$$

and

$$SV_{\lambda,\delta}[U] = \sup_{c\leq t\leq d} SV_{\lambda,\delta;t}[U]$$

with

$$SV_{\lambda,\delta;t}[U] = SV^{(s)}_{[c,t-\delta]}[U^t(s)e^{-\lambda(t-s)}] + SV_{[t-\delta,t]}[U^t] +$$

$$+ SV_{[t,t+\delta]}[U^t] + SV^{(s)}_{[t+\delta,d]}[U^t(s)e^{-\lambda(s-t)}]$$

where, we recall, $SV^{(s)}[Z(t,s)]$ denotes the semivariation calculated with respect to the variable s.

It is immediate that $|||\ |||_{\lambda,\delta}$ is a norm on G^u.

PROPOSITION 1.12. *In* G^u *the norms* $|||\ |||$ *and* $|||\ |||_{\lambda,\delta}$ *are equivalent.*

PROOF. We will show that for every $U \in G^u$ we have

$$\frac{1}{4}|||U|||_{\lambda,\delta} \leqslant |||U||| \leqslant 4e^{\lambda(d-c)}|||U|||_{\lambda,\delta}.$$

a) It is immediate that $\|U\|_{\lambda,\delta} \leqslant \|U\| \leqslant e^{\lambda(d-c)}\|U\|_{\lambda,\delta}$.

b_1) Lemma 1.11 implies that

$$SV^{(s)}_{[c,t-\delta]}[U^t(s)e^{-\lambda(t-s)}] \leqslant SV_{[c,t-\delta]}[U^t]\ e^{-\lambda\delta} + \|U\| \leqslant$$

$$\leqslant SV[U^t] + \|U\|$$

and analogously

$$SV^{(s)}_{[t+\delta,d]}[U^t(s)e^{-\lambda(s-t)}] \leqslant SV[U^t] + \|U\|$$

hence

$$SV_{\lambda,\delta}[U] \leqslant 4 \sup_{c\leqslant t\leqslant d} SV[U^t] + 2\|U\|$$

and therefore $|||U|||_{\lambda,\delta} \leqslant 4|||U|||$.

b_2) Again by Lemma 1.11 we have

$$SV_{[c,t-\delta]}[U^t] = SV^{(s)}_{[c,t-\delta]}[U^t(s)e^{-\lambda(t-s)}\cdot e^{\lambda(t-s)}] \leqslant$$

$$\leqslant SV^{(s)}_{[c,t-\delta]}[U^t(s)e^{-\lambda(t-s)}]e^{\lambda(d-c)} + \|U\|_{\lambda,\delta}e^{\lambda(d-c)} \leqslant$$

$$\leqslant SV_{\lambda,\delta}[U]e^{\lambda(d-c)} + \|U\|_{\lambda,\delta}e^{\lambda(d-c)}.$$

For $SV_{[t+\delta,d]}[U^t]$ we have an analogous majoration; we also have

$$SV_{[t-\delta,t]}[U^t],\ SV_{[t,t+\delta]}[U^t] \leq SV_{\lambda,\delta}[U]$$

hence

$$|||\, U\, ||| \leq 4e^{\lambda(d-c)}\, |||\, U\, |||_{\lambda,\delta}$$

and this completes the proof.

THEOREM 1.13. *There exist* $\lambda > 0$ *and* $\delta > 0$ *such that* $\mathcal{T}$ *is a contraction of* $G^u_{|||\ |||_{\lambda,\delta}}$.

PROOF. Obviously it is enough to prove the same result for the linear transformation $\mathcal{T}_o$ where for $U \in G^u$ we define

$$(\mathcal{T}_o U)(t,s) = \int_s^t d_\sigma K(t,\sigma)\circ U(\sigma,s) \qquad t,s \in [c,d].$$

Let us find an upper bound for $|||\mathcal{T}_o U|||_{\lambda,\delta}$.

I - We begin with $\|\mathcal{T}_o U\|_{\lambda,\delta}$.

a) For $|t-s| \leq \delta$ we have

$$\|(\mathcal{T}_o U)(t,s)\| = \left\|\int_s^t d_\sigma K(t,\sigma)\circ U(\sigma,s)\right\| \leq$$

$$\leq SV_{[s,t]}[K^t]\,\|U_s\|_{[s,t]} \leq SV^\delta[K]\,\|U\|_{\lambda,\delta}.$$

b) For $|t-s| \geq \delta$, let us suppose that $c \leq s \leq t-\delta$; we have

$$\|(\mathcal{T}_o U)(t,s)e^{-\lambda(t-s)}\| = \left\|\int_s^t d_\sigma K^t(\sigma)\circ U(\sigma,s)e^{-\lambda(\sigma-s)}.e^{-\lambda(t-\sigma)}\right\| =$$

$$\leq \left\|\int_s^{t-\delta}\right\| + \left\|\int_{t-\delta}^t\right\|$$

$$\left\|\int_s^{t-\delta}\right\| \leq SV_{[s,t-\delta]}(K^t) \sup_{s\leq\sigma\leq t-\delta} \|U(\sigma,s)e^{-\lambda(\sigma-s)}\|\, e^{-\lambda\delta} \leq$$

$$\leq e^{-\lambda\delta} SV_{[c,d]}[K^t]\,\|U\|_{\lambda,\delta},$$

$$\left\|\int_{t-\delta}^t\right\| \leq SV_{[t-\delta,t]}[K^t]\,\|U\|_{\lambda,\delta} \leq SV^\delta[K]\,\|U\|_{\lambda,\delta}$$

and when $t+\delta \leqslant s \leqslant d$ we have analogous bounds. a) and b) imply that

$$(\alpha) \qquad \|\mathcal{J}_o U\|_{\lambda,\delta} \leqslant \left[e^{-\lambda\delta} SV^u[K] + SV^\delta[K]\right] \|U\|_{\lambda,\delta}.$$

II - In order to find an upper bound for

$$SV_{\lambda,\delta}[\mathcal{J}_o U] = \sup_{c \leqslant t \leqslant d} SV_{\lambda,\delta;t}[\mathcal{J}_o U]$$

we will look separately the 4 terms of the definition of $SV_{\lambda,\delta;t}[\mathcal{J}_o U]$:

a) If we apply (8') of Chapter II (with $\bar{a} = t-\delta$ and $s_o = t$) and afterwards use Lemma 1.11 we get

$$SV^{(s)}_{[c,t-\delta]}\left[(\mathcal{J}_o U)^t(s)e^{-\lambda(t-s)}\right] =$$

$$= SV^{(s)}_{[c,t-\delta]}\left[\int_s^t d_\sigma K^t(\sigma) \circ U(\sigma,s) e^{-\lambda(t-s)}\right] \leqslant$$

$$SV_{[c,t-\delta]}[K^t]\left[\|U\|_\Delta e^{-\lambda\delta} + \sup_{c \leqslant \sigma \leqslant t-\delta} SV^{(s)}_{[\sigma,t-\delta]}\left[U^\sigma(s)e^{-\lambda(\sigma-s)}e^{-\lambda(t-\sigma)}\right]\right] +$$

$$+ SV_{[t-\delta,t]}[K^t] \sup_{t-\delta \leqslant \sigma \leqslant t} SV^{(s)}_{[c,t-\delta]}\left[U^\sigma(s)e^{-\lambda(\sigma-s)} \cdot e^{-\lambda(t-\sigma)}\right] \leqslant$$

$$\leqslant SV_{[c,d]}[K^t]\left[\|U\|_{\lambda,\delta} e^{-\lambda\delta} + SV_{\lambda,\delta}[U] e^{-\lambda\delta}\right] +$$

$$+ SV^\delta[K]\left[\sup_{t-\delta \leqslant \sigma \leqslant t} SV^{(s)}_{[c,\sigma-\delta]}\left[U^\sigma(s)e^{-\lambda(\sigma-s)} \cdot e^{-\lambda(t-\sigma)}\right] +\right.$$

$$\left. + SV^{(s)}_{[\sigma-\delta,t-\delta]}\left[U^\sigma(s)e^{-\lambda(t-s)}\right]\right] \leqslant$$

$$\leqslant e^{-\lambda\delta} SV_{[c,d]}[K^t] |||U|||_{\lambda,\delta} + SV^\delta[K]\left[SV_{\lambda,\delta}[U] + SV_{\lambda,\delta}[U]e^{-\lambda\delta} + \|U\|_{\lambda,\delta}\right] \leqslant$$

$$\leqslant 2\left[e^{-\lambda\delta} SV_{[c,d]}[K^t] + SV^\delta[K]\right] |||U|||_{\lambda,\delta}.$$

b) For $SV^{(s)}_{[t+\delta,d]}\left[(\mathcal{J}_o U)^t(s)e^{-\lambda(s-t)}\right]$ we have the same upper bound.

c) By (7') of Chapter II we have

$$SV_{[t-\delta,t]}[(\mathcal{T}_o U)^t] = SV^{(s)}_{[t-\delta,t]}\left[\int_s^t d_\sigma K^t(\sigma)\circ U(\sigma,s)\right] \leqslant$$

$$SV_{[t-\delta,t]}[K^t]\left[\|U\|_\Delta + \sup_{t-\delta\leqslant\sigma\leqslant t} SV_{[t-\delta,\sigma]}[U^\sigma]\right] \leqslant$$

$$\leqslant SV^\delta[K]\left[\|U\|_{\lambda,\delta} + SV_{\lambda,\delta}[U]\right] = SV^\delta[K]\cdot |||U|||_{\lambda,\delta}.$$

d) For $SV_{[t,t+\delta]}[(\mathcal{T}_o U)^t]$ we have the same upper bound.

From a), b), c) and d) we get

$$SV_{\lambda,\delta;t}[\mathcal{T}_o U] \leqslant \left[4e^{-\lambda\delta}SV_{[c,d]}[K^t] + 6SV^\delta[K]\right] |||U|||_{\lambda,\delta}$$

hence

$$(\beta) \qquad SV_{\lambda,\delta}[\mathcal{T}_o(U)] \leqslant \left[4e^{-\lambda\delta}SV^u[K] + 6SV^\delta[K]\right] |||U|||_{\lambda,\delta}.$$

By (α) and (β) we have

$$(\gamma) \qquad |||\mathcal{T}_o(U)|||_{\lambda,\delta} \leqslant \left[5e^{-\lambda\delta}SV^u[K] + 7SV^\delta[K]\right] |||U|||_{\lambda,\delta}.$$

Since K satisfies (SV^{uo}) there exists $\delta > 0$ such that $7SV^\delta[K] < \frac{1}{4}$; we fix such a $\delta > 0$, then there exists $\lambda > 0$ such that $5e^{-\lambda\delta}SV^u[K] < \frac{1}{4}$, hence $\mathcal{T}_o$ is a contraction in $G^u_{|||\ |||_{\lambda,\delta}}$.

The preceding theorem implies that the resolvent R, solution of (R^*), i.e. the fixed point of $\mathcal{T}$, is an element of G^u; however we want to prove that $R \in G^{uo}$; for this purpose we will show that G^{uo} is a closed subspace of G^u and that $\mathcal{T}G^{uo} \subset G^{uo}$.

PROPOSITION 1.14. G^{uo} *is a closed subespace of* G^u.

PROOF. Let U be in the closure of G^{uo}; then for every $\varepsilon > 0$ there exists $U_\varepsilon \in G^{uo}$ such that $|||U-U_\varepsilon||| \leqslant \varepsilon$ hence for every $t \in [c,d]$ we have $SV_{[c,d]}[U^t-U^t_\varepsilon] \leqslant \varepsilon$. Let $\delta > 0$ be such that

$SV^{\delta}[U_{\varepsilon}] \leqslant \varepsilon$ i.e. $SV_{[s-\delta,s+\delta]}[U^t_{\varepsilon}] \leqslant \varepsilon$ for all $s,t \in [c,d]$; then we have for all $s,t \in [c,d]$ that

$$SV_{[s-\delta,s+\delta]}[U^t] \leqslant SV_{[s-\delta,s+\delta]}[U^t - U^t_{\varepsilon}] + SV_{[s-\delta,s+\delta]}[U^t_{\varepsilon}] \leqslant 2\varepsilon$$

hence $U \in G^{uo}$.

PROPOSITION 1.15. *The transformation* $\mathcal{T}$ *of* G^u *takes* G^{uo} *into* G^{uo}.

PROOF. Obviously it is enough to prove the same result for $\mathcal{T}_o$. If $U \in G^{uo}$ we have by (8') of Chapter II that

$$SV_{[\tau-\delta,\tau+\delta]}[(\mathcal{T}_o U)^t] = SV^{(s)}_{[\tau-\delta,\tau+\delta]}\left[\int_s^t d_{\sigma}K^t(\sigma)\circ U(\sigma,s)\right] \leqslant$$

$$\leqslant SV_{[\tau-\delta,\tau+\delta]}[K^t]\left[\|U\|_{\Delta} + \sup_{\tau-\delta\leqslant\sigma\leqslant\tau+\delta} SV_{[\tau-\delta,\sigma]}[U^{\sigma}]\right] +$$

$$+ SV_{\{t,\tau-\delta\}}[K^t] \sup_{\sigma\in\{t,\tau-\delta\}} SV_{[\tau-\delta,\tau+\delta]}[U^{\sigma}] \leqslant$$

$$\leqslant SV^{\delta}[K]\left(\|U\|_{\Delta} + SV^{\delta}[U]\right) + SV^u[K]\,SV^{\delta}[U]$$

hence the result since K and U satisfy (SV^{uo}).

By Theorem 1.13 and Propositions 1.14 and 1.15 we have immediately

COROLLARY 1.16. *The fixed point* R *of* $\mathcal{T}$ *is in* G^{uo}, *i.e.. for* $K \in G^{uo}$ *there is one and only one* $R \in G^{uo}$ *that satisfies* (R^*); *we have a) and b) of Theorem 1.8.*

Given $K \in G^{uo}$ let us denote for a moment by $\mathcal{T}_K$ the transformation defined by K, and by R_K its resolvent i.e. the fixed point of K. Let us prove that the mapping

$$K \in G^{uo} \longmapsto R_K \in G^{uo}$$

is continuous.

Indeed: let $|||\ |||_{\lambda,\delta}$ be the norm of G^{uo} such that $\mathcal{T}_K$ is a contraction in this norm with contraction constant c_K given by (γ) of Theorem 1.13

$$c_K = 5e^{-\lambda\delta}SV^u[K] + 7SV^{\delta}[K] < \tfrac{1}{2}\,.$$

It is immediate (Cf. the proof of Proposition 1.14) that if $K \in G^{uo}$ then for all $\hat{K}$ sufficiently close to K we also have $c_{\hat{K}} < \frac{1}{2}$, hence there is a neighborhood V of K such that the familly of contractions $(\mathcal{T}_{\hat{K}})_{\hat{K}\in V}$ is uniform; since for every $U \in G^{uo}$ the mapping

$$K \in G^{uo} \longmapsto \mathcal{T}_K U \in G^{uo}$$

is continuous ($||| \mathcal{T}_K U ||| \leqslant SV^u[K] \, ||| U |||$: we have trivially

$$\| \mathcal{T}_K U \| \leqslant SV^u[K] \, \| U \|$$

and by (3) of Chapter II we have $SV^u[\mathcal{T}_K U] \leqslant SV^u[K] SV^u[U]$) it follows from Theorem 0.3 that the fixed point R_K is a continuous function of K, i.e., we have the

COROLLARY 1.17. *The mapping that to each* $K \in G^{uo}$ *associates its resolvent* $R \in G^{uo}$, *solution of*

$$(R^*) \qquad R(t,s) = I_X - \int_s^t d_\sigma K(t,\sigma) \circ R(\sigma,s) \qquad s,t \in [c,d]$$

is a continuous function.

b) of Theorem 1.8 and Corollary 1.17 imply the

COROLLARY 1.18. *For* $K \in G^{uo}$, $x \in X$ *and* $f \in G([c,d],X)$ *the solution* $y \in G([c,d],X)$ *of*

$$y(t) - x + \int_{t_o}^t d_\sigma K(t,\sigma) \cdot y(\sigma) = f(t) - f(t_o)$$

depends continuously on K, x *and* f.

Let us now prove that if we consider only normalized elements $K \in G^{uo}$ (i.e. with $K(t,t) \equiv 0$) then the mapping of Corollary 1.17 is injective.

Indeed: Let $K_1, K_2 \in G^{uo}$ be normalized and have the same resolvent R. Given $y \in G([c,d],X)$ we define

$$f_i(t) = y(t) - y(t_o) + \int_{t_o}^t d_\sigma K_i(t,\sigma) \cdot y(\sigma), \qquad i = 1,2.$$

By Theorem 1.8 $y(t) = R(t,t_o)y(t_o) + \int_{t_o}^t R(t,s)df_1(s)$ satisfies

$$y(t) - y(t_o) + \int_{t_o}^t d_\sigma K_i(t,\sigma)y(t) = f_1(t), \qquad i = 1,2$$

and the same applies to f_2 hence $f_1 = f_2 = f$. Hence by subtraction we obtain that

$$\int_{t_o}^{t} d_\sigma \left[K_2(t,\sigma) - K_1(t,\sigma)\right] \cdot y(\sigma) = 0$$

for all $y \in G([c,d],X)$ and every $t \in [c,d]$. If we take then $x \in X$, $\tau \in [t_o,t]$ and $y = \chi_{[\tau,t]}x$ we obtain

$$[K_2(t,t) - K_1(t,t)]x - [K_2(t,\tau) - K_1(t,\tau)]x = 0.$$

The normalization and the fact that $x \in X$ is arbitrary imply that $K_2(t,\tau) \equiv K_1(t,\tau)$ for all $\tau \in [t_o,t]$; since t_o is arbitrary, or by Remark 2, we have $K_2 \equiv K_1$, i.e. we proved that

COROLLARY 1.19. *The continuous mapping* $K \in G^{uo} \longmapsto R \in G^{uo}$ *when restricted to normalized elements, i.e. such that* $K(t,t) \equiv 0$, *is injective.*

E - We will now complete the proof of Theorem 1.5.

THEOREM 1.20. *Given* $K \in G^{uo}$ *such that* $K(t,t) \equiv 0$ *and* R *its resolvent, we have*

$$(R_*) \qquad R(t,s) = I_X + \int_s^t R(t,\sigma) \circ d_\sigma K(\sigma,s) \quad \text{for all} \quad s,t \in [c,d]$$

$$(R_{**}) \qquad K(t,s) = R(t,s) - I_X + \int_s^t d_\sigma R(t,\sigma) \circ K(\sigma,s)$$

$$\text{for all} \quad s,t \in [c,d].$$

PROOF. Let us first remark that the integral in (R_*) makes sense because $R^t \in SV([c,d],L(X))$ (since $R \in G^{uo}$ by Corollary 1.16) and $K_s \in G([c,d],L(X))$. By (R^*) we have

$$\int_s^t R(t,\sigma) \circ d_\sigma K(\sigma,s) = \int_s^t \left[I_X - \int_\sigma^t d_\tau K(t,\tau) \circ R(\tau,\sigma)\right] \circ d_\sigma K(\sigma,s) =$$

$$= K(t,s) - \int_s^t \left[\int_\sigma^t d_\tau K(t,\tau) \circ R(\tau,\sigma)\right] \circ d_\sigma K(\sigma,s) \overset{(D)}{=\!=}$$

$$\overset{(D)}{=\!=} K(t,s) - \int_s^t d_\tau K(t,\tau) \circ \left[\int_s^\tau R(\tau,\sigma) \circ d_\sigma K(\sigma,s)\right] =$$

$$= - \int_s^t d_\tau K(t,\tau) \circ \left[I_X + \int_s^\tau R(\tau,\sigma) \circ d_\sigma K(\sigma,s)\right]$$

where in $\overset{(D)}{=\!=}$ we applied II.1.13. Hence we proved that the function

$$S(\tau,s) = I_X + \int_s^\tau R(\tau,\sigma)\circ d_\sigma K(\sigma,s)$$

satisfies the equation

$$S(t,s) = I_X - \int_s^t d_\tau K(t,\tau)\circ S(\tau,s), \text{ i.e.,}$$

(R^*), whose only solution is R; therefore we have $S = R$, i.e. (R_*). We get (R_{**}) from (R_*) using integration by parts.

THEOREM 1.21. *Given* $R\in G^{uo}$ *with* $R(t,t) \equiv I_X$ *there is one and only one* $K\in G^{uo}$ *with* $K(t,t) \equiv 0$ *such that*

$$(R^*) \qquad R(t,s) = I_X - \int_s^t d_\sigma K(t,\sigma)\circ R(\sigma,s) \quad \text{for all} \quad s,t\in [c,d]$$

and the (non linear) mapping $R\in G^{uo} \longmapsto K\in G^{uo}$ *is continuous.*

PROOF. The unicity of K satisfying (R^*) follows from Corollary 1.19. Let us prove initially that there is one and only one $K\in G^{uo}$ with $K(t,t) \equiv 0$ such that (R_*) or, equivalently

$$(R_{**}) \qquad K(t,s) = R(t,s) - I_X + \int_s^t d_\sigma R(t,\sigma)\circ K(\sigma,s)$$

i.e. such that K is the fixed point of the affine transformation $\mathcal{R}$, where for $U\in G^{uo}$ we define

$$(\mathcal{R}U)(t,s) = R(t,s) - I_X + \int_s^t d_\sigma R(t,\sigma)\circ U(\sigma,s).$$

The linear part of $\mathcal{R}$ is analogous to $\mathcal{Y}_o$ defined in Theorem 1.13 and Proposition 1.15; hence apply the same conclusions of these theorems to the transformation $\mathcal{R}$ (that is, the analogous of Corollaries 1.16 and 1.17).

b) We still have to prove that K defined in this way, i.e., satisfying (R_*) also satisfies (R^*): using integration by parts in (R^*) we obtain

$$(R^{**}) \qquad K(t,s) = R(t,s) - I_X - \int_s^t K(t,\sigma)d_\sigma R(\sigma,s)$$

and it is sufficient to prove (R^{**}). By (R_{**}) we have

$$\int_s^t K(t,\sigma)\circ d_\sigma R(\sigma,s) = \int_s^t \left[R(t,\sigma)-I_X+\int_\sigma^t d_\tau R(t,\tau)\circ K(\tau,\sigma)\right]\circ d_\sigma R(\sigma,s).$$

If in the second integral we use integration by parts for the first two summands and apply II.1.13 to the third we obtain

$$\int_s^t K(t,\sigma)\circ d_\sigma R(\sigma,s) = \int_s^t d_\tau R(t,\tau)\circ\left[I_X - R(\tau,s)+\int_s^\tau K(\tau,\sigma)\circ d_\sigma R(\sigma,s)\right]$$

hence if we define

$$S(\tau,s) = -I_X + R(\tau,s) - \int_s^\tau K(\tau,\sigma)\circ d_\sigma R(\sigma,s)$$

we have just proved that

$$-S(t,s) - I_X + R(t,s) = -\int_s^t d_\tau R(t,\tau)\circ S(\tau,s)$$

i.e. S satisfies the equation (R_{**}) whose only solution (by part a)) is K; hence $S = K$ i.e. we have (R^{**}). QED

If we denote by G_o^{uo} the subspace of those $K\in G^{uo}$ that satisfy $K(t,t) \equiv 0$ and by G_I^{uo} the subspace of those that satisfy $R(t,t) = I_X$, then if we group the preceding results we have

THEOREM 1.22 - *The mapping that to every* $K\in G_o^{uo}$ *associates its resolvent* $R\in G_I^{uo}$ *is one to one and bicontinuous from* G_o^{uo} *onto* G_I^{uo}*; in every one of the equations* (R^*) *and* (R_*), K *determines uniquely* R *and* R *determines uniquely* K.

THEOREM 1.23. *1)* R_s *is discontinuous to the left (right) at the point* t *only if for some* $\sigma\in\{s,t\}$ K_σ *is discontinuous to the left (right) at* t.

2) y, *solution of* (K) *is discontinuous to the left (right) at the point* t *only if* f *is discontinuous to the left (right) at* t, *or for some* $s\in\{t_o,t_1\}$ K_s *(or* R_s*) is discontinuous to the left (right) at* t.

PROOF. 1) By (R^*) and by (15') of Chapter II we have

$$R_s(t-) = I_X - \int_s^t d_\sigma K(t-,\sigma)\circ R_s(\sigma)$$

hence

$$R_s(t) - R_s(t-) = -\int_s^t d_\sigma [K(t,\sigma)-K(t-,\sigma)] \circ R_s(\sigma)$$

and this implies 1).

2) By (ρ') of Theorem 1.8 we have

$$y(t) = f(t) + R(t,t_o)[x-f(t_o)] - \int_{t_o}^t d_s R(t,s)\cdot f(s);$$

then (15') of Chapter II implies that

$$y(t-) = f(t-) + R(t-,t_o)[x-f(t_o)] - \int_{t_o}^t d_s R(t-,s)\cdot f(s),$$

hence

$$y(t) - y(t-) = f(t) - f(t-) + [R(t,t_o)-R(t-,t_o)][x-f(t_o)] + \\ - \int_{t_o}^t d_s [R(t,s)-R(t-,s)]\cdot f(s)$$

which implies the assertion in 2) for R; for K it follows from 1).

F - We will now prove that if the kernel K satisfies certain additional properties the same is true for R and reciprocally.

DEFINITIONS. We denote by $\mathcal{E} = \mathcal{E}([c,d]\times[c,d],L(X))$ the closed subspace of G formed by the continuous functions (i.e. $\mathcal{E} = \mathcal{C}([c,d]\times[c,d],L(X))$). $\mathcal{E}^u = \mathcal{E}^u([c,d]\times[c,d],L(X))$ denotes the closed subspace of G^u formed by those elements of G^u that are continuous functions. $\mathcal{E}^{uo} = \mathcal{E}^u \cap G^{uo}$. $\mathcal{E}^{co}$ denotes the subspace of those elements $U \in G^{uo}$ that have the property

$$(SV^c) \qquad \lim_{t\to t_1} |||U^t - U^{t_1}||| = 0 \quad \text{for every} \quad t_1 \in [c,d]$$

where $|||U^t||| = \|U^t\| + SV[U^t]$.

PROPOSITION 1.24. *The elements of* $\mathcal{E}^{co}$ *are continuous functions and* $\mathcal{E}^{co}$ *is closed subspace of* $\mathcal{E}^{uo}$

PROOF. We have

$$\|K(t_1,s_1)-K(t_2,s_2)\| \leq \|K(t_1,s_1)-K(t_2,s_1)\| + \\ + \|K(t_2,s_1)-K(t_2,s_2)\| \leq \|K^{t_1}-K^{t_2}\| + SV_{[s_1,s_2]}[K^{t_2}]$$

hence the continuity of K follows from (SV^c) and (SV^o).

In order to prove that $\mathcal{E}^{co}$ is a closed subspace of $\mathcal{E}^{uo}$ it is enough to prove that every element K of the closure of $\mathcal{E}^{co}$ belongs to $\mathcal{E}^{co}$; if $K \in \overline{\mathcal{E}^{co}}$ for every $\varepsilon > 0$ there is $K_\varepsilon \in \mathcal{E}^{co}$ such that $|||K-K_\varepsilon||| \leqslant \varepsilon$. Since we have

$$|||K^t-K^{t_1}||| \leqslant |||K^t-K_\varepsilon^t||| + |||K_\varepsilon^t-K_\varepsilon^{t_1}||| + |||K_\varepsilon^{t_1}-K^{t_1}||| \leqslant$$

$$\leqslant 2\varepsilon + |||K_\varepsilon^t-K_\varepsilon^{t_1}|||$$

the result follows.

REMARK 8. In the Appendix of this § we will prove that if U satisfies (SV^c) and (SV^o) it satisfies (SV^{uo}).

THEOREM 1.25. *Given* $K \in \mathcal{E}^{uo}$, *with the notations of Proposition 1.10, for every* $U \in \mathcal{E}$ *we have* $\mathcal{T}U \in \mathcal{E}$.

PROOF. We have

$$\|(\mathcal{T}U)(t_1,s_1)-(\mathcal{T}U)(t_2,s_2)\| =$$

$$= \left\|\int_{s_1}^{t_1} d_\sigma K(t_1,\sigma)\circ U(\sigma,s_1) - \int_{s_2}^{t_2} d_\sigma K(t_2,\sigma)\circ U(\sigma,s_1)\right\| \leqslant$$

$$\leqslant \left\|\int_{s_1}^{t_1} d_\sigma\left[K^{t_1}(\sigma)-K^{t_2}(\sigma)\right]\circ U_{s_1}(\sigma)\right\| + \left\|\int_{s_2}^{s_1} d_\sigma K^{t_2}(\sigma)\circ U_{s_2}(\sigma)\right\| +$$

$$+ \left\|\int_{s_1}^{t_1} d_\sigma K^{t_2}(\sigma)\circ\left[U_{s_2}(\sigma)-U_{s_1}(\sigma)\right]\right\| + \left\|\int_{t_1}^{t_2} d_\sigma K^{t_2}(\sigma)\circ U_{s_2}(\sigma)\right\|;$$

by I.5.9 the first summand goes to 0 if $t_2 \longrightarrow t_1$ since we have $SV[K^t] \leqslant SV^u[K]$ for all t and $K(t_2,\sigma) \longrightarrow K(t_1,\sigma)$ by the continuity of K; the second summand is bounded by $SV_{[s_1,s_2]}[K^{t_2}]\,\|U\|$ which goes to 0 if $s_2 \longrightarrow s_1$ since K satisfies (SV^{uo}); for the fourth summand we have analogous result; the third summand is bounded by $SV^u[K]\,\|U_{s_1}-U_{s_2}\|$ which goes to 0 if $s_2 \longrightarrow s_1$ since U is continuous. Hence we have $(\mathcal{T}U)(t_2,s_2) \longrightarrow (\mathcal{T}U)(t_1,s_1)$ if $(t_2,s_2) \longrightarrow (t_1,s_1)$, i.e., $\mathcal{T}U$ is continuous.

By Theorem 1.25 and Proposition 1.15 we have

COROLLARY 1.26. *The transformation* $\mathcal{T}$ *takes* $\mathcal{E}^{uo}$ *into* $\mathcal{E}^{uo}$.

It follows that if $K \in \mathcal{E}^{uo}$ then the fixed point of $\mathcal{T}$, i.e., the resolvent R is in $\mathcal{E}^{uo}$ too and Theorem 1.21 shows that reciprocally if $K \in G^{uo}$ and its resolvent is in $\mathcal{E}^{uo}$ then $K \in \mathcal{E}^{uo}$.

We define $\mathcal{E}^{uo}_{o} = \mathcal{E} \cap G^{uo}_{o}$ and $\mathcal{E}^{uo}_{I} = \mathcal{E} \cap G^{uo}_{I}$ then by Theorem 1.22 we have

THEOREM 1.27. *The mapping defined in Theorem 1.22 when restricted to* $\mathcal{E}^{uo}_{o}$ *is injective and bicontinuous from* $\mathcal{E}^{uo}_{o}$ *onto* $\mathcal{E}^{uo}_{I}$.

THEOREM 1.28. *If* $K \in \mathcal{E}^{co}$ *then for every* $U \in \mathcal{E}^{u}$, $\mathcal{T}U$ *satisfies* (SV^{c}).

PROOF. We have to show that if $t_2 \to t_1$ then

$$|||(\mathcal{T}U)^{t_2} - (\mathcal{T}U)^{t_1}||| = \|(\mathcal{T}U)^{t_2} - (\mathcal{T}U)^{t_1}\| + \\ + SV[(\mathcal{T}U)^{t_2} - (\mathcal{T}U)^{t_1}] \longrightarrow 0;$$

this is obvious for the first summand since $\mathcal{T}U$ is a continuous function. For the second summand we have

$$SV\left[(\mathcal{T}U)^{t_2}-(\mathcal{T}U)^{t_1}\right]=SV^{(s)}\left[\int_s^{t_2} d_\sigma K^{t_2}(\sigma)\circ U(\sigma,s)-\int_s^{t_1} d_\sigma K^{t_1}(\sigma)\circ U(\sigma,s)\right] \leqslant$$

$$\leqslant SV(s)\left[\int_s^{t_2} d_\sigma [K^{t_2}(\sigma)-K^{t_1}(\sigma)]\circ U(\sigma,s)\right]+SV^{(s)}\left[\int_{t_1}^{t_2} d_\sigma K^{t_1}(\sigma)\circ U(\sigma,s)\right].$$

By (9') and (3) of Chapter II the first and second summands are bounded respectively by

$$SV[K^{t_2}-K^{t_1}]\left[\|U\| + 2SV^{u}[U]\right] \quad \text{and} \quad SV_{[t_1,t_2]}[K^{t_1}]SV^{u}[U]$$

which go to 0 if $t_2 \to t_1$ since K has the properties (SV^{c}) and (SV^{uo}). QED

By Corollary 1.26 we then have

COROLLARY 1.29. *If* $K \in \mathcal{E}^{co}$ *then* $\mathcal{T}$ *takes* $\mathcal{E}^{uo}$ *into* $\mathcal{E}^{co}$.

We define

$$\mathcal{E}_o^{co} = \mathcal{E}^{co} \cap G_o^{uo} \quad \text{and} \quad \mathcal{E}_I^{co} = \mathcal{E}^{co} \cap G_I^{uo} \; ;$$

then in the same way as Theorem 1.27 one proves the

THEOREM 1.30. *The mapping defined in Theorem 1.22 when restricted to* $\mathcal{E}_o^{co}$ *is injective and bicontinuous from* $\mathcal{E}_o^{co}$ *onto* $\mathcal{E}_I^{co}$.

REMARK 9. One can still impose other restrictions on K and prove that R satisfies the same restrictions and reciprocally. For instance, we denote by

$$G\mathcal{B}V^{uo} = G\mathcal{B}V^{uo}([c,d] \times [c,d], L(X))$$

the space of all functions $U: [c,d] \times [c,d] \longrightarrow L(X)$ that are regulated as a function of the first variable and which as functions of the second variable satisfy

(BV^{uo}) - For every $\varepsilon > 0$ there exists $\delta > 0$ such that $V_{[s-\delta,s+\delta]}[U^t] \leqslant \varepsilon$ for all $s,t \in [c,d]$.

Then we have that $K \in G\mathcal{B}V_o^{uo}$ if and only if $R \in G\mathcal{B}V_I^{uo}$; this correspondence is bicontinuous with respect to the obvious natural norms.

The same is true if we consider the restriction to the subspace $\mathcal{G}\mathcal{B}V^{uo}$ of those functions of $G\mathcal{B}V^{uo}$ that are continuous. In an analogous way we can define $\mathcal{G}\mathcal{B}V^{co}$, etc..

REMARK 10. As we explained at the beginning of this item B, we did reduce the study of the solutions of the equation (K) in $]a,b[$ to their study in closed intervals $[c,d] \subset]a,b[$. In this way all the results for the existence and unicity of the solutions of (K), of the resolvent etc. are true for $]a,b[$. The topological results, i.e., the results that use the topology defined on the spaces of functions over $[c,d]$ or $[c,d] \times [c,d]$ are easily extended to $]a,b[$ if we introduce in the corresponding spaces the topology defined by the corresponding seminorms on the intervals $[a_n,b_n]$ where $a_n \downarrow a$ and $b_n \uparrow b$. For instance in $G^{uo}(]a,b[\times]a,b[, L(X))$ we consider the locally convex topology defined by the sequence of seminorms $|||\ \ |||_{[a_n,b_n]}$ of the spaces

$$G^{uo}([a_n,b_n]\times[a_n,b_n],L(X)).$$

The locally convex spaces we obtain in this way are Frechet spaces and it is immediate that the continuity and bicontinuity of the mappings in the theorems on $[c,d]$ imply the continuity and bicontinuity in the corresponding theorems on $]a,b[$.

APPENDIX

THEOREM 1.31. *If* $K: [c,d]\times[c,d] \longrightarrow L(X)$ *satisfies the properties*

(SV^c) $\lim\limits_{t\to t_1}\left[\|K^t-K^{t_1}\|+SV[K^t-K^{t_1}]\right] = 0$ *for every* $t_1\in[c,d]$.

(SV^o) $\lim\limits_{\delta\downarrow 0} SV_{[s-\delta,s+\delta]}[K^t] = 0$ *for all* $s,t\in[c,d]$;

then K *satisfies the property*

(SV^{uo}) $\lim\limits_{\delta\downarrow 0} \sup\{SV_{[s-\delta,s+\delta]}[K^t] \mid s,t\in[c,d]\} = 0.$

PROOF. For every $\delta > 0$ we consider the function

$$V_\delta: (t,s)\in[c,d]\times[c,d] \longmapsto V_\delta(t,s) = SV_{[s-\delta,s+\delta]}[K^t]\in \mathbb{R}_+.$$

a) V_δ is upper semicontinuous i.e. if we have

$$V_\delta(t_1,s_1) < c$$

for some point (t_1,s_1) the same is true for all points (t,s) of a neighborhood of (t_1,s_1). Indeed: if

$$V_\delta(t_1,s_1) = SV_{[s_1-\delta,s_1+\delta]}[K^{t_1}] < c$$

then by (SV^o) there exists $\varepsilon_1 > 0$ such that

$$SV_{[s_1-\delta-\varepsilon_1,s_1+\delta+\varepsilon_1]}[K^{t_1}] < c$$

and by (SV^c) there exists $\varepsilon_2 > 0$ such that for $|t-t_1| < \varepsilon_2$ we have $SV_{[s_1-\delta-\varepsilon_1, s_1+\delta+\varepsilon_1]}[K^t] < c$; if $|s-s_1| < \varepsilon_1$, $|t-t_1| < \varepsilon_2$ we have $[s-\delta, s+\delta] \subset [s_1-\delta-\varepsilon_1, s_1+\delta+\varepsilon_1]$ and therefore

$$SV_{[s-\delta,s+\delta]}[K^t] \leqslant SV_{[s_1-\delta-\varepsilon_1, s_1+\delta+\varepsilon_1]}[K^t] < c$$

b) By (SV^o) we have $V_\delta(t,s) \downarrow 0$ if $\delta \downarrow 0$ for every (t,s); hence by the theorem of Dini V_δ converges uniformly to 0 i.e. given $\varepsilon > 0$ there exists $\delta_\varepsilon > 0$ such that for $0 < \delta < \delta_\varepsilon$ we have $V_\delta(t,s) < \varepsilon$ for all $s,t \in [c,d]$. Q.E.D.

REMARK 11. In an analogous way one proves that V_δ is lower semicontinuous, hence continuous.

§2 - *Integro-differential equations and harmonic operators*

In this § we will study the example A of §1 i.e. the integro-differential equation

$$\text{(L)} \qquad y(t) - y(s) + \int_s^t dA(\sigma)\cdot y(\sigma) = f(t) - f(s) \qquad s,t \in]a,b[$$

where $y,f \in G(]a,b[,X)$, and $A \in \mathfrak{G}SV^{loc}(]a,b[,L(X))$ (i.e. A is continuous and $A \in SV([c,d],L(X))$ for every $[c,d] \subset]a,b[$) satisfies

$$(SV^o) \qquad \lim_{\delta \downarrow 0} SV_{[s-\delta,s+\delta]}[A] = 0 \quad \text{for every} \quad s \in]a,b[.$$

We don't know if every element $A \in \mathfrak{G}SV^{loc}(]a,b[,L(X))$ has this property; if X is reflexive this is true.

We denote by $\mathcal{A} = \mathcal{A}(]a,b[,L(X))$ the set of all $A \in \mathfrak{G}SV^{loc}(]a,b[,L(X))$ that satisfy (SV^o).

A - We recall that (L) is a particular instance of (K) from §1, with $K(t,s) = A(s)$ or $K(t,s) = A(s)-A(t)$, if K is normalized (i.e. $K(t,t) \equiv 0$) and therefore all the results of §1 apply to (L). K defined by A obviously has the properties (SV^{uo}) and (SV^c) on every interval $[c,d] \subset]a,b[$ (see Theorem 1.31) and by Theorem 1.30 we have

$$R \in \mathcal{E}_I^{co} = \mathcal{E}_I^{co}(]a,b[\times]a,b[,L(X)),$$

where R is the resolvent associated to A.

DEFINITION. For $U:]a,b[\times]a,b[\longrightarrow L(X)$ we consider the following properties:

(SV_{uo}) - For every $[c,d] \subset]a,b[$ and every $\varepsilon > 0$ there exists $\delta > 0$ such that

$$SV_{[t-\delta,t+\delta]}[U_s] \leqslant \varepsilon \quad \text{for all} \quad s,t \in [c,d].$$

(SV_o) - $\lim\limits_{\delta \downarrow 0} SV_{[t-\delta,t+\delta]}[U_s] = 0$ for all $s,t \in]a,b[$.

(SV_c) - For every $[c,d] \subset]a,b[$ we have

$$\lim_{\delta \to 0} \|\|U_{s+\delta} - U_s\|\|_{[c,d]} = 0$$

for all $s \in [c,d]$.

The properties (SV_{uo}), (SV_o), (SV_c) are the analogous for the first variable of U of the properties (SV^{uo}), (SV^o), (SV^c) which are formulated with respect to the 2nd variable of U. In an analogous way we define (SV_u), etc..

The fundamental results of this § are contained in the Theorems 2.1 and 2.3.

THEOREM 2.1. *Given* $A \in \mathcal{A}$ *i.e.* $A \in \mathcal{G}SV^{loc}(]a,b[,L(X))$ *satisfying* (SV^o) *we have:*

I - There is one and only one $R \in \mathcal{E}$, *the resolvent of* A, *such that*

$$(R^*) \qquad R(t,s) = I_X - \int_s^t dA(\sigma) \circ R(\sigma,s) \quad \textit{for all} \quad s,t \in]a,b[.$$

$\bar{I}$ - R satisfies

$$(\bar{R}^*) \qquad R(t,s) = R(\tau,s) - \int_\tau^t dA(\sigma) \circ R(\sigma,s) \quad \textit{for all} \quad s,\tau,t \in]a,b[.$$

II - $R \in \mathcal{E}_I^{co}$ *i.e.* R *satisfies* (SV^c) *and* (SV^{uo}), *and,* $R(t,t) \equiv I_X$.

II' - R satisfies (SV_{uo}) *and* (SV_c).

III - For every $t_o \in]a,b[$, $f \in G(]a,b[,X)$ *and* $x \in X$ *the equation*

(L) $$y(t) - y(s) + \int_s^t dA(\sigma)\cdot y(\sigma) = f(t) - f(s)$$

has one and only one solution $y \in G(]a,b[,X)$ *such that* $y(t_o) = x$*; this solution is given by*

(ρ) $$y(t) = R(t,t_o)x + \int_{t_o}^t R(t,s)df(s)$$

and depends continuously on f *and* x *(and* A*);* y *is continuous if and only if* f *is continuous.*

IV - $R(t,\tau)\circ R(\tau,s) = R(t,s)$ *and* $R(\tau,t) = R(t,\tau)^{-1}$ *for all* $s,\tau,t \in]a,b[$.

V - *For* $u,v \in]a,b[$ *we have*

$$A(u) - A(v) = \int_u^v d_t R(t,s)\circ R(s,t)$$

for any $s \in]a,b[$.

VI - R *satisfies*

(R_*) $$R(t,s) = I_X - \int_s^t R(t,\tau)dA(\tau) \quad \text{for all} \quad s,t \in]a,b[$$

($\bar{R}_*$) $$R(t,s) = R(t,\sigma) + \int_\sigma^s R(t,\tau)d\,A(\tau) \quad \text{for all} \quad s,\sigma,t \in]a,b[.$$

PROOF. I and III follow immediately from the analogous results of §1 (see I and III of Theorem 1.5 and 1.3.b); $\bar{\text{I}}$ follows from I; II was proved at the beginning of this item.

II': Let us take $[c,d] \subset]a,b[$, $c \leq t_1 < t_2 \leq d$ and $s \in [c,d]$. By (R^*) we have

$$SV_{[t_1,t_2]}[R_s] = SV^{(t)}_{[t_1,t_2]}\left[\int_s^t dA(\sigma)\circ R(\sigma,s)\right].$$

By I.5.2 and II.1.9 we have

$$SV_{[t_1,t_2]}[R_s] =$$

$$= \sup\{\|\int_{t_1}^{t_2} d_t\left[\int_s^t dA(\sigma)\circ R(\sigma,s)\right]\cdot f(t)\| \mid f \in G([t_1,t_2],X), \|f\| \leq 1\} =$$

$$= \sup_{\|f\|\leq 1} \|\int_{t_1}^{t_2} dA(t)\circ R(t,s)\cdot f(t)\| \leq SV_{[t_1,t_2]}[A]\,\|R_s\|_{[t_1,t_2]}.$$

If we take $[t_1,t_2] = [t-\delta,t+\delta]$ we prove (SV_o). If we replace R_s by $R_{s+\delta}-R_s$ and take $[t_1,t_2] = [c,d]$ we obtain

$$SV_{[c,d]}[R_{s+\delta}-R_s] \leq SV_{[c,d]}[A]\,\|R_{s+\delta}-R_s\|_{[c,d]}$$

hence (SV_c) since R is continuous. By Theorem 1.31 we have then (SV_{uo}).

IV: $(\bar{R}^*)$ and (L) show that $R(t,s)$ is the value at the point t of the solution of $(\bar{R}^*)$ which takes the value I_X at the point s. At the point τ this solution takes the value $R(\tau,s)$. On the other hand if we apply (ρ) to functions with values in $L(X)$, with $f \equiv 0$, $t_o = \tau$ and $x = R(\tau,s)$ we see that $R(t,\tau)\circ R(\tau,s)$ is the value at the point t of the solution of $(\bar{R}^*)$ which takes the value $R(\tau,s)$ at the point τ. Hence the functions $t \longmapsto R(t,s)$ and $t \longmapsto R(t,\tau) \circ R(\tau,s)$ satisfy the same equation $(\bar{R}^*)$ and take the same value, $R(\tau,s)$, at τ. By the unicity of the solution we have

$$R(t,\tau)\circ R(\tau,s) = R(t,s).$$

If we take $s = t$ in this equality and if we recall that $R(t,t) = I_X$ we get $R(t,\tau)\circ R(\tau,t) = I_X$; analogously we have $R(\tau,t)\circ R(t,\tau) = I_X$ hence $R(\tau,t) = R(t,\tau)^{-1}$.

V: If we apply sucessively (R^*), II.1.9 and IV we have

$$\int_u^v d_t R(t,s)\circ R(s,t) = \int_u^v d_t\Big[I_X - \int_s^t dA(\sigma)\circ R(\sigma,s)\Big]\circ R(s,t) =$$

$$= -\int_u^v dA(t)\circ R(t,s)\circ R(s,t) = -\int_u^v dA(t) = A(u) - A(v).$$

VI: It follows from IV of Theorem 1.5 (we recall that K in IV of Theorem 1.5 is normalized and therefore we have to take $K(\sigma,s) = A(s) - A(\sigma)$).

B - Obviously (L) does not change if we replace A by $A+c$, where $c \in L(X)$; hence we may fix a point $\bar{o} \in \,]a,b[$ and suppose that $A(\bar{o}) = 0$. We write $\mathcal{A}_{\bar{o}} = \{A \in \mathcal{A} \mid A(\bar{o}) = 0\}$.

We say that a mapping $R: \,]a,b[\,\times\,]a,b[\, \longrightarrow L(X)$ is *harmonic* or an *harmonic operator* if R satisfies (SV^{uo}), (SV^c),

(SV_{uo}), (SV_c) and

(□) $R(t,t) = I_X$, $R(t,\tau)\circ R(\tau,s) = R(t,s)$ for all $s,\tau,t \in]a,b[$.

Then we have obviously $R(\tau,t) = R(t,\tau)^{-1}$.

We denote by $\mathcal{H} = \mathcal{H}(]a,b[\times]a,b[,L(X))$ the set of all harmonic operators.

THEOREM 2.2. *If* $R:]a,b[\times]a,b[\longrightarrow L(X)$ *satisfies* (□) *and* (SV_o) *then* $R\in\mathcal{H}$ *and* R *is the resolvent of* A, *where*

$$A(u) = \int_u^{\bar{o}} d_t R(t,s)\circ R(s,t),$$

the definition being independent of the particular $s\in]a,b[$.

PROOF. R is continuous as a function of the first variable since it satisfies (SV_o). R is also continuous as a function of the second variable because if $(t,s_n) \longrightarrow (t,s)$ then by (□) we have

$$\|R(t,s_n)-R(t,s)\| = \|R(s_n,t)^{-1}-R(s,t)^{-1}\|$$

and this expression goes to zero when $n \longrightarrow \infty$ because R is continuous in the first variable and the mapping

$$R(\sigma,\tau) \longmapsto R(\sigma,\tau)^{-1}$$

is continuous.

Hence we have

$$R_s \in \mathcal{G}SV^{loc}(]a,b[,L(X)) \quad \text{and} \quad R^s\in \mathcal{G}(]a,b[,L(X))$$

and therefore

$$A(u) = \int_u^{\bar{o}} d_t R(t,s)\circ R(s,t)$$

is well defined. By (□) we have

$$A(u) = \int_u^{\bar{o}} d_t [R(t,\tau)\circ R(\tau,s)]\circ R(s,t) = \int_u^{\bar{o}} d_t R(t,\tau)\circ R(\tau,t)$$

i.e. the definition of A is independent of the particular $s\in]a,b[$.

From

$$SV_{[u_1,u_2]}[A] \leqslant SV_{[u_1,u_2]}[R_s]\,\|R^s\|_{[u_1,u_2]}$$

it follows that A satisfies (SV^o). We will now prove that R satisfies (R^*) i.e. R is the resolvent of A and is therefore harmonic. By II.1.9 we have

$$\int_s^t dA(\sigma)\circ R(\sigma,s) = \int_s^t d_\sigma\left[\int_\sigma^{\bar{o}} d_t R(t,s)\circ R(s,t)\right]\circ R(\sigma,s) =$$

$$= -\int_s^t d_\sigma R(\sigma,s)\circ R(s,\sigma)\circ R(\sigma,s) = -\int_s^t d_\sigma R(\sigma,s) = -R(t,s) + I_X.$$

QED

We recall that the topology on $\mathcal{A}$ is defined by the seminorms

$$A\in\mathcal{A} \longmapsto |||A|||_{[c,d]} = \|A\|_{[c,d]} + SV_{[c,d]}[A]$$

where $[c,d]$ runs over all closed subintervals of $]a,b[$. $\mathcal{A}$ is a Frechet space and $\mathcal{A}_{\bar{o}}$ is a closed subspace of $\mathcal{A}$.

$\mathcal{H}^{co}$ denotes $\mathcal{H}$ with the topology induced by $\mathcal{E}^{co}$ or G^{uo} i.e. with the topology defined by the seminorms

$$R\in\mathcal{H} \longmapsto |||R|||_{[c,d]} = \|R\|_{[c,d]} + SV^u_{[c,d]}[R] \qquad [c,d]\subset\,]a,b[$$

where, we recall,

$$\|R\|_{[c,d]} = \sup\{\|R(t,s)\| \mid s,t\in[c,d]\}$$

and

$$SV^u_{[c,d]}[R] = \sup\{SV_{[c,d]}[R^t] \mid t\in[c,d]\}.$$

We denote by $\mathcal{E}_{co}$ the set of all

$$U:\ ]a,b[\times]a,b[\longrightarrow L(X)$$

that satisfy (SV_c) and (SV_o) (and hence (SV_{uo}) by a result analogous to Theorem 1.31). On $\mathcal{E}_{co}$ we consider the topology defined by the seminorms

$$U\in\mathcal{E}_{co} \longmapsto |||U|||^{[c,d]} = \|U\|_{[c,d]} + SV_{u,[c,d]}[U],\quad [c,d]\subset\,]a,b[$$

where

$$SV_{u,[c,d]} = \sup\{SV_{[c,d]}[U_s] \mid s\in[c,d]\}.$$

We define $\mathcal{E}^I_{co} = \{U \in \mathcal{E}_{co} \mid U(t,t) \equiv I_X\}$. $\mathcal{H}_{co}$ denotes the set $\mathcal{H}$ with the topology induced by $\mathcal{E}_{co}$.

THEOREM 2.3. *On $\mathcal{H}$ the topologies of $\mathcal{H}^{co}$ and $\mathcal{H}_{co}$ coincide and the mapping $A \in \mathcal{A}_{\bar{o}} \longmapsto R \in \mathcal{H}$ is injective bicontinuous (non linear) from the first space onto the second.*

PROOF. We denote by R_A the resolvent associated to A and for $R \in \mathcal{H}$ we denote by A_R the element of $\mathcal{A}_{\bar{o}}$ defined in Theorem 2.2. The result will follow from the following facts that we shall prove sucessively:

1) For every $A \in \mathcal{A}_{\bar{o}}$ we have $K_A \in \mathcal{E}^{co}$ and the mapping $A \longmapsto K_A$ is obviously linear and continuous.

2) $K_A \in \mathcal{E}^{co} \mid A \in \mathcal{A}_{\bar{o}}\}$ is a closed vector subspace of $\mathcal{E}^{co}$ and the mapping $A \longmapsto K_A$ is bicontinuous.

Indeed, we have

$$\{K_A \in \mathcal{E}^{co} \mid A \in \mathcal{A}_{\bar{o}}\} =$$

$$= \{K \in \mathcal{E}^{co} \mid K(t,s) = K(\bar{o},s) - K(\bar{o},t) \quad \text{for all} \quad s,t \in]a,b[\} =$$

$$= \{K \in \mathcal{E}^{co} \mid \Phi_{t,s}(K) = \Phi_s(K) - \Phi_t(K) \quad \text{for all} \quad s,t \in]a,b[\},$$

where $\Phi_{t,s}(K) = K(t,s)$ and $\Phi_\sigma(K) = K(\bar{o},\sigma)$; the $\Phi_{t,s}$ and Φ_σ are linear continuous operators and therefore the vector subspace defined above is closed. The mapping $A \longmapsto K_A$ is obviously one-to-one and continuous (by 1)) hence bicontinuous by the interior mapping principle.

3) The mapping $K \in \mathcal{E}^{co}_{o} \longrightarrow R \in \mathcal{E}^{co}_{I}$ is injective, bicontinuous and onto.

Indeed, this was proved in Theorem 1.30.

From 2), 3) and Theorem 2.2 it follows that

4) The mapping $A \in \mathcal{A}_{\bar{o}} \longmapsto R_A \in \mathcal{H}^{co}$ is injective, bicontinuous and onto.

5) The mapping $R \in \mathcal{H}_{co} \longmapsto A_R \in \mathcal{A}_{\bar{o}}$ is injective and continuous.

Indeed, in Theorem 2.2 we saw that the mapping is injective. Let us prove that it is continuous. For $R_1, R \in \mathcal{H}$ we write $A_1 = A_{R_1}$ and $A = A_R$. We have

$$A_1(u)-A(u) = \int_u^{\bar{o}} d_t R_1(t,s) \circ R_1(s,t) - \int_u^{\bar{o}} d_t R(t,s) \circ R(s,t) =$$

$$= \int_u^{\bar{o}} d_t \left[R_1(t,s)-R(t,s)\right] \circ R_1(s,t) + \int_u^{\bar{o}} d_t R(t,s) \circ \left[R_1(s,t)-R(s,t)\right]$$

hence

$$\|A_1(u)-A(u)\| \leq SV_{(\bar{o},u)}\left[R_{1,s}-R_s\right] \|R_1^s\|_{(\bar{o},u)} + SV_{(\bar{o},u)}[R_s] \|R_1^s-R^s\|_{(\bar{o},u)}$$

which implies

$$\|A_1-A\|_{(c,d)} \leq SV_{(c,d)}[R_{1,s}-R_s] \|R_1^s\|_{(c,d)} + SV_{(c,d)}[R_s] \|R_1^s-R^s\|_{(c,d)}.$$

In the same way one proves

$$SV_{(c,d)}[A_1-A] \leq SV_{(c,d)}[R_{1,s}-R_s] \|R_1^s\|_{(c,d)} + SV_{(c,d)}[R_s] \|R_1^s-R^s\|_{(c,d)}$$

hence

$$A \xrightarrow{\mathcal{A}_{\bar{o}}} A_1 \quad \text{if} \quad R \xrightarrow{\mathcal{H}_{co}} R_1.$$

6) The mapping $A \in \mathcal{A}_{\bar{o}} \longmapsto R_A \in \mathcal{H}_{co}$ is continuous.

PROOF. a) By 4) the mapping $A \in \mathcal{A}_{\bar{o}} \longmapsto R_A \in \mathcal{E}$ is continuous.
b) We still have to prove that given $A_1 \in \mathcal{A}_{\bar{o}}$ for $A \in \mathcal{A}_{\bar{o}}$ sufficiently close to A_1, $SV_{u,(c,d)}[R_1-R]$ becomes arbitrarily small. In the proof of II' of Theorem 2.1 we saw that

$$SV_{(c,d)}[R_s] \leq SV_{(c,d)}[A] \|R_s\|_{(c,d)}$$

and if we proceed as in 5) we have

$$SV_{(c,d)}[R_{1,s}-R_s] \leq SV_{(c,d)}[A_1-A] \|R_{1,s}\|_{(c,d)} +$$
$$+ SV_{(c,d)}[A] \|R_{1,s}-R_s\|_{(c,d)}$$

hence

$$SV_{u,(c,d)}[R_1-R] \leq SV_{(c,d)}[A_1-A] \|R_1\|_{(c,d)} +$$
$$+ SV_{(c,d)}[A] \|R_1-R\|_{(c,d)}$$

and therefore, since for $A \longrightarrow A_1$ by a) we have

$$\|R_1-R\|_{[c,d]} \longrightarrow 0$$

it follows that $SV_{u,[c,d]}[R_1-R] \longrightarrow 0$ hence b).

By 5) and 6) the mapping $A \in \mathcal{A}_{\bar{o}} \longmapsto R_A \in \mathcal{H}_{co}$ is injective, bicontinuous and onto and with 4) this shows that

7) On $\mathcal{H}$ the topologies of $\mathcal{H}^{co}$ and $\mathcal{H}_{co}$ coincide.

This completes the proof of the theorem.

§3 - *Equations with linear constraints*

In this § we study the solutions of the system (K), (F) (see the introduction of this chapter) when we have unicity of the solutions and we find the Green function. We recall that F is called a linear constraint. In A we give examples of the main linear constraint s . We suppose that K is continuous (i.e. $K \in \mathcal{E}^{uo}$); in B we make a preliminar algebraic study where it is enough to suppose that $K \in G^{uo}$. The analytic results of C will allow us to transform the formulas of B in formulas of the Green function type (D and E).

A - In what follows we give the main examples of linear constraints that appear in Analysis, i.e., of opertators $F \in L[G(]a,b[,X),Y]$ or $F \in L[G([a,b],X),Y]$.

1 - Initial conditions: we take $Y = X$ and $t_o \in]a,b[$; $F[y] \equiv y(t_o)$.

We recall that when we have a linear differential equation of order n

$$\text{(N)} \qquad N[z] \equiv z^{(n)} + a_1(t)z^{(n-1)} + \ldots + a_n(t)z = b(t)$$

where, for instance, $z \in \mathcal{C}^{(n)}(]a,b[,Z)$ and $b, a_i \in \mathcal{C}(]a,b[,Z)$, with initial conditions

$$z(t_o) = c_1,\ z'(t_o) = c_2, \ldots,\ z^{(n-1)}(t_o) = c_n ,$$

then we take $X = Z^n$ and $y_i(t) = z^{(i-1)}(t)$, $i = 1,2,\ldots,n$, and the n-order equation is transformed into the system

$$\begin{aligned} &y_1'(t) - y_2(t) = 0 \\ &y_2'(t) - y_3(t) = 0 \\ &\cdots\cdots\cdots\cdots \\ &y_{n-1}'(t) - y_n(t) = 0 \\ &y_n'(t) + \sum_{i=1}^{n} a_i(t) y_{n-i}(t) = b(t) \end{aligned}$$

that is, of the form

$$y'(t) + A(t)y(t) = f(t), \qquad y(t_o) = c.$$

2 - Boundary conditions: we take $Y = X$ and $[a,b]$; $F[y] \equiv Ay(a) + By(b)$ where $A,B \in L(X)$.

We recall that if we have the n-order equation (N) and boundary conditions

$$F_i[z] \equiv \sum_{j=1}^{n} \left[\alpha_{ij} z^{(j-1)}(a) + \beta_{ij} z^{(j-1)}(b)\right] = c_i \qquad i=1,2,\ldots,n$$

where α_{ij}, $\beta_{ij} \in L(Z)$, by the transformation given in 1 we get an example of the type 2.

3 - Periodicity conditions: we take $]a,b[\, = \mathbb{R}$, $Y = G(\mathbb{R},X)$; given $p > 0$ (the *period*) we define

$$F[y](t) \equiv y(t+p) - y(t), \qquad t \in \mathbb{R}.$$

4 - Left discontinuity: We take $Y = X^2$, $t_o \in\,]a,b[$ and $F[y] \equiv (y(t_o), y(t_o-))$.

5 - Multiple point conditions (the Nicoletti problem): We give $t_1,\ldots,t_m \in\,]a,b[$ and $A_1,\ldots,A_m \in L(X,Y)$;

$$F[y] \equiv \sum_{i=1}^{m} A_i y(t_i).$$

If for the n-order equation (N) we give

$$F_i[z] \equiv \sum_{j=1}^{m} \sum_{h=1}^{n} \alpha_{ijh} z^{(h-1)}(t_j) \qquad i=1,\ldots,n, \quad \alpha_{ijh} \in L(Z)$$

the transformation of example 1 gives us an example of type 5.

6 - Conditions at infinite points: We give a sequence $t_n \in [a,b]$, $n = 1,2,\ldots$ and $u = (u_n)_{n\in\mathbb{N}} \in s(\mathbb{N},L(X,Y))$ (see B of §5 of Chapter I) and $F[y] \equiv \sum_{n\in\mathbb{N}} u_n y(t_n)$.

7 - Integral conditions: We give $\alpha \in SV_{oo}(]a,b[,L(X,Y))$ and $F[y] \equiv \int_a^b \cdot d\alpha(t)\cdot y(t)$.

8 - Interface conditions: We give $t_o \in]a,b[$ and $A, A_-, A_+ \in L(X,Y)$; $F[y] \equiv A_- y(t_o-) + Ay(t_o) + A_+ y(t_o+)$.

9 - Integral equations: We take $Y = G(]c,d[,Z)$ and $A \in G(]c,d[,SV^{\sigma}_{oo}(]a,b[,L(X,Z)))$, $F[y](t) \equiv \int_a^b d_\sigma A(t,\sigma)\cdot y(\sigma)$ (see (I.6.10)).

B - We will now make an algebraic study of the resolution of the system (K), (F); we recall that $K \in G^{uo}$ and hence by II of Theorem 1.5 we have $R \in G^{uo}$ hence for every $s \in]a,b[$ we have $R_s \in G(]a,b[,L(X))$. Given $F \in L[G(]a,b[,X),Y]$ by I.6.8 we have $F = F_\alpha + F_u$. We recall that

3.1. F, F_α *and* F_u *have natural extensions as linear continuous mappings from* $G(]a,b[,L(X))$ *in* $L(X,Y)$.

PROOF. Given $U \in G(]a,b[,L(X))$ for every $x \in X$ we define $F[U]x = F[Ux]$. We have $Ux \in G(]a,b[,X)$ and hence $F[Ux]$ is well defined and depends obviously linearly and continuously on x. For $q \in \Gamma_Y$ there exist $[c,d] \subset]a,b[$ and $c_q > 0$ such that $q[F(f)] \leqslant c_q \|f\|_{[c,d]}$ and hence

$$q[F(U)x] \leqslant c_q \|Ux\|_{[c,d]} \leqslant c_q \|U\|_{[c,d]} \|x\|$$

i.e. $q[F[U]] \leqslant c_q \|U\|_{[c,d]}$, which proves the continuity of the mapping $U \longmapsto F[U]$. For F_α and F_u we have analogous proofs.

DEFINITION. For every $s \in]a,b[$ we define $J_s = J(s) = F_t[R(t,s)] = F[R_s]$, $J_\alpha(s) = F_\alpha[R_s]$, $J_u(s) = F_u[R_s]$.

By 3.1 we have

3.2. $J(s),\ J_\alpha(s),\ J_u(s)\in L(X,Y)$ *for every* $s\in\,]a,b[$.

3.3. $J_\alpha\in SV^{loc}(]a,b[,L(X,Y))$ *and*

$$\lim_{\delta\downarrow 0} SV_{q,[s-\delta,s+\delta]}[J_\alpha] = 0$$

for every $s\in\,]a,b[$ *and* $q\in\Gamma_Y$.

PROOF. By definition we have

$$J_\alpha(s) = \int_a^b d\alpha(t)\circ R(t,s);$$

given $q\in\Gamma_Y$, let $]a_q,b_q[$ contain the q-support of f_α; by (3) of §1 of Chapter II (and Remark 8 of that §) we have

$$SV_{q,[s_1,s_2]}[J_\alpha] \leqslant SV_{q,[a_q,b_q]}[\alpha] \sup_{a_q\leqslant t\leqslant b_q} SV_{[s_1,s_2]}[R^t]$$

which implies all the assertions if we recall that $R\in G^{uo}$.

3.4. *If* K *is continuous we have* $J = J_\alpha$ *and* $J_u = 0$.

PROOF. If K is continuous so is R_s, hence $J_u[R_s] = 0$.

THEOREM 3.5. *For the equation* (L) J *satisfies the adjoint equation*

$$J(t) - J(s) - \int_s^t J(\sigma)dA(\sigma) = 0 \quad \textit{for all} \quad s,t\in\,]a,b[.$$

PROOF. By $(\bar{R}_*)$ of Theorem 2.1 we have

$$R(\tau,t) - R(\tau,s) = \int_s^t R(\tau,\sigma)dA(\sigma),$$

hence, if we recall that by 3.4 we have $J = J_\alpha$, we obtain

$$J(t) - J(s) = \int_a^b d\alpha(\tau)\circ\left[\int_s^t R(\tau,\sigma)\cdot dA(\sigma)\right] =$$

$$= \int_s^t\left[\int_a^b d\alpha(\tau)\circ R(\tau,\sigma)\right]\circ dA(\sigma) = \int_s^t J(\sigma)\circ dA(\sigma)$$

where we did apply (5) of §1 of Chap. II and Remark 1 of that §.

We now define

$$K[y](t) \equiv y(t) - y(t_o) + \int_{t_o}^t d_\sigma K(t,\sigma)\cdot y(\sigma)$$

and we write $K[y] = f$ if $K[y](t) = f(t) - f(t_o)$.

We define

$$Y_o = F[K^{-1}(0)] = \{F[y] \mid y(t)-y(t_o) + \int_{t_o}^{t} d_\sigma K(t,\sigma)\cdot y(\sigma) \equiv 0\} \subset Y.$$

THEOREM 3.6. *Given the system* (K), (F) *the following properties are equivalent:*

(i) $y \equiv 0$ *is the only solution of* $K[y] \equiv 0$, $F[y] = 0$.

(ii) For every $c \in Y_o$ *the system* $K[y] \equiv 0$, $F[y] = c$ *has exactly one solution.*

(iii) The mapping $y \in K^{-1}(0) \longmapsto F[y] \in Y_o$ *is one-to-one onto.*

(iv) $J(t_o): X \longrightarrow Y_o$ *is one-to-one onto (but not bicontinuous).*

PROOF. (i) $\Longrightarrow$ (ii). Given $c = F[y_1] \in Y_o$ with $K[y_1] \equiv 0$ if there were a $y_2 \neq y_1$ with $K[y_2] \equiv 0$ and $F[y_2] = c$ then $y = y_1 - y_2 \neq 0$ would be a solution of $K[y] \equiv 0$, $F[y] = 0$ in contradiction to (i).

(ii) $\Longrightarrow$ (i) is obvious.

(ii) $\Longleftrightarrow$ (iii) is immediate.

(iii) $\Longleftrightarrow$ (iv). Let y_x be the solution of $K[y] \equiv 0$, $y(t_o) = x$ (by III of Theorem 1.5). Hence the mapping

$$x \in X \longmapsto y_x \in K^{-1}(0)$$

is a Banach space isomorphism. Therefore the mapping

$$y \in K^{-1}(0) \longmapsto F[y] \in Y_o$$

is one-to-one onto if and only if the composed mapping

$$x \in X \longmapsto F[y_x] = F[R_{t_o} x] = J(t_o)x \in Y_o$$

is one-to-one onto.

REMARK 1. In the case of the example (L) of §2 we may take as t_o any point $s \in]a,b[$ and then the properties above are still equivalent to the following ones:

(iv') - For every $s \in]a,b[$, $J(s): X \longrightarrow Y_o$ is one-to-one onto.

(v') - There exists $s \in \left]a,b\right[$ such that $J(s): X \longrightarrow Y_o$ is one-to-one onto.

FROM NOW ON WE SUPPOSE THAT THE EQUIVALENT PROPERTIES OF THEOREM 3.6 ARE SATISFIED

For every $t \in \left]a,b\right[$ we define

$$\bar{J}(t) = R(t,t_o) \circ J(t_o)^{-1} : Y_o \longrightarrow X.$$

3.7. *a)* $\bar{J}(t)$ *is linear (not continuous in general).*

b) $\bar{J}(t)$ *is injective if and only if* $R(t,t_o)$ *is injective.*

c) $\bar{J}(t)$ *is continuous if* $J(t_o)^{-1}$ *is continuous.*

d) If $J(t_o)^{-1}$ *is continuous,* Y_o *is a Banach space and is closed in* Y.

e) In the example (L) *of §2 we have* $R(t,s) = J(t)^{-1} \circ J(s)$ *and* $\bar{J}(t) = J(t)^{-1}$.

f) In the example (L) *of §2,* $\bar{J}(t)$ *is bijective and if* $\bar{J}(t)$ *is continuous for some* $t \in \left]a,b\right[$ *it is continuous for every* $t \in \left]a,b\right[$.

PROOF. a), b) and c) are obvious by the definition of $\bar{J}(t)$.

d) If $J(t_o)^{-1}$ is continuous then $J(t_o)$ is bicontinous, hence Y_o is isomorphic to the Banach space X and therefore complete, hence closed in every separated LCS.

e) By Remark 1 for every $t \in \left]a,b\right[$ there exists $J(t)^{-1}$ and in order to prove that $R(t,s) = J(t)^{-1} \circ J(s)$ it is enough to show that $J(t) \circ R(t,s) = J(s)$: by (IV) of Theorem 2.1 we have

$$J(s) = F_\tau[R(\tau,s)] = F_\tau[R(\tau,t) \circ R(t,s)] =$$
$$= F_\tau[R(\tau,t)] \circ R(t,s) = J(t) \circ R(t,s).$$

The second assertion follows from

$$\bar{J}(t) = R(t,t_o) \circ J(t_o)^{-1} = [J(t)^{-1} \circ J(t_o)] \circ J(t_o)^{-1} = J(t)^{-1}.$$

f) follows immediately from e).

3.8. *For every* $c \in Y_o$ *the function*

$$t \in]a,b[\longmapsto \bar{J}(t)c \in X$$

is regulated (continuous if K *is continuous).*

PROOF. We have $\bar{J}(t)c = R(t,t_o)J(t_o)^{-1}c$; hence the result follows from the fact that the function R_{t_o} is regulated (continuous if K is continuous).

THEOREM 3.9. *The function* $\bar{J}$ *has the following properties:*

a) $\bar{J}(t)c - \bar{J}(t_o)c + \int_{t_o}^{t} d_\sigma K(t,\sigma)\cdot\bar{J}(\sigma)c = 0$ *for every* $c \in Y_o$, $t \in]a,b[$.

b) $F_t[\bar{J}(t)c] = c$ *for every* $c \in Y_o$.

PROOF. We have $\bar{J}(t)c = R(t,t_o)J(t_o)^{-1}c$; by ($R^*$) of Theorem 1.5 we have

$$R(t,t_o) - I_X + \int_{t_o}^{t} d_\sigma K(t,\sigma)\, R(\sigma,t_o) = 0$$

and if we apply this to $J(t_o)^{-1}c$ we get a).

By

$$F_t[\bar{J}(t)c] = F_t[R(t,t_o)\cdot J(t_o)^{-1}c] =$$

$$= F_t[R(t,t_o)]J(t_o)^{-1}c = J(t_o)\cdot J(t_o)^{-1}c = c$$

we have b).

COROLLARY 3.10. *The solution* y_c *of* $K[y] \equiv 0$, $F[y] = c$ *where* $c \in Y_o$ *is given by* $y_c(t) = \bar{J}(t)c$, $t \in]a,b[$.

b) The linear mapping $c \in Y_o \longmapsto y_c \in G(]a,b[,X)$ *is continuous if and only if* $J(t_o)^{-1}$ *is continuous (and hence* $J(t_o)$ *is bicontinuous).*

DEFINITIONS

$$S_{K,F} = \{(f,c) \in G(]a,b[,X) X Y \mid \exists\, y \in G(]a,b[,X) \text{ such that } K[y] = f,\ F[y] = c\}$$

$$S^{\mathcal{G}}_{K,F} = \{(g,c) \in \mathcal{G}(]a,b[,X) X Y \mid y \in G(]a,b[,X) \text{ such that } K[y] = g,\ F[y] = c\}$$

In the case of the example (L) of §2 we write $S_{L,F}$ and $S^{G}_{L,F}$.

Given $(f,c)\in S_{K,F}$ if $K[y] = f$ and $F[y] = c$ by (ρ) of Theorem 1.5 we have

$$(1)\qquad y(t) = R(t,t_o)y(t_o) + \int_{t_o}^{t} R(t,\sigma)df(\sigma).$$

For $f\in G(]a,b[,X)$ we define

$$\hat{f}(t) = \int_{t_o}^{t} R(t,\sigma)df(\sigma),$$

$t\in]a,b[$; by b) of II.1.14 we have $\hat{f}\in G(]a,b[,X)$, hence $F(\hat{f})$ is well defined. If we apply F to (1) we obtain

$$c = F[y] = J(t_o)y(t_o) + F[\hat{f}],$$

hence

$$y(t_o) = J(t_o)^{-1}[c - F(\hat{f})]$$

and if we replace this value in (1) we obtain

$$y(t) = R(t,t_o)\circ J(t_o)^{-1}[c-F(\hat{f})] + \int_{t_o}^{t} R(t,\sigma)\cdot df(\sigma).$$

This proves the first part of

THEOREM 3.11. *a) For every* $(f,c)\in S_{K,F}$ *the solution* y *of* $K[y]=f$, $F[y] = c$ *is given by*

$$(2)\qquad y(t) = \int_{t_o}^{t} R(t,\sigma)\cdot df(\sigma) + \bar{J}(t)[c-F(\hat{f})].$$

b) Reciprocally, if $(f,c)\in G(]a,b[,X)\mathrm{X}Y$ *is such that* $c-F(\hat{f})\in Y_o$ *then the system* $K[y] = f$, $F[y] = c$ *has a solution* y *given by* (2) *(hence* $(f,c)\in S_{K,F}$*)*.

Proof of b: immediate since we may "go back" through the transformations we made in the proof of a).

REMARK 2. In (2) we cannot write

$$\bar{J}(t)[c-F(\hat{f})] = \bar{J}(t)c - \bar{J}(t)F(\hat{f})$$

because, in general, we don't have c, $F(\hat{f})\in Y_o$ hence $\bar{J}(t)c$ and $\bar{J}(t)F(\hat{f})$ are not defined.

If K is continuous so is R hence by b) of II.1.14 $\hat{g}$

is continuous if g is continuous and therefore $F(\hat{g})=F_\alpha(\hat{g})$; by 3.8 we then have

THEOREM 3.12. *Let* K *be continuous.*

a) For $(g,c)\in S^{\mathcal{C}}_{K,F}$ *the solution* $y\in G(]a,b[,X)$ *of* $K[y] = g$, $F[y] = c$ *is a continuous function and is given by*

$$(3)\qquad y(t) = \int_{t_o}^{t} R(t,\sigma)dg(\sigma) + \bar{J}(t)\left[c-\int_a^b d\alpha(\tau)\left[\int_{t_o}^{\tau} R(\tau,\sigma)dg(\sigma)\right]\right].$$

b) Reciprocally if $(g,c)\in \mathcal{C}(]a,b[,X)\times Y$ *is such that*

$$c - \int_a^b d\alpha(\tau)\left[\int_{t_o}^{\tau} R(\tau,\sigma)dg(\sigma)\right]\in Y_o$$

the system $K[y] = g$, $F[y] = c$ *has a solution given by* (3).

Using integration by parts in (1) we obtain

$$(4)\qquad y(t) = f(t)+R(t,t_o)[y(t_o)-f(t_o)] - \int_{t_o}^{t} d_\sigma R(t,\sigma)\cdot f(\sigma).$$

For $f\in G(]a,b[,X)$ we define $\tilde{f}(t) = \int_{t_o}^{t} d_\sigma R(t,\sigma)\cdot f(\sigma)$, $t\in]a,b[$, and by a) of II.1.14 we have $\tilde{f}\in G(]a,b[,X)$ and $\tilde{f}$ is continuous if K (and hence R) is continuous; therefore $F(\tilde{f})$ is well defined. If we apply F to (4) we obtain $c = F[y] = F[f] + J(t_o)[y(t_o)-f(t_o)] - F(\tilde{f})$, hence

$$y(t_o) - f(t_o) = J(t_o)^{-1}[c-F(f)+F(\tilde{f})]$$

and if we replace this expression in (4) we get

$$y(t) = f(t)+R(t,t_o)\cdot J(t_o)^{-1}[c-F(f)+F(\tilde{f})] - \int_{t_o}^{t} d_\sigma R(t,\sigma)\cdot f(\sigma)$$

i.e.

THEOREM 3.13. *a) For every* $(f,c)\in S_{K,F}$ *the solution* y *of* $K[y] = f$, $F[y] = c$ *is given by*

$$(5)\qquad y(t) = f(t) - \int_{t_o}^{t} d_\sigma R(t,\sigma)\cdot f(\sigma) + \bar{J}(t)[c-F(f)+F(\tilde{f})].$$

b) Reciprocally, if $(f,c)\in G(]a,b[,X)\times Y$ *is such that* $c - F(f) + F(\tilde{f})\in Y_o$ *then the system* $K[y] = f$, $F[y] = c$ *has a solution given by* (5) *(hence* $(f,c)\in S_{K,F}$*).*

If K is continuous, so is R and then by a) of II.1.14 $\tilde{f}$ is continuous too, hence $F(\tilde{f}) = F_\alpha(\bar{f})$; therefore we have

3.14. *Let* K *be continuous. For every* $(f,c) \in S_{K,F}$ *the solution* y *of* $K[y] = f$, $F[y] = c$ *is given by*

$$(6) \qquad y(t) = f(t) - \int_{t_0}^{t} d_\sigma R(t,\sigma)\cdot f(\sigma) +$$

$$+ \bar{J}(t)\Big[c - F(f) + \int_a^b d\alpha(\tau)\Big[\int_{t_0}^{\tau} d_\sigma R(\tau,\sigma)\cdot f(\sigma)\Big]\Big].$$

(6) is a *regularizing formula* since all functions of the second member, but f, are continuous (by 3.8 and because $\tilde{f}$ is continuous); hence we see that y and f have the same kinds of discontinuities and at the same points.

C - The theorem that follows will allow us to make further transformations of the formulas (2), (3), (5) and (6).

We recall that if X is a Banach space, Y a SSCLCS and $u \in L(X,Y)$, for every $q \in \Gamma_Y$ we define

$$q[u] = \sup_{\|x\| \leq 1} q(u(x)).$$

LEMMA 3.15. *Given* $\beta \in SV_{oo}(]a,b[,L(X,Y))$, $q \in \Gamma_Y$ *and* $a_q \in]a,b[$ *such that for every* $x \in X$ *we have* $q[\beta(t)x] = 0$ *for* $t \leq a_q$, *then*

$$q\Big[\int_a^t \beta(s)\cdot dg(s) - \int_{a_q}^t \beta(s)\cdot dg(s)\Big] = 0$$

for every $g \in \mathcal{G}(]a,b[,X)$.

PROOF. It is immediate since for $s_{i-1} \leq \xi_i \leq s_i \leq a_q$ we have

$$q\Big[\beta(\xi_i)[g(s_i)-g(s_{i-1})]\Big] \leq q[\beta(\xi_i)]\|g(s_i)-g(s_{i-1})\| = 0$$

because $q[\beta(\xi_i)] = 0$ if $\xi_i \leq a_q$.

THEOREM 3.16. *Given* $K \in \mathcal{E}^{uo}$, R *its resolvent and*

$$J(s) = F[R_s] = F_\alpha[R_s]$$

we define

$$H(t,s) = \int_a^s d\alpha(\tau)\circ R(\tau,s) - Y(s-t)J(s);$$

we have

a) $H^t \in SV_{oo}(]a,b[,L(X,Y))$ *and* $H(t,b-) = 0$ *for every* $t \in]a,b[$.

b) $\int_a^b d\alpha(\tau)\int_\tau^t R(\tau,s)\cdot dg(s) = \int_a^b H(t,s)\cdot dg(s)$ *for every* $g \in \mathfrak{G}(]a,b[,X)$.

c)
$$H(t,s) + Y(s-t)J(s) + \int_a^s [H(t,\sigma) + Y(\sigma-t)J(\sigma)]\, d_\sigma K(\sigma,s) = \alpha(s)$$

for all $s,t \in]a,b[$.

PROOF. a) We want to show that for every $q \in \Gamma_Y$ there is a $[a_q,b_q] \subset]a,b[$ such that:

(i) For every $x \in X$ we have $q[H^t(s)x] = 0$ if $s \leq a_q$ or $s \geq b_q$,

(ii) $SV_{q,[a_q,b_q]}[H^t] < \infty$.

(i) We take the q-support $[a_q,b_q]$ of H^t and decrease a_q or increase b_q in such a way that $t \in [a_q,b_q]$. Then for $s \leq a_q$ we have

$$H^t(s) = \int_a^s d\alpha(\tau)\circ R(\tau,s)$$

and

$$q[H^t(s)x] = q\left[\int_a^s d\alpha(\tau)\circ R(\tau,s)x\right] = 0$$

for every $x \in X$ since $SV_{q,]a,a_q]}[\alpha] = 0$. Analogously for $s \geq b_q$ we have

$$H^t(s) = \int_a^s d\alpha(\tau)\circ R(\tau,s) - \int_a^b d\alpha(\tau)\circ R(\tau,s) = -\int_s^b d\alpha(\tau)\circ R(\tau,s)$$

and

$$q[H^t(s)x] = q\left[-\int_s^b d\alpha(\tau)\circ R(t,s)x\right] = 0$$

for every x since $SV_{q,[b_q,b)}[\alpha] = 0$.

(ii) By I.6.2 we have

$$SV_{q,(a_q,b_q)}[H^t] = \sup\{q\Big[\int_{a_q}^{b_q} ds\Big[\int_a^s d\sigma(\tau)\circ R(\tau,s) -$$

$$- Y(s-t)\int_a^t d\alpha(\tau)\circ R(\tau,s)\Big]\cdot f(s)\Big] \mid f\in G((a_q,b_q),X),\ \|f\|\leqslant 1\}.$$

Hence

$$SV_{q,(a_q,b_q)}[H^t] \leqslant \sup_{\|f\|\leqslant 1} q\Big[\int_{a_q}^{t} d_s\Big[\int_{a_q}^{s} d\alpha(\tau)\circ R(\tau,s)\Big]\cdot f(s)\Big] +$$

$$+ \sup_{\|f\|\leqslant 1} q\Big[\int_{t}^{b_q} d_s\Big[\int_{s}^{b_q} d\alpha(\tau)\circ R(\tau,s)\Big]\cdot f(s)\Big].$$

If we apply (7) of II.1.6 and recall that $R(t,t)\equiv I_X$, we obtain

$$SV_{q,(a_q,b_q)}[H^t] \leqslant SV_{q,(a_q,t)}[\alpha]\Big[1 + \sup_{a_q\leqslant\tau\leqslant t} SV_{(\tau,t)}[R^\tau]\Big] +$$

$$+ SV_{q,(t,b_q)}[\alpha]\Big[1 + \sup_{t\leqslant\tau\leqslant b_q} SV_{(t,\tau)}[R^\tau]\Big].$$

b) From the definition of H it follows that

$$H(t,s) = \int_a^b \cdot d\alpha(\tau)\circ sg(t-\tau)\chi_{(\tau,t)}(s)R(\tau,s)$$

hence

$$\int_a^b H(t,s)dg(s) = \int_a^b\Big[\int_a^b \cdot d\alpha(\tau)\circ sg(t-\tau)\chi_{(\tau,t)}(s)R(\tau,s)\Big]dg(s).$$

We define $h(\tau,s) = sg(t-\tau)\chi_{(\tau,t)}(s)R(\tau,s)$; the functions α, h and g satisfy the hypothesis of Theorem 2.6 of Chapter II hence, by (7) of this theorem, the last integral is equal to

$$\int_a^b \cdot d\alpha(\tau)\int_\tau^t R(\tau,s)dg(s).$$

c) By the definition of H we have

$$H(t,\sigma) + Y(\sigma-t)J(\sigma) = \int_a^\sigma d\alpha(\tau)\circ R(\tau,\sigma);$$

by Theorem 2.7 of Chapter II we have

$$(*)\quad \int_a^s \left[\int_a^\sigma d\alpha(\tau)\circ R(\tau,\sigma)\right]\circ d_\sigma K(\sigma,s) = \int_a^s d\alpha(\tau)\left[\int_\tau^s R(\tau,\sigma)\circ d_\sigma K(\sigma,s)\right]$$

and by (R_*) of Theorem 1.5 we have

$$\int_\tau^s R(\tau,\sigma)\circ d_\sigma K(\sigma,s) = I_X - R(\tau,s);$$

if we replace this in the second member of $(*)$ we obtain c).

D - We give now a first form of the integral formulas of Green function type.

THEOREM 3.17. *For* $K \in \mathcal{E}^{uo}$ *we have*

a) For every $(g,c) \in S^{\mathfrak{G}}_{K,F}$ *there is one and only one solution* y *of* $K[y] = g$, $F[y] = c$*; the solution* y *is continuous and is given by*

$$(7)\qquad y(t) = \int_{t_o}^t R(t,\sigma)dg(\sigma) + \bar{J}(t)\left[c + \int_a^b H(t_o,\sigma)dg(\sigma)\right].$$

b) Reciprocally if $(g,c) \in \mathfrak{G}(]a,b[,X)\times Y$ *is such that*

$$c + \int_a^b H(t_o,\sigma)dg(\sigma) \in Y_o$$

then the system $K[y] = g$, $F[y] = c$ *has a solution* y *given by* (7).

PROOF. It follows immediately from (3) by b) of Theorem 3.12.

In the case of the example (L) of §2 for each $t \in]a,b[$ we take $t_o = t$ in (7):

THEOREM 3.18. *For every* $(g,c) \in S^{\mathfrak{G}}_{L,F}$ *the solution* y *of* $L[y] = g$, $F[y] = c$ *is continuous and is given by*

$$(7')\qquad y(t) = J(t)^{-1}\left[c + \int_a^b H(t,\sigma)\cdot dg(\sigma)\right].$$

THEOREM 3.19. *For* $K \in \mathcal{E}_o^{uo}$ *we have*

a) *For every* $(f,c) \in S_{K,F}$ *the solution* y *of* $K[y] = f$, $F[y] = c$ *is given by*

(8) $$y(t) = f(t) - \int_{t_o}^{t} d_\sigma R(t,\sigma)\cdot f(\sigma) + $$
$$+ \bar{J}(t)\Big[c - F(f) - \int_a^b H(t_o,\sigma)\cdot d_\sigma\Big[\int_{t_o}^{\sigma} d_s K(\sigma,s)\cdot f(s)\Big]\Big].$$

b) *Reciprocally, if* $(f,c) \in G(]a,b[,X) \times Y$ *is such that*

$$c - F(f) - \int_a^b H(t_o,\sigma) d_\sigma\Big[\int_{t_o}^{\sigma} d_s K(\sigma,s)\cdot f(s)\Big] \in Y_o$$

then the system $K[y] = f$, $F[y] = c$ *has a solution* y *given by* (8).

PROOF. $K[y] = f$ may be written as

$$(y-f)(t) - (y-f)(t_o) + \int_{t_o}^{t} d_\sigma K(t,\sigma)[(y-f)(\sigma)] = g(t)$$

where

$$g(t) = -\int_{t_o}^{t} d_\sigma K(t,\sigma)\cdot f(\sigma)$$

and by a) of II.1.14 we have $g \in \mathcal{G}(]a,b[,X)$; hence by Theorem 3.17 we have

$$y(t) - f(t) = -\int_{t_o}^{t} R(t,\sigma)\cdot d_\sigma\Big[\int_{t_o}^{\sigma} d_\tau K(\sigma,\tau)\cdot f(\tau)\Big] +$$
$$+ \bar{J}(t)\Big[F[y-f] - \int_a^b H(t_o,\sigma) d_\sigma\Big[\int_{t_o}^{\sigma} d_\tau K(\sigma,\tau)\cdot f(\tau)\Big]\Big].$$

We have $F[y-f] = c - F[f]$ and we still have to prove that

$$\int_{t_o}^{t} R(t,\sigma) d_\sigma\Big[\int_{t_o}^{\sigma} d_\tau K(\sigma,\tau)\cdot f(\tau)\Big] = \int_{t_o}^{t} d_\tau R(t,\tau)\cdot f(\tau).$$

Indeed, using first integration by parts in the first integral above, then applying (6') of Chapter II (and recalling that $K(t,t) \equiv 0$) and using afterwards (R_{**}) of Theorem 1.20 we obtain

$$\int_{t_o}^{t} R(t,\sigma) d_\sigma\Big[\int_{t_o}^{\sigma} d_\tau K(\sigma,\tau)\cdot f(\tau)\Big] =$$

$$= \int_{t_o}^{t} d_\tau K(t,\tau)\cdot f(\tau) - \int_{t_o}^{t} d_\sigma R(t,\sigma)\cdot \int_{t_o}^{\sigma} d_\tau K(\sigma,\tau)\cdot f(\tau) =$$

$$= \int_{t_o}^{t} d_\tau K(t,\tau)\cdot f(\tau) - \int_{t_o}^{t} d_\tau \Big[\int_{\tau}^{t} d_\sigma R(t,\sigma)\cdot K(\sigma,\tau)\Big] f(\tau) =$$

$$= \int_{t_o}^{t} d_\tau K(\sigma,\tau)\cdot f(\tau) + \int_{t_o}^{t} d_\tau [R(t,\tau)-K(t,\tau)-I_X]\cdot f(\tau) =$$

$$= \int_{t_o}^{t} d_\tau R(t,\tau)\cdot f(\tau).$$

QED

REMARK 3. (8) is a regularizing formula (see the comment after 3.14).

In the case of the example (L) of §2 for each $t \in \,]a,b[$ we may take $t_o = t$; we recall that in Theorem 3.19 K is normalized hence we have $K(\sigma,s) = A(s)-A(\sigma)$ and we obtain

Theorem 3.20 - *For every* $(f,c)\in S_{L,F}$ *the system* $L[y] = f$, $F[y] = c$ *has a solution* y *given by*

$$(8')\qquad y(t) = f(t)+J(t)^{-1}\Big[c-F(f)-\int_a^b H(t,\sigma)\cdot d_\sigma\Big[\int^{\sigma} dA(s)\cdot f(s)\Big]\Big].$$

E - In this item we give conditions in order that the solutions of the problem $K[y] = g$, $F[y] = c$ with $g\in \mathcal{G}(]a,b[,X)$ may be written in the form

$$(9)\qquad y(t) = \bar{J}(t)c + \int_a^b G(t,s)\cdot dg(s).$$

We will show that then y depends continuously on g. We extend these results to the general problem $K[y] = f$, $F[y]=c$.

THEOREM 3.21. *Let* K *and* F *be such that*

1) The solution y *of* $K[y] = g$, $F[y] = c$ *where* $g\in\mathcal{G}(]a,b[,X)$ *may be written in the form* (9).

2) For any $c\in Y_o$ *and* $g\in \mathcal{G}(]a,b[,X)$, y *given by* (9) *is the solution of* $K[y] = g$, $F[y] = c$.

Then: a) $S^{\mathcal{G}}_{K,F} = \mathcal{G}(]a,b[,X)\times Y_o$ *b)* $F[\mathcal{G}(]a,b[,X)] = Y_o$.

PROOF. a) If $(g,c)\in S^{\mathcal{G}}_{K,F}$ is such that the solution y of $K[y] = g$, $F[y] = c$ may be written in the form (9) then c has to be in the domain of definition of $\bar{J}(t)$, in particular of $\bar{J}(t_o) = J(t_o)^{-1}$, i.e., $c\in Y_o$, hence $S^{\mathcal{G}}_{K,F}\subset \mathcal{G}(]a,b[,X)\times Y_o$ and by 2) we have the other inclusion.

b) We have $K^{-1}(0)\subset \mathcal{G}(]a,b[,X)$, hence

$$Y_o = F[K^{-1}(0)] \subset F[\mathcal{G}(]a,b[,X)]$$

and by 2) we have the other inclusion.

DEFINITION: $Y_\alpha = F_\alpha[G(]a,b[,X)]$.

In what follows we will prove that if $Y_\alpha = Y_o$ then we have 1) and 2) of Theorem 3.21. The example 3 at the end of this § shows that b) of Theorem 3.21 does not necessarily imply that $Y_\alpha = Y_o$.

THEOREM 3.22. *If* $Y_\alpha = Y_o$ *then* $S^{\mathcal{G}}_{K,F} = \mathcal{G}(]a,b[,X)\times Y_o$.

PROOF. It is immediate that $S^{\mathcal{G}}_{K,F}\subset \mathcal{G}(]a,b[,X)\times Y_o$; reciprocally, given $(h,d)\in \mathcal{G}(]a,b[,X)\times Y_o$ we want to prove that the system $K[y] = h$, $F[y] = d$ has a solution. By Theorem 1.5 there exists a $\bar{y}\in G(]a,b[,X)$ such that $K[\bar{y}] = h$ and by a) of Theorem 3.12 $\bar{y}$ is continuous, hence $F[\bar{y}] = F_\alpha[\bar{y}]\in Y_o$ and therefore $d - F_\alpha[\bar{y}]\in Y_o$; then by b) of Theorem 3.16, applied to $g \equiv 0$ and $c = d - F_\alpha[\bar{y}]$, there exists $z\in \mathcal{G}(]a,b[,X)$, solution of $K[z] = 0$, $F[z] = d - F_\alpha[\bar{y}]$; if we take $y = z + \bar{y}$ we have $K[y] = K[\bar{y}] = h$ and

$$F[y] = F[z] + F[\bar{y}] = d - F_\alpha[\bar{y}] + F_\alpha[\bar{y}] = d.$$

QED

3.23. *If* $Y_\alpha = Y_o$ *then for every* $g\in \mathcal{G}(]a,b[,X)$ *there exists*

$$\int_a^b H(t_o,s)\cdot dg(s)\in Y_o.$$

PROOF. By Theorem 3.22 we have $(g,0)\in S^{\mathcal{G}}_{K,F}$ hence, by Theorem 3.17 the solution of $K[y] = g$, $F[y] = 0$ is given by

$$y(t) = \int_{t_o}^t R(t,s)\cdot dg(s) + \bar{J}(t)\int_a^b H(t_o,s)\cdot dg(s);$$

this implies the result if we take $t = t_o$ and recall that Y_o is the domain of definition of $\bar{J}(t_o) = J(t_o)^{-1}$.

Since $J(t_o)$ is a (continuous) linear bijection from X onto Y_o we may use it to transfer to Y_o the Banach space norm of X. We denote by Y_X the vector space of Y_o endowed with this new norm, i.e., for $c \in Y_X$ we define

$$\|c\|_X = \|J(t_o)^{-1}c\| .$$

Obviously $\bar{J}(t) = R(t,t_o) \circ J(t_o)^{-1}: Y_X \longrightarrow X$ is continuous for every $t \in]a,b[$.

3.24. *If* $Y_\alpha = Y_o$ *then for all* $s,t \in]a,b[$ *we have*

a) $H(t,s) \in L(X,Y_o)$.

b) $H(t,s) \in L(X,Y_X)$.

PROOF. a) We have

$$H(t,s) = \int_a^s d\alpha(\tau)\cdot R(\tau,s) - Y(s-t)J(s) =$$

$$= \int_a^b d\alpha(\tau)\cdot Y(s-\tau)R(\tau,s) - Y(s-t)\int_a^b d\alpha(\tau)\cdot R(\tau,s) =$$

$$= \int_a^b \cdot d\alpha(\tau)\cdot\left[Y(s-\tau) - Y(s-t)\right]R(\tau,s) =$$

$$= \int_a^b \cdot d\alpha(\tau)\cdot \rho_{s,t}(\tau) = F_\alpha[\rho_{s,t}]$$

where $\rho_{s,t} \in G(]a,b[,L(X))$ with

$$\rho_{s,t}(\tau) = \left[Y(s-\tau)-Y(s-t)\right]R(\tau,s).$$

For every $x \in X$ we have

$$H(t,s)x = F_\alpha[\rho_{s,t}x] \in F_\alpha[G(]a,b[,X)] = Y_\alpha,$$

hence $H(t,s) \in L(X,Y_o)$.

b) By a) the graph of $H(t,s)$ in $X \times Y_o$ is closed, hence a fortiori the graph is closed in $X \times Y_X$; then we have b) by the closed graph theorem.

THEOREM 3.25. *If* $Y_\alpha = Y_o$ *then*

a) $F_\alpha \in L[G(]a,b[,X),Y_X]$.

b) $\alpha \in SV_{oo}(]a,b[,L(X,Y_X))$.

c) $\alpha \in SV_{oo}(]a,b[,L(X,Y_o))$.

d) For every $t \in]a,b[$ *we have* $H^t \in SV_{oo}(]a,b[,L(X,Y_X))$.

e) For every $t \in]a,b[$ *we have* $H^t \in SV_{oo}(]a,b[,L(X,Y_o))$.

f) For every $t \in]a,b[$ *there is* $[a_t,b_t] \subset]a,b[$ *such that* $H(t,s) = 0$ *for all* $s < a_t$ *or* $s > b_t$.

PROOF. a) By $Y_\alpha = Y_o$ we have $F_\alpha \in L[G(]a,b[,X),Y_o]$; hence the graph of F_α in $G(]a,b[,X)XY_o$ is closed and a fortiori it is closed in $G(]a,b[,X)XY_X$; the result follows from the closed graph theorem.

b) follows from a).

c) follows from $\alpha \in SV_{oo}(]a,b[,L(X,Y))$ and the fact that α takes its values in Y_o.

d) By b) of 3.24 we have $H(t,s) \in L(X,Y_X)$ for every $s \in]a,b[$ hence the result follows from a) of Theorem 3.16 applied to the Banach space Y_X (instead of Y) since by b) we have $\alpha \in SV_{oo}(]a,b[,L(X,Y_X))$.

e) follows directly from a) of Theorem 3.16.

f) follows from a) of Theorem 3.16 and from d).

3.26. *If* $Y_\alpha = Y_o$ *then for every* $g \in \mathcal{G}(]a,b[,X)$ *there exists*

$$\bar{J}(t)\cdot\int_a^b H(t_o,s)\cdot dg(s) = \int_c^b \bar{J}(t)H(t_o,s)\cdot dg(s)$$

and the first integral exists both in Y_X *and* Y_o.

PROOF. By d) of Theorem 3.25 the first integral exists in Y_X (hence in Y_o since $Y_X \hookrightarrow Y_o$ is continuous) therefore the first member is well defined. Again by d) of Theorem 3.25 and since $\bar{J}(t) \in L(Y_X,X)$ we have

$$\bar{J}(t)H^{t_o} \in SV_{oo}(]a,b[,L(X)),$$

hence the second integral exists. The equality follows from the continuity of $\bar{J}(t)$ in Y_X.

FROM NOW ON WE SUPPOSE THAT $Y_\alpha = Y_o$

DEFINITION. For every $s,t \in]a,b[$ we write

$$G(t,s) = \bar{J}(t) \circ H(t_o,s) + [Y(s-t_o)-Y(s-t)]R(t,s)$$

and G is called the *Green function* of the system (K), (F). By b) of 3.24 and since $\bar{J}(t) \in L(Y_X,X)$ (and $R(t,s) \in L(X)$) we have

3.27. $G(t,s) \in L(X)$ *for all* $s,t \in]a,b[$.

REMARK 4. The theorems that follow are the fundamental theorems of this §. We don't know if they are true without the hypothesis $Y_\alpha = Y_o$, i.e. we ignore if the necessary conditions 1) and 2) of Theorem 3.21 imply that $Y_\alpha = Y_o$. If $\alpha \in BV^{loc}(]a,b[,L(X,Y))$ the necessary condition

$$F[\mathcal{G}(]a,b[,X)] = Y_o$$

(see Theorem 3.21) implies that $Y_\alpha = Y_o$.

THEOREM 3.28. *If* K *and* F *are such that* $Y_\alpha = Y_o$ *then*

a) The system $K[y] = g$, $F[y] = c$ *has a solution* $y \in \mathcal{G}(]a,b[,X)$ *if and only if* $(g,c) \in \mathcal{G}(]a,b[,X) \times Y_o$*; then this solution is given by*

$$y(t) = \bar{J}(t)c + \int_a^b G(t,s)\cdot dg(s) \qquad t \in]a,b[$$

b) For every $(f,c) \in S_{K,F}$ *the system* $K[y] = f$, $F[y] = c$ *has one and only one solution given by*

$$y(t) = f(t)+\bar{J}(t)\Big[c-F(f)\Big] - \int_a^b G(t,s)d_s\Big[\int_{t_o}^s d_\sigma K(s,\sigma)\cdot f(\sigma)\Big].$$

PROOF. a) By (7) and 3.23 $\bar{J}(t)c$ and

$$\bar{J}(t)\int_a^b H(t_o,s)\cdot dg(s)$$

are well defined and if we recall that

$$\int_{t_o}^t R(t,s)\cdot dg(s) = \int_a^b [Y(s-t_o)-Y(s-t)]R(t,s)\cdot dg(s)$$

the result follows from the definition of G.

b) We may write

$$y(t) - f(t) + \int_{t_o}^{t} d_\sigma K(t,\sigma)[y(\sigma)-f(\sigma)] = g(t)$$

where

$$g(t) = -\int_{t_o}^{t} d_\sigma K(t,\sigma)\cdot f(\sigma).$$

By a) of II.1.14 g is continuous and if we apply a) we have

$$y(t) - f(t) = \bar{J}(t)F[y-f] + \int_a^b G(t,s)d_s\int_{t_o}^{s} d_\sigma K(s,\sigma)\cdot f(\sigma)$$

hence the result.

THEOREM 3.29. *The Green function*

$$G: \left]a,b\right[\times \left]a,b\right[\longrightarrow L(X)$$

has the following properties:

(G_o) $F[G_s] = 0$ *for every* $s \in \left]a,b\right[$.

(G_1) $$G_s(t)-G_s(t_o) + \int_{t_o}^{t} d_\sigma K(t,\sigma)\circ G_s(\sigma) = [-Y(s-t)+Y(s-t_o)]I_X \qquad s,t \in \left]a,b\right[.$$

(G_2) $$G(t,s) + Y(s-t)R(t,s) + Y(s-t_o)[\bar{J}(t)J(s)-R(t,s)] +$$
$$+\int_a^s \Big[G(t,\sigma)+Y(\sigma-t)R(t,\sigma)+Y(\sigma-t_o)[\bar{J}(t)J(\sigma)-R(t,\sigma)]\Big]d_\sigma K(\sigma,s) =$$
$$= \bar{J}(t)\alpha(s).$$

(G_3) *For every* $s \in \left]a,b\right[$ G_s *is continuous at* $t \neq s$ *and left-continuous at* $t = s$.

(G_4) *For every* $t \in \left]a,b\right[$ $G^t \in SV_{oo}(\left]a,b\right[,L(X))$ *and* $G^t(s) = 0$ *if* $s < \inf[t,t_o,a_o]$ *or* $s > \sup[t,t_o,b_o]$ *where* (a_o,b_o) *denotes the support of* $J(t_o)^{-1}H^{t_o}$; G *is locally uniformly of bounded semivariation in the second variable.*

PROOF. (G_o). By the definitions of G and H we have

$$G(t,s) = \bar{J}(t)\int_a^s d\alpha(\tau)\circ R(\tau,s) -$$
$$- Y(s-t_o)\bar{J}(t)\circ J(s) + Y(s-t_o)R(t,s) - Y(s-t)R(t,s),$$

and by Theorem 3.9 we have

$$F[G_s] = \int_a^s d\alpha(\tau)\circ R(\tau,s) -$$

$$- Y(s-t_o)J(s) + Y(s-t_o)J(s) - \int_a^s d\alpha(t)\circ R(t,s) = 0.$$

(G_1). By definition

$$G(t,s) = \bar{J}(t)H(t_o,s) + [Y(s-t_o)-Y(s-t)]R(t,s)$$

and by a) of Theorem 3.9 the first summand satisfies the homogeneous equation. For the second summand we have to prove that

$$[Y(s-t_o)-Y(s-t)]R(t,s) + \int_{t_o}^t d_\sigma K(t,\sigma)[Y(s-t_o)-Y(s-\sigma)]R(\sigma,s) =$$

$$= [Y(s-t)-Y(s-t_o)]I_X.$$

which is obvious for $s \notin \{t_o,t\}$ since then everything is zero; for $t_o \leqslant s < t$ the equation reduces to

$$R(t,s) + \int_\sigma^t d_\sigma K(t,\sigma)\circ R(\sigma,s) = I_X$$

i.e., to the equation of the resolvent ((R^*) of Theorem 1.5) and analogously for $t < s \leqslant t_o$.

(G_2) follows immediately from c) of Theorem 3.16 and from the definition of G.

(G_3) follows from the definition of G.

(G_4). By d) of Theorem 3.25 we have

$$H^{t_o} \in SV_{oo}(]a,b[,L(X,Y_X))$$

and there exists $[a_o,b_o] \subset]a,b[$ such that $H(t_o,s) = 0$ for $s < a_o$ or $s > b_o$; the same is true for $J(t)\circ H^{t_o}$, hence it follows from the definition of G that $G(t,s) = 0$ for $s < \inf[t,t_o,a_o]$ or $s > \sup[t,t_o,b_o]$. The rest is obvious.

REMARK 5. In the case of example (L) of §2 (G_2) takes the form

(G_2')
$$G(t,s) + Y(s-t)R(t,s) -$$
$$- \int_a^s [G(t,\sigma) + Y(\sigma-t)R(t,\sigma)]\,dA(\sigma) = J(t)^{-1}\alpha(s).$$

Indeed in the case of example (L) we have

$$\bar{J}(t)J(\sigma) - R(t,\sigma) \equiv 0$$

(by c) of Theorem 3.9); for every s we may take $t_o = s$ and we have $K(\sigma,s) = A(s) - A(\sigma)$.

REMARK 6. (G_1) says that G_s satisfies the equation $\frac{d}{dt}K(G_s)=\delta_{(s)}$ in the sense of Theory of Distributions i.e.

$$\frac{d}{dt} G_s(t) + \frac{d}{dt}\int_{t_o}^t d_\sigma K(t,\sigma)\circ G_s(\sigma) = \delta_{(s)}(t).$$

THEOREM 3.30. *a) The mapping*

$$g \in \mathcal{G}(]a,b[,X) \longmapsto \mathcal{G}g \in \mathcal{G}(]a,b[,X)$$

is continuous, where

$$(\mathcal{G}g)(t) = \int_a^b G(t,s)\,dg(s), \qquad t \in]a,b[.$$

b) The mapping $c \in Y_X \longmapsto y_c \in \mathcal{G}(]a,b[,X)$ *is continuous, where* $y_c(t) = \bar{J}(t)c$.

c) The following properties are equivalent:

(i) The mapping $c \in Y_o \longmapsto y_c \in \mathcal{G}(]a,b[,X)$ *is continuous.*

(ii) $J(t_o)^{-1}: Y_o \longrightarrow X$ *is continuous.*

(iii) Y_o *is a Banach space.*

PROOF. By (G_4) G^t has compact support, hence

$$\int_a^b G(t,s)\,dg(s) = -\int_a^b d_s G(t,s)\cdot g(s).$$

The continuity of $\mathcal{G}$ follows from

$$\sup_{c\leq t\leq d} \left\| \int_a^b d_s G(t,s)\cdot g(s)\right\| \leq \sup_{c\leq t\leq d} SV_{[\bar{a},\bar{b}]}[G^t]\, \|g\|_{[\bar{a},\bar{b}]}$$

where $\bar{a} = \inf[c,t_o,a_o]$ and $\bar{b} = \sup[d,t_o,b_o]$ (cf. (G_4)).

b) Follows from b) of Corollary 3.10 applied to Y_X.

c) Follows from b) of Corollary 3.10 and d) of 3.7.

THEOREM 3.31. *The mapping*

$$f \in G(]a,b[,X) \longmapsto \mathcal{G}_K f \in \mathcal{G}(]a,b[,X)$$

is continuous where

$$(\mathcal{G}_K f)(t) = \int_a^b G(t,s)\, d_s\left[\int_{t_o}^s d_\sigma K(s,\sigma)\cdot f(\sigma)\right], \qquad t\in\,]a,b[.$$

PROOF. The mapping $f \longmapsto \mathcal{G}_K f$ is the composition of the continuous mappings

$$f \in G(]a,b[,X) \longmapsto \mathcal{k} f \in \mathcal{G}(]a,b[,X)$$

and

$$g \in \mathcal{G}(]a,b[,X) \longmapsto \mathcal{G} g \in \mathcal{G}(]a,b[,X),$$

where

$$(\mathcal{k} f)(s) = \int_{t_o}^s d_\sigma K(s,\sigma)\cdot f(\sigma), \qquad s\in\,]a,b[,$$

and $\mathcal{G}$ is defined in Theorem 3.30.

EXAMPLES

1. We take $X = Y = \mathbb{R}$ and consider the equation

$$y' + A'y = f',$$

more precisely the integro-differential equation

$$\text{(L)} \qquad y(t) - y(s) + \int_s^t dA(\sigma)\cdot y(\sigma) = f(t)-f(s) \qquad s,t\in\,]a,b[$$

where $y,f \in G(]a,b[)$ and $A \in \mathcal{G}BV^{loc}(]a,b[)$.

The resolvent of (L) is $R(t,s) = \exp[-A(t)+A(s)]$ and the general solution of (L) is

$$y(t) = y(s)\exp[-A(t)+A(s)] + \int_s^t \exp[-A(t)+A(\sigma)]\cdot df(\sigma).$$

If we take now a linear constraint $F\in G(]a,b[)'$

$$\text{(F)} \qquad F[y] = c$$

by I.6.8 there exist $\alpha\in BV_{oo}(]a,b[)$ and $u\in s_{oo}(]a,b[)$ (i.e., u is zero outside an interval $[\bar{a},\bar{b}]\subset]a,b[$ and $u\in \ell_1([\bar{a},\bar{b}])$) such that

$$F[y] = \int_a^b y(t)d\alpha(t) + \sum_{a<t<b} u(t)[y(t)-y(t-)].$$

We have

$$J(s) = F[R_s] = \int_a^b exp[-A(t)+A(s)]\cdot d\alpha(t) = e^{A(s)}\int_a^b e^{-A(t)}d\alpha(t);$$

hence

$$H(t,s) = \int_a^s exp[-A(\tau)+A(s)]d\alpha(\tau) + Y(s-t)e^{A(s)}\int_a^b e^{-A(\tau)}d\alpha(\tau).$$

The condition for the existence of the Green function is $J(s)\neq 0$, i.e.

$$\int_a^b e^{-A(t)}d\alpha(t) \neq 0.$$

If $J(s)\neq 0$ the Green function is given by

$$G(t,s) = J(t)^{-1}H(t,s) =$$

$$= -\left[\int_a^b e^{-A(\tau)}d\alpha(\tau)\right]^{-1} \times \begin{cases} \int_s^b e^{-A(\tau)}d\alpha(\tau) & \text{if} \quad s \geqslant t \\ \int_a^s e^{-A(\tau)}d\alpha(\tau) & \text{if} \quad s < t \end{cases}$$

hence the solution y of the problema (L), (F) is given by

$$y(t) = f(t) + \left[\int_a^b e^{-A(\tau)}d\alpha(\tau)\right]e^{-A(t)}[c-F(f)] -$$

$$-\int_a^b G(t,s)d_s\int^s f(\sigma)dA(\sigma).$$

2. $Y = X^2$ and $F[y] = (y(t_o),y(t_o-))$; for any equation (K) we have

$$Y_\alpha = Y_o = \Delta_X = \{(x,x)\in X^2 \mid x\in X\}$$

hence if $J(t_o)$ is injective (i.e., if $y \equiv 0$ is the only solution of the system $K[y] \equiv 0$, $F[y] = 0$ - see Theorem 3.6) the problema (K), (F) has a Green function (and $J(t_o)$ is bicontinuous).

3. $Y = X^2$ and $F[y] = (y(t_o), y(t_o+))$; then we have

$$\alpha(t)x = F[\chi_{]a,t]}x] = (\chi_{]a,t]}(t_o)x, \chi_{]a,t]}(t_o+)x = \begin{cases} (x,x) & \text{if} \quad t > t_o \\ (x,0) & \text{if} \quad t = t_o \\ (0,0) & \text{if} \quad t < t_o \end{cases}$$

$$u(t)x = F[\chi_{\{t\}}x] = (\chi_{\{t\}}(t_o)x, \chi_{\{t\}}(t_o+x)) = \begin{cases} (x,0) & \text{if} \quad t = t_o \\ (0,0) & \text{if} \quad t \neq t_o \end{cases}$$

hence

$$F_u[y] = \sum_{a<t<b} u(t)[y(t)-y(t-)] = (y(t_o)-y(t_o-), 0)$$

and

$$F_\alpha[y] = F[y] - F_u[y] = (y(t_o), y(t_o+)) - (y(t_o)-y(t_o-), 0) = $$
$$= (y(t_o-), y(t_o+)).$$

Therefore

$$Y_\alpha = F_\alpha[G(]a,b[,X)] = X^2 \supsetneqq \Delta_X = Y_o = F[K^{-1}(0)] = F[\mathcal{G}(]a,b[,X)]$$

for any K.

If we take now $L[y] \equiv y'$ we have the resolvent $R(t,s) = I_X$ and

$$J(s)x = F[R_s x] = (R_s(t_o)x, R_s(t_o+)x) = (x,x).$$

We have

$$\int_a^s d\alpha(\tau) \circ R(\tau,s) = F_\alpha[\chi_{]a,s]} R_s] \notin L(X, Y_o)$$

since

$$F_\alpha[X]a,s]R_s x] = \begin{cases} (x,x) & \text{if} \quad s > t_o \\ (x,0) & \text{if} \quad s = t_o \\ (0,0) & \text{if} \quad s < t_o \end{cases}$$

hence $H(t,s) \notin L(X,Y_o)$ and there cannot exist the Green function of the problem (L), (F).

4. We take $]a,b[= \mathbb{R}$, $Y = G(\mathbb{R},X)$ and

$$F[y](\sigma) = y(\sigma+1) - y(\sigma), \qquad \sigma \in \mathbb{R}.$$

We have $F_\alpha[f] = F[I\_f]$, hence $Y_\alpha = G\_(\mathbb{R},X)$ which is a Frechet space and **thus** (by the closed graph theorem) has no finer Banach space topology hence for no K can we have $Y_\alpha = Y_o$, so there never exists a Green function with the properties of Theorem 3.29. Hence for any $K \in \mathcal{E}^{uo}(\mathbb{R}\times\mathbb{R},X)$ there never exists a function $G: \mathbb{R}\times\mathbb{R} \longrightarrow L(X)$ with the properties (G_o) to (G_4) such that the continuous periodic solutions of period 1 of

$$y(t) - y(t_o) + \int_{t_o}^{t} d_\sigma K(t,\sigma)\cdot y(\sigma) = g(t) - g(t_o)$$

are exactly the functions of the form

$$y(t) = \int_{-\infty}^{\infty} G(t,s)\cdot dg(s).$$

5. We take $X = Y = G([a,b],Z)$ where Z is a Banach space and define

$$F[f](\sigma) = \int_a^\sigma f(\tau)(\tau)d\tau, \qquad \sigma \in [a,b],$$

for every $f \in G([a,b],X) = G([a,b],G([a,b],Z))$.

a) In order to show that $F(f)$ is well defined we will prove that the function $\tau \in [a,b] \longmapsto f(\tau)(\tau) \in Z$ is regulated; this follows from the fact that for $0 < \varepsilon < \delta$ and $\tau \in [a,b-\delta]$ we have

$$\|f(\tau+\delta)(\tau+\delta) - f(\tau+\varepsilon)(\tau+\varepsilon)\| \leqslant$$

$$\leqslant \|f(\tau+\delta)(\tau+\delta)-(\tau+\varepsilon)(\tau+\delta)\| + \|f(\tau+\varepsilon)(\tau+\delta)-f(\tau+\varepsilon)(\tau+\varepsilon)\| \leqslant$$

$$\leqslant \|f(\tau+\delta)-f(\tau+\varepsilon)\|_{[a,b]} + \|f(\tau+\varepsilon)(\tau+\delta) - f(\tau+\varepsilon)(\tau+\varepsilon)\|$$

since f and $f(\tau+\varepsilon)$ are regulated.

b) We have $F_u = 0$: $u(t)x = F[\chi_{\{t\}}x]$ where $x \in X$; hence

$$F = F_\alpha = F[\chi_{\{t\}}x](\sigma) = \int_a^\sigma [\chi_{\{t\}}(\tau)x](\tau)d\tau =$$

$$= \int_a^\sigma \chi_{\{t\}}(\tau)x(\tau)d\tau = 0;$$

therefore we have $F = F_\alpha$.

c) We have

$$Y_o = G_a^{(1)}([a,b],Z) = \{g \in G^{(1)}([a,b],Z) \mid g(a) = 0\}$$

that is not a closed subspace of $Y = G([a,b],Z)$ but that allows a finer Banach space norm given by

$$\|g\|^{(1)} = \|g\| + \|g'\|.$$

d) If we take $L[y] \equiv y'$ we have $L^{-1}(0) = X$, the space of constant functions $(\tau \longmapsto \hat{x}(\tau) = x)$ and

$$Y_o = F[L^{-1}(0)] = Y_\alpha;$$

indeed: given $f \in G([a,b],G([a,b],Z))$ we take

$$\hat{x}_f \in X = G([a,b],Z)$$

such that $\hat{x}_f(\tau)(\sigma) = f(\sigma)(\sigma)$ for all $\tau,\sigma \in [a,b]$, hence the function $\hat{x}_f$ is constant $(\hat{x}_f(\tau_1) = \hat{x}_f(\tau_2)$ for any $\tau_1,\tau_2 \in [a,b])$ and we have $F[\hat{x}_f] \in Y_o$ and $F[\hat{x}_f] = F[f]$.

e) $L[y] = 0$ and $F[y] = 0$ imply $y = 0$; indeed: if $L[y] = 0$ we have $y = \hat{x}$ a constant function, hence

$$0 = F[y](\sigma) = \int_a^\sigma y(\tau)(\tau)d\tau = \int_a^\sigma \hat{x}(\tau)d\tau$$

for every $\sigma \in [a,b]$ implies $\hat{x}(\tau) = 0$ i.e. $\hat{x} = 0$. Therefore $J(s)\colon X \longrightarrow Y_o = Y_\alpha$ is injective continuous and onto but not bicontinuous; if however we consider on Y_o the Banach space structure defined in c) $J(s)$ becomes bicontinuous.

f) We have $R(t,s) = I_X$ and $J(s)(\sigma) = (\sigma-a)I_X$;

$$[\alpha(t)x](\sigma) = F[\chi_{]a,t]}x](\sigma) =$$

$$= \int_a^\sigma \chi_{]a,t]}(\tau)x(\tau)d\tau = \int_a^{\sigma\wedge t} x(\tau)d\tau.$$

REFERENCES

[B] - H.E.BRAY, *Elementary properties of Stieltjes integral*, Ann. of Math., 20(1918-19), 177-186.

[B-T] - S.BOCHNER and A.E.TAYLOR, *Linear functionals on certain spaces of abstractly-valued functions*, Ann. of Math. 39(1938), 913-944.

[C] - H.CARTAN, Calcul Différentiel, Hermann, Paris (1967).

[Ca] - C.S. CARDASSI, *Dependência diferenciável das soluções de equações integro-diferenciais em espaços de Banach*, Master Thesis, Instituto de Matemática e Estatística da Universidade de S.Paulo, 1975.

[D] - N.DINCULEANU, Vector Measures, Pergamon Press, Oxford (1967).

[G] - M.GOWURIN, *Über die Stieltjes Integration abstrakter Funktionen*, Fund.Math., 27(1936), 254-268.

[H] - S.Z. HERSCOWITZ, *Classes de funções associadas pela integral de Riemann-Stieltjes*, Master Thesis, Instituto de Matemática e Estatística da Universidade de S.Paulo, 1975.

[H-ie] - T.H.HILDEBRANDT, *On systems of linear differentio-Stieltjes integral equations*, Illinois J.Math., 3(1959),352-373.

[H-ti] - T.H.HILDEBRANDT, Introduction to the theory of integration, Academic Press, 1963.

[H-BAMS] - C.S.HÖNIG, *The Green function of a linear differential equation with a lateral condition*, Bull. Amer. Math. Soc., 79(1973),587-593.

[H-IME] - C.S.HÖNIG, *The abstract Riemann-Stieltjes integral and its applications to Linear Differential Equations with generalized boundary conditions*, Notas do Instituto de Matemática e Estatística da Universidade de S.Paulo, Série Matemática nº1, 1973.

[H-BAMS$_2$] - C.S.HÖNIG, *Volterra-Stieltjes integral equations with linear constraints and discontinuous solutions*, Bull. Am. Math. Soc. **81**(1975).

[H-DS] - C.S.HÖNIG, *The formulas of Dirichlet and of Substitution for Riemann-Stieltjes integrals in Banach spaces*, To appear.

[H-OP] - C.S.HÖNIG, *Open problems in the theory of differential equations with linear constraints*, Coleção Atas, vol. nº5(1974), 161-199, Sociedade Brasileira de Matemática, Rio de Janeiro.

[H-R]- C.S. HÖNIG, *An unified representation theory for linear continuous operators between function spaces*, To appear.

[K] - H.S.KALTENBORN, *Linear functional operations on functions having discontinuities of the first kind*, Bull. Amer. Math. Soc., 40(1934), 702-708.

[M] - J.S.MAC-NERNEY, *Stieltjes integrals in linear spaces*, Ann. of Math., 61(1955), 354-367.

[R] - G.C. da ROCHA FILHO, *Incompatibilities in general Riemann-Stieltjes integration theories*. To appear.

[S] - M.I. de SOUZA, *Equações diferencio-integrais do tipo Riemann-Stieltjes em espaços de Banach com soluções descontínuas*, Master thesis, Instituto de Matemática e Estatística da Universidade de São Paulo, 1974.

[W] - H.S.WALL, *Concerning harmonic matrices*, Arch. Math., 5(1954),160-167.

SYMBOL INDEX